Mary
May your ride through
life be filled with
joy, good health and
forgiveness.
Nancy Jasin

The Tire Swing

A Memoir of Survival

Nancy Jasin Ensley

PublishAmerica
Baltimore

First printing

PublishAmerica has allowed this work to remain exactly as the author intended, verbatim, without editorial input.

Softcover 9781462667765
PUBLISHED BY PUBLISHAMERICA, LLLP
www.publishamerica.com
Baltimore

Printed in the United States of America

The Tire Swing

A Memoir of Survival

Nancy Jasin Ensley

"Take this special gift into every journey in your life"

Artwork by my dear sister,
Ethel Cousino (called Erin in this story)

INTRODUCTION

The wind pushes the tire swing back and forth ever so slightly. The thick hemp rope tied with a special sailor's knot to the old tractor tire makes a whistling sound like the loons swooping over the marshes near the shore. Nancy tells this story from her own experiences, perceived or imagined. When the tale becomes hazy or too painful she may tell it as though she were watching the scenes as a spectator.

Life, from diapers to Depends, becomes a dilemma for her and for many of the people who enter her life. Her stormy relationship with her father affects her relationships not only with men but also with her work and with other women.

Moving from her home in New Jersey at age eleven seems to add insult to injury as she gazes through the car window at endless farm fields, manufacturing plants, with not a single hill or mountain. People talked with their mouths wide open in the Midwest, and there are hardly any passenger trains carrying interesting people to the city. She misses her grandmother terribly and could hardly understand her seven- year- old sister who can be so oblivious to this drastic change in their lives. Their father had been transferred from Raritan Arsenal in New Jersey to another arsenal in Rossford, Ohio. He will be taking photographs of whatever he takes photographs of. Nancy prays to her own special guardian angel that her father will be happier and nicer to her mother, herself, and---yes----even her kid sister who wrinkles her nose up like a bunny when she laughs.

Throughout her life, she will encounter women who have a special quality, this amazing gift of unconditional love. They struggle against pain, disappointment, and fear with humility and bravery. Even when they are knocked down by inequality and prejudice, anger and brutality, disease and frustration, they dust themselves off, put on their lipstick and carry on with tenderness and forgiveness. Her mother, Ethelyn, is one of those women. An accomplished pianist, graduate of Julliard School of Music, and following a job in New York City as a governess, she meets Walter at a dance. She has moved in with her aunts in Atlantic Highlands after losing her mother to leukemia. Walter seems enamored with the pretty, well-mannered, young lady from East Orange, New Jersey. They court and marry. Walter restrains his innate passion for women and his temper until they both rear there ugly heads very shortly after the marriage. Ethelyn finds him romancing the lady who colors his photographs just three weeks into the marriage. Instead of an apology she receives the first of many verbal beatings and experiences the madness of his rage. This later transcends from verbal to physical abuse. She stays because she is pregnant and excuses his transgressions for many years. She finds some solace in the lilting concertos she plays for a handful of piano students in the town and from some talent shows she and Walter participate in for the fire department and the Sea Scouts. Walter can whistle any tune with finesse. The townspeople love the shows and marvel at Ethelyn's feathery touch on the keys.

Years of verbal and physical abuse were hidden from the world. They both remain on stage and in costume outside of their home. The only cathartic relief from the charade for Nancy's mother is her sudden trips away from home. A tiny note is left on their dresser or on the kitchen table.

I need to go away for a while.
I will be home soon, don't worry.
I love you both
Mom

The impact of being left with an unpredictable father who could surge into volcanic rages at any moment was indescribable. Their guts tighten into a ball of fear. They try, at all costs, to obey and go unnoticed. They look out the window or down the street anxiously awaiting their mother's return but fearing that one of these times she will not return. She always does, but the fear never leaves them.

There are also many good times. Ethelyn takes them on trips to New York and California. She loves to travel and to experience the world. Walter never likes any of that, or perhaps.......perhaps he is never invited to come along. Nancy doesn't know him. She wants to love him. She wants him to love her. She never seems to do the right thing. Over the years, she yearns to be noticed, to be applauded, to be loved. Never able to love herself enough to see that she is indeed loved, she turns to alcohol, poor relationships, and other obsessions in search of a feeling of completeness and peace.

This is the story of her ride on the tire swing------the story of her life.

ACKNOWLEDGEMENTS

This memoir is possible because of the amazing women and men who have shaped my life. Their influence in the shaping of this story has been the driving force in the long pursuit of finalization of this book.

I offer my endearing thanks to my mother and my sisters for their encouragement and examples of strength and dignity. To my husband and friends, my children and grandchildren my heartfelt appreciation and love for their patience and support. To my teachers over the years who bolstered this shy, frightened child's damaged ego enough to realize God indeed had given me a gift.

The Tire Swing has been a twenty year project that often became buried under life's commitments, mistaken priorities, and years of alcohol abuse. I would find its tattered handwritten pages tugging at my heart to continue but would shove them away in a dark corner of my desk or a box similar to the way I dealt with portions of my life.

My mother was a pianist and a writer. Her fingers on those ivory keys were gentle and confident. She wrote poetry and short stories that were never published. She played concertos with the finesse of a master but without the applause she so deserved. She withstood poverty and ridicule, abuse and illness, with strength and humility. This book is dedicated to her memory, to her artistic talent, and to her influence in so many lives.

If this book helps anyone in their struggles with life, with abuses of any kind or makes you laugh or cry, I have unending praise for my Higher Power who stood by my side and held my pen to the page.

ix

PREFACE

I was born June 28, 1941 in Long Branch, New Jersey. The Merry-Go-Round on the boardwalk nearby the hospital sent its music from the calliope into the window of my mother's hospital room. The war had ended but mine had just begun. My mother used to tell me that I would spin through life like the horses fixed to the platform of the carousel always reaching for the brass ring but never quite grabbing it. Never needing more than a few hours sleep I saw more and experienced more of life than perhaps I should.

My father was a photographer. His photographs were in black and white in those days. Any color had to be craftily painted in by an artist. He was tall and slim, very handsome and quite a dancer. He was known to whisk a lady around the dance floor almost swooping her into the air at times. He and mom had met at a dance and he had swept her off her feet, literally. Something had happened to him after a year or two of marriage. Mom always told me he had been attacked by a robber and hit on the head leaving him with violent headaches and an even more violent temper.

My mother came from an upper middle class family. She was the only child of Herman, a successful Pharmacist and Elizabeth Westphal , an insatiably dedicated Registered Nurse. Mary, the Westphal's governess was in charge of the growth and development of their daughter. A shy child, Ethelyn immersed herself into perfecting her innate talent for music with hours of practice on the Westphal's grand piano. At fifteen years of age she was accepted to Julliard Academy of Music – a very rare and prestigious opportunity for one so young. Had she not been swept away by Walter, the photographer, she may have had an amazing career playing concerts for audiences and bowing as they stood to applaud her performance.

Conjecture can be the source of inner pain that leads to nothing but resentment, anger, self doubt, and withdrawal. Time spent on "what could have been" may be bittersweet at first but often leads to disaster if it consumes you.

I think that both my parents' regrets played a large part in the instability of our family. My father had the ability to capture the character and mood of those he photographed. Poor business decisions, a volcanic temper, and his skirt chasing overshadowed his talent and lead to financial and emotional troubles for all of us. My mother fought battles with an enemy she could not see nor overcome. When fighting hit a brick wall she would flee, retreat, or disappear for periods of time.

Please do not think that I resent my parents, nor do I regret the things we struggled through. Circumstances and choices, wrong or right, affect us and our loved ones. We make mistakes – big ones, little ones. We loose sight of God, who tells us in subtle ways the paths He wishes us to choose; we often choose the clatter of life over His soft lullabies. My parents did their best. They gave each of us some amazing traits and abilities. I might not have had to ability to write this with the emotion that pushes me to tears had I not experienced the highs and lows of my upbringing. I might not have had the empathy and caring that my patients need for their pain and suffering. I might not have come to treasure every moment I awaken to another day. I might not have recognized this amazing "gift without a name" that women possess. I might not have met those women had my life been the daydream I often fell into, a perfect life without any struggles or needs.

The tire swing was in my Nanny's (my grandmother's) side yard. It hung by a thick hemp rope from a large tree that bordered her neighbor's yard. I always thought the tree was massive with branches reaching high into the clouds until we visited that house and yard this year, sixty one years later. The tree barely reached the level of the second floor of the house on Garfield Ave. The tire swing was gone, but the house had changed very little. The owners were on vacation. One of the neighbors living across the street from that old house told us they were very lovely people. We explained to him we were not trespassing, just reminiscing. I looked up at the attic window that used to lead to my uncle Alfred and aunt Betty's apartment. When Uncle Alfred left for the Navy the apartment became mine and my sister's bedroom.

Of what importance could a tire swing be to a woman's memoir, you might ask? It was a place I would go when I was sad and lonely. It encircled me and felt like it was protecting me from feelings I could not understand, from events I could not understand. It was a release of the energy produced by my restless adrenal glands. I could use all my strength to soar as high as gravity would allow and then some. I could twirl until the world spun around me and looked different, blurred, not so overwhelming. Though I think it was an oak tree from which the swing was suspended there must have been an apple tree nearby as there were always green apples I would gather and eat until my tummy wretched in painful consequence. Self punishment, obsessive-compulsiveness, seeking excitement and love became part of my nature. That time in my life was so pivotal that the tire swing swung through the pages gathering indelible memories.

My wish for anyone who spends time with me in these pages is that you realize every person you meet, even for a few moments, effects you and is put in your path for a reason.

When I tell the story of my life I tell it in the third person as though I were the storyteller reporting happenings that I could not reveal to anyone. Therefore, join Nancy on a ride on the tire swing told in the only way she could make sense of it.

CONTENTS

I dedicate the pages of this story to my mother, Ethelyn
Her music lives on in my heart

Chapter 1

The Tire Swing

There are moments in our lives that have a significant impact on the path we take and the people we travel with on the journey.

Nancy felt safe and confident when she was surrounded by the tire swing in her grandmother's yard. Her mother and father had been gone for over four months. She stared as far as she could down Garfield Avenue hoping to see the old DeSoto racing home to her and her little sister. Each time the familiar car didn't appear, her tummy tied into a knot that pushed on her chest and tugged at her seven- year-old heart. It was the same feeling that she always had just before his big hands pounded her arms and back, sending her across the floor or against furniture. She wondered why a part of her missed him, too. It all left her confused, frightened, and wondering what she had done to cause them to leave her.

When she settled herself into the opening of the tire swing, though, she could feel the knot in her little belly give way to the excitement of swinging high enough that she might go over the limb of the oak tree. Gravity always snapped her back just as she stretched her legs as far as she could toward the sky and bent them as far as she could behind her to achieve her goal. If one of her friends was available to push, she could get even with the branch faster and with less personal effort.

Some days she would twirl the swing as far as she could, hop onto the belly of the tire, and watch the world spin by her as she gripped the rough hemp rope tightly so she wouldn't fall. The years she and her sister spent at their grandmother's home demonstrated to them that no matter how painful or confusing life's journey may be, the people who you encounter, even for a moment, impact that ride and mold the person you become.

The tire swing hung from a tree
It beckoned them "come ride with me"

The rubber seat would bruise your thigh
But no one cared
When soaring high
Above the ground –then touch the sky
If you pull and push
Oh my
You may be brave and try to fly
Thus is life the tire swing
It beckons us to do great things
Sometimes we soar – sometimes we fall
It makes us dizzy when we twirl
Out of control
But all in all
We have the choice to ride

Nancy's mother, Ethelyn, had never pictured a life like this for herself and especially for her, or especially, her children. Lynn, as her father had lovingly dubbed her, imagined that her parents, Herman and Irene, would be aghast at the treatment of their only daughter. They would have rescued her long ago.....if they were alive and not too busy.

Chapter 2

Ethelyn

Ethelyn Elizabeth Westphal was the only child of Herman and Irene Westphal an upper- middle- class family in an upper- middle-class home in a sedate section of East Orange, New Jersey.

Ethelyn's mother, Irene, was a registered nurse, with the vision of many in the medical profession--- who labored through the hours of tedious study and clinical tribulation and humiliation---- that she alone could save the injured and needy of the world, or at least her world. She worked long hours at a New York City hospital scrubbing wounds, feeding starving children, watching people die alone and abandoned; she saw alcoholics chained to their beds in jaundiced confusion, the gaping wounds of those injured in street battles, the malnourished homeless people reeking of urine and the garbage and vomit dried on their tattered clothes. At the tender age of nineteen she felt she had lived fifty years and had seen humanity at its worst and at its best. Taking short sabbaticals to her home town in New Jersey, she would find herself walking around the campus of the local college watching young lovers kissing behind their books in the pretence of study, and sitting by a lazy stream in the park near the medical center.

It was there that Irene began a friendship with a young pharmacy student. They engaged in long conversations about the philosophy of life, nature, medical infirmities, politics and poetry. Herman was stricken with Irene's confidence and beauty. He fell in love with her the first day he saw her musing over a book of Shakespeare's sonnets. He wrote poems to her from his heart, flamboyantly transmitting feelings to words on paper that he was to shy to express verbally.

Thus they married. Irene continued to work at the hospital in New York while Herman finished his schooling and opened a small apothecary in East Orange. Herman was a diligent worker and a wise businessman. The apothecary flourished and Irene's dream of changing the world became more realistic as she opened the first free clinic in the Bowery just east of Central Park. The clinic served the poor, the homeless, the hungry and the lost. It became her life. Even after her marriage and the birth of her only child, Ethelyn, it continued to be the fulfillment of her dreams and the focus of her energy. Herman's love for her changed from poetic romance to respectful ambivalence. Ethelyn, or Lynn, as her father fondly addressed her, grew up with a governess and an unidentified sense of loss. She wasn't sure what was missing but she knew there was something.

Herman was well respected in the community. In the early 1900s the pharmacist was looked upon by many families as the family physician is today. There were few doctors who could make enough house calls to cover a town, so the pharmacist gave advice and potions for many minor ailments and even some chronic diseases. Federal and state regulations were almost nonexistent, so the health care field monitored itself without outside scrutiny and oversight. Herman was a crisp, stalwart and austere man – a product of his parent's roots in northern Germany. Irene was obsessed with her clinic. She rode the train from East Orange to New York every day at four in the morning and proudly walked several miles through Central Park and across town to the halfway house and clinic. There she saw all forms of suffering related to poverty and hopelessness. Dysentery, malnutrition, infections, tuberculosis, schizophrenia, non-healing wounds, and death were routine events in her day. She would put in thirteen to fifteen hours a day before trudging----- through snow, rain, heat, and some beautiful days alike----- to the train station and the hour-long ride home.

Irene could never hope to change the faces of those saddened by poverty and crime. No matter how hard she worked, no matter how many times she would bind their wounds they would return in a few weeks with more---- or never return at all. She took her compulsion with her through Central Park each day, with her as she rode the train home each night, exhausted mentally and physically. Though she could not change the imperfections she saw in humanity, she was determined to have a perfect home. On the surface, it *was* perfect. No angry words were uttered, no dust dared to linger as it was whisked away with a cloth, no object wandered out of place.

She had a respectable husband, an obedient child, trustworthy servants, and a degree of independence that few women enjoyed during those times. Was it loneliness rather than freedom? She and Herman slept in separate bedrooms. His clothes never touched her starched uniforms and tasteful suits. There was little touching at all. After all, she had to touch and give fourteen hours a day to everyone else. It was not that she did not love her husband and child---- it was that she had little left for those two people who needed her touch more than all the rest.

Until the day she died from a form Leukemia at fifty-four years old Irene remained dedicated to service and healing. Lynn attempted to fit into the pristine, orderly world of her parents, but rarely thought she did.

The Westphals hired a governess named Mary whose primary responsibility was to oversee Ethelyn's daily needs and to teach her to be a proper lady. Though Mary was strict and quite unaffectionate, Lynn could soften her and get her own way, though she rarely could do the same with her parents. One spring afternoon, Irene announced that the family was taking a vacation together in the month of June, 1925. Ethelyn could hardly believe her ears, as the word "vacation" was barely whispered in the Westphal household. Every day she would mark a big X on the calendar in her room and her heart would beat faster as the middle of June began to disappear. Mary watched her excitement and prayed that the event would truly take place, even though she had her doubts. Mary had been with the family since Lynn was three months old, and this was the first actual announcement of some event other than work that she could recall. The last week in June was exceedingly hot, and Ethelyn was sure that this would be the most opportune time to travel to the shore. She hinted at this in many ways by humming songs about the ocean and playing tunes on the piano that were light and airy. She even had her little suitcase packed and hidden under her bed, just so she would be ready when the actual day arrived. The thirtieth of June was a Sunday, and that morning Lynn tiptoed down the mahogany stairway that emptied onto the polished marble floor of the vestibule. Her mother was sitting in her chair with her bamboo fan moving back and forth in front of her aquiline face. She wore a soft blue chiffon dress that revealed her strong, trim figure much more than the starched uniform and cape that was her usual attire. Lynn had her tiny carpetbag suitcase in her hand. As she approached her mother she hid it behind one of the huge planters that adorned the staircase on either side. She had scrubbed her face and nails meticulously that morning, pulled her blond curly hair into a clasp at the back of her head, and put on a fresh skirt and crisp white blouse. She did not see any other trunks or bags sitting by the heavy double doors that graced the entrance to there home, as she thought would have been present when one takes a trip.

Perhaps they are in the buggy already, she pondered.

She stood at the arched opening to the sitting room that was filled with a flowered yellow, green, and blue loveseat and two green velvet high- back chairs facing a gold inlayed coffee table. None of these were worn or fingerprinted in any way, as Ethelyn was neither allowed to sit on the loveseat or either of the chairs nor touch the beautifully etched table. In fact, it was rare to see anyone in that elegant room with its immense fireplace adorned with hand painted tiles flown in from Germany and the sparse but tasteful sculptures and figurines. The housekeeper and cook, Belinda, would move gingerly between the furniture, with her feather duster in hand, once or twice a week lest any dust dare to settle on them.

A small ray of sunshine mixed with the tiny breeze came quietly in through the tall windows on the east side of the room. Ethelyn tried to run into it so the tiny beads of sweat forming on her brow would not taint her sterile appearance as she approached her mother. Demonstration of affection in this seemingly perfect family were limited to occasional smiles or nods of approval, but rarely a hug, a kiss, or a touch. Herman and Irene loved their daughter and each other, but had tucked away the passion of their courtship and their pride in their only child into a neatly closed box tied with ribbons of apathy and professional achievement. Ethelyn stood a respectful distance from her mother and cleared her throat. Deep inside her chest, she felt that sinking feeling you feel when you know the answer to a question you are about to ask and don't really want to hear the answer. The other part of her – the part that would shine no matter how dark the moment or dismal the circumstances--- held on to the hope that there would be a glimmer of sunshine that could somehow part the shadows.

"M-m-m-mother." Her voice could barely be heard above the ticking of the grandfather clock across the room. "Mother, is there going to be a vacation as you announced in May?" her voice was filled with the tiniest speck of assurance. "I have cleaned my room and packed my bag as I did not want to delay anyone". She stepped close enough to Irene that she could hear the fan making whooshing sounds as her mother moved it back and forth.

"That announcement was made in haste, my dear. There is much too much work to be done here." Irene looked straight into Ethelyn's deep brown eyes, and stood up slowly rising above her daughter to reach the austere posture of a general in command of his troops. "I know that is a disappointment for you, my dear. Some work will push that away." Irene walked into the pantry as Lynn stood melting in her crisp blue holiday skirt and white blouse. As Lynn gulped back the cry that was welling up in her throat, Irene returned with polishing cloths and polish. She pointed to the dining room table with its massive oak legs and tabletop.

"When you have finished perhaps we will go to see your father at the apothecary and get an ice cream. Don't get your outfit soiled. Do a good job."

Irene walked regally from the room without a backward glance at the little girl holding the polishing cloths and polish limply in her hands. The nurse who gently healed the wounds of so many lost souls could not find it in her heart to realize the wounds that could be inflicted with broken promises and lack of affection.

Lynn sat under the dark shadow of the table holding the tools that were supposed to heal her broken heart. Salty tears ran down her meticulously scrubbed cheeks as she began pour polish on the soft white cloth. She heard a rustle behind her and quickly wiped the tears away, thinking it might be the "general" back to see if the task was being carried out. Two warm hands pulled her close to a starched white apron covering an ample bosom.

Mary whispered softly, "Now, now….there will be a time for many vacations, so don't you fret". They sat there, the two of them, under the oak table with the massive oak legs surrounding them, holding on to one another. In a few moments they were laughing as they had a contest to see who could make their polished oak leg shiny enough to see her face in it.

The piano was Lynn's escape as well as her mental vacation. It took her to distant lands with magic candy lined streets and streams made of chocolate and whipped cream. She imagined herself a sparrow gliding above gardens filled with roses and lullabies. The notes filled the emptiness of an only child with distracted parents.

The hours of practice since she was four years old, the worn out metronomes and stacks of music, prompted Lynn's mother to schedule an interview with Julliard School of Music. This renowned institute offered entrance to only the most gifted musicians. The applicants were talented prodigies with intractable dedication and discipline. Ethelyn certainly was used to being obedient and had the passion for her music that fostered dedication. It was rare that anyone under the age of eighteen would even be granted an interview, let alone a fifteen year old, skinny, shy ingénue.

She never forgot how terrified she was the day of her audition with the school's headmaster. Being fifteen years old and very shy added to her nervousness, as well as the other forces tugging at her body far removed from her artistic drive. She was to play Wagner's "Concerto in C-Minor", a very difficult selection with challenging runs of sixteenth notes. The long, dimly lit hallway of the revered academy smelled of old mahogany and manuscripts piled in boxes. She passed tiny rooms from which music from various instruments surrounded her and moved her along the hallway to a grand piano, its ivory keys smiling at her and beckoning her slim fingers to join it in concert.

Professor Engler stood unceremoniously in militaristic attendance near the beautiful instrument. His face was somber, and he scowled at the young girl with perfectly coiffed golden curls and conservative starched white blouse and blue skirt as though he had a sentence to pass rather than an appraisal. For a moment she wanted to disappear, but the outline of her mother standing in the doorway left no means of escape other than to disappear, and she was no magician. Sheepishly she slid onto the smooth surface of the piano bench, placed the music on the ornate stand of the fabulous piano, laid her slim fingers on the cold ivory keys, took a big breath, and waited for a signal from the professor to beg

"Miss Westphal! Your nails are atrocious!" he growled as he pulled a pair of scissors that looked like a machete from his waistcoat and bent toward the small hands of the trembling Ethelyn. He proceeded to cut her nails to the quick. Tiny raw areas where the scissors cut into the skin brought tears to her eyes, but she blinked them back as quickly as they came, all the while praying for a storm or other diversion to end this moment. After depositing the weapon back into the pocket of his coat, he cleared his throat with a "humpf, humpf" and gestured the wounded child to begin to play.

Lynn's heart was pounding so loudly she could only pray that it was in the tempo of the composition she had to play perfectly. She wanted to make her mother proud. She needed the embrace of this woman's approval, though she longed for the embrace of affection. So she played. The arpeggio and allegro of the somber concerto whirled about the room. Her touch was a caress. She embraced each note as lovers embrace when they part. She lingered, oh so gently, on the stanzas of reverie and sadness typical of the composer's work. Tiny drops of blood fell upon the keys from her magical fingers to mix with the passion and the crescendo to the finale. Lynn became the music. She was lifted above anyone in the room, lifted above her loneliness, above shyness and uncertainty.

In the moments following the final note time seemed to stop. Professor Engler stood above her as she stared into his dark piercing eyes for a glimmer of hope that she had found favor. He pulled a handkerchief from the breast pocket of his coat and wiped what might have been a tear from his face. His eyes fixed on her fingers as they lifted from the keys and folded gently into her lap. Letting out a deep sigh, he straightened suddenly and seemed to transpose into the stern and rigid figure he had shed for a brief moment.

"She will need to be here at seven o'clock every morning, not a minute later. Perhaps someday she may become a true pianist." he announced as he turned abruptly and left the room.

Lynn's heart leaped into her throat, and she could barely speak. She had made it! She was to be the youngest student at Julliard Academy of Music! She ran across the room and wrapped herself around Irene, laying her head against her mother's chest, listening to her heart beating rapidly. Irene cautiously embraced her daughter and buried her nose into the soft blond curls, breathing in the smell of freshly washed tresses and the rose petals brushed into them early that morning by a very encouraging governess. Irene kissed Lynn's injured fingers and stood looking victoriously at the piano. They walked past the music flowing from the practice rooms. It seemed more like a concert now, every note carrying them along as though they were on a magic carpet.

Another special event was the yearly trip to New York City to see the Barnum and Bailey circus at Madison Square Garden.

Lynn rarely had bonding moments with her busy mother and looked forward to this occasion with the enthusiasm of a child's first Christmas. It was June, and Lynn was eight years old. Irene was no stranger to the ride to Grand Central Station, but it was always and adventure for her enthusiastic daughter. Lynn loved watching the faces of the passengers, some distant and detached, some dozing with heads bobbing to the rhythm of the train moving over the tracks, children (not nearly as obedient as she) being scolded for running in the aisles, ladies attempting to breath in there girdles cinching their waists to a mere nineteen inches, patting the tiny perfumed sweat beads from their brows with lace hankies; stern faced conductors able to stand erect without stumbling as the train rocked back and forth, testing their equilibrium. There was music in every part of life she surmised. Something inside her reached out and collected every sound, transmitting it to the keyboard ever present in her mind.

Grand Central echoed footsteps in a staccato aria, voices accompanied the opera with chords both soprano and tenor, the train sounds provided the percussion section as the doors opened onto the stage of the "Big Apple". The city enveloped the passengers and dispersed them to their destinations. Ethelyn took in every sound, every face, from the vagrant huddled in the alley, to the fur-swaddled elite pointing their noses toward the sky so as not to notice the serfs and peasants.

Fascinating! She could describe it in no other way. Perhaps, if she practiced very hard she could write an operetta encompassing the sounds and sights of this amazing city.

Irene held her hand tightly, guiding her through the crowds until they reached the front of the arena. Smells of peanuts roasting and popcorn popping waved the passers-by toward the ticket booth and the huge doors opening into the arena. Lights on the marquis flashed with names of famous tightrope artists and clowns waiting in the wings of the Big Top to dazzle the crowd. To the left of the ticket booth there was a small cage with a sign warning those who approached not to put their hands near the bars of the cage. "Dangerous Gorilla!" it blared, as children and adults cautiously stood a fair distance from the cage to catch a glimpse of the beast. Lynn begged Irene to step out of the ticket line so she could see the animal in the cage. Irene stood her ground and purchased a red balloon from a clown passing by the line for her pleading child in hopes this would pacify her.

"Go over there where that post is, and do not move. You can see the cage from there and I can watch you until I purchase the tickets" Irene directed.

Lynn happily clutched her red balloon and stood near the pole obediently.

The beast's eyes mesmerized her. The sadness and hollowness touched her heart. He sat in the back corner of his prison, his hairy humanlike hands sifting through rancid banana peels and peanut shells being thrown into the cage by the crowd. He was too large for the cage and had to sit hunched over, almost touching the top with his furry head. A massive belly protruded over his legs crossed Indian-style. Every once in a while he would lunge toward the bars exhaling a fierce growl which drove the crowd back with a rehearsed- sounding gasp.

Lynn looked into those eyes, and a tear ran down her cheek as she somehow felt the same – caged by tradition and neatness, surrounded by the debris of a lost relationship, lonely and confused. She wanted to open the cage's huge lock and free the poor soul. She knew she shouldn't, but she felt compelled to take a few steps toward the cage.

The beast followed the girl holding the red balloon with his eyes. Her eyes met the gorilla's pleading gaze and she was drawn across the yellow caution line dangerously close to the cage.

Someone in the crowd noticed the red balloon and the mesmerized girl attached to it. Suddenly, her shoulders were grabbed by strong hands and she was sucked into the crowd like a piece of dust in a sweeper. Lynn tried to part the sea of bodies as they tired of watching the caged animal and began to move away from the arena. The bodies were much larger than hers. She clutched her balloon wrapping the string around her hand several times. After traveling some distance from the circus, the crowd began to disperse and Lynn could see the city looming ahead of her. The ticket booth was nowhere to be seen, nor could she see the cage of her new found friend. She was on a corner with autos and trolley cars, buildings towering above her on all sides, horses and carriages weaving there way through the traffic.

Where was her mother? She felt that panicky flutter in her tummy reaching up into her chest and throat. A trolley pulled up in front of her and the conductor opened the door. "Ride, Ma'am?" he asked her unemotionally.

"N-n-n-no thanks, but co---" Lynn began to ask, but the door slammed shut and the trolley pulled away! She tried to remember from which direction the crowd had ambushed her. As panic took over, she became more disoriented.

"What a beautiful balloon," a deep, kind voice fell upon her terribly lost ears.

"Are you waiting for someone? Perhaps I can help." the voice said.

Lynn turned and looked into ice blue eyes, a mustache, and a mesmerizing smile, surrounded by a kind face.

"Please don't be frightened but I am lost and I saw you standing here with this red balloon. You looked so confident and sure of yourself that I thought perhaps you could tell me where you are going and it might be the same place I am going," The man smiled, and his smile radiated assurance and friendliness.

"I----I am going the Barnum and Bailey circus. My mother is waiting there buying tickets and I, well, I was just checking with the trolley conductors to make sure we don't miss our trolley to the train station when the show is over." Lynn fabricated somewhat dramatically.

"The circus! That is exactly where I was going! Imagine that, finding you to guide me," the gentleman with the ice blue eyes fabricated as well. "Would you allow me to accompany you, ma'am?"

"I'm not sure my mother would approve as she has cautioned me not to speak to strangers, but she is a nurse and always is helping others. I am sure she would want me to be helpful."

Lynn's heart and stomach had gone back into place and she felt safe and relieved, even though she had told a lie. She would go to the pastor at church tomorrow and confess.

The gentleman was tall and handsome, dressed in a fine suit. He held a briefcase in his hand, and his shoes were polished. He reached for Lynn's balloon free hand and turned in the opposite direction.

"I believe it is a couple of blocks in this direction. Do you concur?" he asked his newfound guide.

"Oh, yes. I do believe I was…. it is down this way, sir," Lynn said confidently. They walked across a busy intersection and headed toward a large building with a domed roof. Several flags on top of the dome waved occasionally as if to say, "This way, this way."

"Ethelyn Elizabeth! Oh, my God, Ethelyn!!" a familiar voice shouted a short distance behind them.

"Unhand my daughter, you terrible man!! Unhand her!! The voice grew louder and someone grabbed Lynn's hand from the gentleman's.

"How dare you!! I am reporting you to the police as soon as I can find one! You should be ashamed of yourself!"

"But, mother...." Lynn looked up into her mother's red face. Irene's hair, usually slicked back tightly in a bun, had fallen in ringlets against her moist red cheeks. "He was not taking me away. I had wandered too far .... I was looking for the trolley to see what the sched....Oh, really I had gotten lost watching the sad gorilla. Then I was pushed along by the crowd and this nice gentleman was just trying to help me find you." Lynn expounded, coming clean with the actual story.

Irene had bent down level with her daughter's eyes "Are you telling me the truth. This...this man....er....um gentleman was not kidnapping you?"

The gentleman with the ice blue eyes was watching Irene....all of Irene. He watched her auburn hair touching her flawless skin. The blush of her cheeks and the fire in her eyes, the rise and fall of her breast beneath her sparkling white blouse, the tiny waist and the long fingers holding tightly to her daughter's shoulders.

"I turned to find you after purchasing the tickets, and you were nowhere to be found. I stopped everyone in the area, but no one had seen you. I ran up and down the streets near the arena and there were so many people....I thought I d lost you forever! Then I saw the red balloon bobbing up and down about a block away. My heart leaped out of my chest. You don't know how frightened I was, Lynn... so frightened!" Irene hugged her smiling daughter as she had never hugged her before. A real dynamo of a hug! No stiffness. No hesitancy. A real hug!

She called me Lynn! Ethelyn mused as her small arms tightened around her mother's shoulders.

Irene stood holding Lynn's hand and looked at the "would be kidnapper" now turned hero. His eyes were compelling. They sparkled with confidence and kindness at the same time. The corners of his full lips turned into a pleasant smile beneath an ample dark mustache. He was gallantly handsome and dressed impeccably and richly. He put out his hand to hers and it was strong, lingering a little while after the handshake.

"I am so sorry if I caused you any more anguish than you were already experiencing. It must be unspeakably horrifying to find your child is missing. I can only imagine. Please accept my apologies, ma'am"

"Oh, my dear sir, it is I who should apologize. I was frantic, and when I saw you walking with my daughter, I lost my senses and assumed you were abducting her. You must think I am a demon for yelling at you," Irene cast her eyes down, her long lashes covering her eyes.

"Now that we have both done penance would you allow me to treat you two lovely ladies to some ice cream at the fountain across the way? I'm sure it is too late to attend this first showing of the circus, and the next show is not for an hour. It is very warm, and we all have had a rush of emotion, so please join me," the kind gentleman, rescuer, handsome man with ice blue eyes pleaded.

"Please, mother. Please. I will stay right with you every minute. You love ice cream, Mother, please?" Lynn begged hoping her mother would be lost in this moment of adulation for the remainder of the day.

"Very well. That is the least I can do to thank you for rescuing my daughter, sir"

"Call me Ben. 'Sir' sounds like you are addressing the teller at the bank. What may I call you both?"

"I am Irene Westphal and this is Ethelyn"

Irene felt a her heart skip a beat as the gentleman took her arm and guided her toward the Eighth Avenue Soda Shoppe.

A long white counter with red stools lined the east wall where people sat and starred into the huge mirror behind the counter. The walls were soft blue with windows all around the remaining walls, framing the buildings, like pictures in a gallery. The tinkle of fountain glasses and the sweet smell of scrumptious confections and creamy delights surrounded the customers as they became like children entering a magic kingdom. White wrought-iron chairs encircled small round tables covered with red and white checkered table cloths. The red balloon entered the doorway and bounced happily toward a table that overlooked a small garden planted in a small patch of earth near the cold asphalt below one of the windows. Daisies and petunias of gold and purple waved their perfume into the warm city air. Irene and their new found friend talked and talked as their ice cream sodas melted. Lynn was making slurping noises with her straw as she finished her strawberry soda and was eyeing her mother's untouched one. Irene pulled herself away from the conversation long enough to notice the slurping noises. She moved Lynn's empty glass and replaced it with her full one. Lynn was amazed, as she was seldom allowed to have more than one desert. Irene smiled at her in a way she had not seen before as she turned her attention back to Ben. Lynn finished her second soda and watched the clock on the wall as it passed the hour for the second showing of the circus. She kept still as she was content to watch her mother enjoying herself with this man who had rescued her.

There is always next year, she thought to herself.

The summer was hazy and drenched with the humidity so familiar to the East Coast. The parks were filled with ladies in creamy dresses fanning themselves and swatting the bees that hummed about their sweet perfume. Soft curls brushed their necks and tiny droplets of sweat sparkled in the sun glowing on their faces. Laughter floated in the air mixed with the shouts of children jumping into tiny puddles left by the early morning shower.

A lady with soft green eyes and a handsome gentleman with strong shoulders and a sureness in his step that let you know he had confidence in the path he had chosen in life strolled along a flowered path in Central Park, close to the lake that mirrored the big city. She wore a uniform, starched and shining white, covered with an apron of dark blue that outlined her full bosom and tiny waist. Her auburn hair was drawn back from her determined face and ringlets bounced around her cheeks as she laughed and starred coyly into the gentleman's ice blue eyes. He took her arm, gently guiding her toward a majestic oak tree close to the water's edge. Tiny ducklings turned in circles making ripples among the saw grass and lily pads. He spread his coat for her on the cool grass beneath the tree. The old tree had seen many a lover, business deal, lonely vagrant, argument, and parting over its many years. Its limbs seemed like arms embracing the human experience, both joyful and tragic. The lady sat lost in her thoughts, oblivious to the sounds around her. She knew in her heart that this was not where she should be, but it was where she needed to be right now. She closed her eyes and sighed, waiting for one of them to speak. Neither wanted to say what they knew they must say. Nor could they find the right words to express the many emotions rolling around in their minds and hearts. They eased themselves down on the makeshift blanket and, for a moment, held on to each other in poignant reverie. A small boy awakened them, looking for a lost ball hit beyond the foul line of the tree.

The gentleman held the lady's hand in his strong fingers. He traced the life line in her palm and drew it to his lips to breathe in her perfume this one last time. Two months since their chance meeting on the sidewalk near the circus had been filled with poetry, stolen walks in the park between the demands of the business world and the sorrow of the Bowery clinic. They had shared long talks about life's iniquities, a friendship blossoming like the seed of flower nurtured by a tender stolen kiss and the warmth of the excitement of fresh love. As it most certainly would grow to be much more than a friendship should they both continue to cultivate it, they knew it must end.

So it did under the embrace of the old oak tree in Central Park on a very hot day in August of 1923.

Almost eleven years later, Irene was laid beneath the cool grass on a hot summer day in July of 1934, in the midst of the Great Depression. She took with her the memory of that wonderful summer; a tiny locket from her sweet daughter, Ethelyn, and a love poem from Herman, her stern but loving husband. She left thousands of fevered foreheads cooled by her kind hand and babies nourished lovingly with the milk she brought to the clinic purchased with her own allowance. She walks through many parks with brave ladies dressed in white uniforms in their tireless struggle to heal the sick and weary.

Nancy never knew her grandmother, yet she felt a part of her from the stories her mother, Ethelyn, used to whisper late at night while they hid in a room from the ghosts that haunted them. Ethelyn used to tell Nancy she was so much like Irene –spirited and compulsive. Maybe Nancy did know her better than she ever could imagine.

The next several chapters describe Nancy's childhood. Those childhood moments, both tragic and joyful, evolve from the womb to the metamorphosis, the moment when she felt she could fill the holes within her inner self and become a person who mattered. That moment begins with a tragic event in her life. Though she sometimes resorted to dangerous and destructive actions to complete herself as a woman, they all sculpted the woman she could look at in the mirror each day and love.

Chapter 3

Soldiers

Sirens wailed like the mournful cry of a baby wolf that has lost its mother. Everything was dark except for an occasional beam from a flashlight as it danced back and forth, up and down outside the window searching wildly for -----something. Occasionally you could see the faces behind the lights, looking like masks eerily painted with the same solemn expressions. The lights ran in front of the men, whose fatigues and boots darted in and out of doorways and alleys playing the games of war, dancing to the music of the sirens and their boot-sounds on the pavement.

The couch was sculpted with mahogany and deep red velvet, hardly something one should be standing on. But when you are just three years old and infatuated with the scene outside the window that is the only way one can see---- standing on the furniture. Her mother held Nancy as she jumped up and down whenever she saw the lights dart past the window. It must have been a bay window as it seemed to be quite a distance from the couch and had windows that wrapped to each side of the main one. The child knew very little about anything in this world except that everyone had to be very quiet and not turn on the lights when the sirens wailed.

When Nancy told anyone that her first real action filled memory on this earth took place when she was barely three, they looked at her with that look that people get when they are trying to be polite and pretend they believe you but they most certainly do not.

Who cares? She said to herself. *I do remember that scene exactly*!

It was 1943 and the war was far away. Yet it seemed very near when the air raid sirens wailed, the lights went out, and faces were grim and eyes were hollow.

Life seemed to contradict the lessons they were learning in school and at home. Parents taught their children to tell the truth; work hard;

be kind to everyone, no matter what color they were nor what language they spoke; avoid fighting; study lessons before play; and respect authority. Yet what the children saw of the adult world - massacres of human beings because they were not "pure", gangsters cheating and injuring innocent people for their own profit, our own forms of prejudice against those who happened to be born with darker skin or were of the "weaker" gender, unions battling with employers---- was not at all what they were told. All of this gave them mixed messages. It wasn't the easiest of times for their parents and their friends. Many men had gone to war and either not returned or returned with masked faces and tortured souls. Some returned without limbs, others without hope.

There she was watching history run by the bay window with the velvet couch supporting her jumping up and down, and her mother's hand steadying her wiggles and giggles in the dark while the sirens wailed.

Nancy's mom, Ethelyn Elizabeth Westphal, was a soldier. She went to battle every day, though she had been raised to be proper, mindful of her place, demure, and reserved. She gave so much more to life than she ever took from it. No matter how difficult and painful life was she somehow found the humor in it and the joy.

Decades later, on May 11, 2006, Nancy would write this letter to her mother:

Dear Mom,

I was listening to the radio on the way home from a long day at work. A woman was telling the story of a time just after her mother had passed away when she and her sister were cleaning out cupboards in her mother's kitchen and she found an old measuring cup with most all of the red marks for measuring worn away. In that moment, days flashed through her mind – her mother giving advice that, at the time, seemed like she was giving orders. "Sit down and have some juice and a sandwich before going to that meeting." "Make sure you always wear clean underwear as you may be in an accident", and on, and on, and on...... Somehow, that advice always made things turn out better though it wasn't recognized as such at the time nor was it appreciated. Not even the unthinkable "thank you" was offered. Staring at that cup in that special moment when time stands still, all the cookies and pancakes baked with measures of ingredients from that cup, all those birthday cakes and formulas mixed with love and unselfish giving, poured from the corners of her heart. In that moment the sisters felt the special part of a mother no one can replace.

I remember how you taught me what silent courage was, how amazing a person can be and yet receive no applause. How unselfish you were when we had no money and you wore faded house dresses so we could go to school with a new outfit for the first day. How you never said an unkind word about anyone even when they hurt you. How you put aside your amazing musical gift to tie our shoes, wipe our noses, and protect us. Your sense of adventure and ability to look at life's humorous side, even when you were abused and degraded, gave us the tools to deal with life as it comes and manage to laugh a little.

I have an awful habit of driving a little too fast usually lost in thought and trying to go over in my mind what I forgot to do that day. I often laid my right hand on the car seat. Whenever you would ride with me you would put your warm hand on mine and quietly whisper, "Slow down, dear"----and I do, because I know you are there, watching over me. .

I miss your smiles, the elegance of your renditions of Mozart and Chopin, your scrumptious meat loaf, your sneaking a "smoke" in our tiny bathroom and trying to cover it up with a half a can of deodorant spray, your nylons rolled down to your ankles, the surprise trips in our old jalopy to amazing places after you pawned the projector to get money for gas! I miss your poems, your letters with writing all around the edges of the pages, your kindness, your patience, your love.

Most of all, I miss holding your warm hand in mine and not having to let go.

.

Chapter 4

Photographs-Pictures of Nancy
Three to Six Years

Her father sat in his chair with the throw covering the grease spots on the head rest. The newspaper slipped from his lap onto the floor as his head bobbed between sleep and awareness. His feet rubbed together restlessly, and toes would peek out through the holes in his socks. They lived in the three rooms over the photography/variety store on Main Street in the small town of Atlantic Highlands, New Jersey. As you came up the stairs from the store you entered the studio room that doubled as the living room. Large windows lined the south wall so that maximum light could enter the room for picture taking. A small cot was against the wall across from the windows. That was her father's bed. There were two dilapidated armchairs and a bench in the studio. On the East wall was a backdrop with a faded painting of a garden that once was beautiful. The kitchen held a small gas stove and an ice box with a drip pan that played marching music especially in the hot summer when the ice would melt much faster. A small table with three chairs purchased at an auction sat against the wall and another cot covered with a green army blanket sat adjacent to the table. That cot soon became her mother's bed when the crib was placed in the tiny bedroom. Nancy thought for a long time that all parents slept in different beds after they were finished having children. For a short time while Nancy slept in the same bed with her mother, her father would come into the room in the darkness and she would hear her mother say, "No Walter, you will wake the girls".

He would leave the room muttering "Jesus Christ" under his breath. Nancy wished she and Erin could make themselves invisible so their mom and dad could be together. Maybe dad wouldn't be so angry then.

The bathroom had a toilet with a broken seat that pinched your butt if you didn't sit on in just the right way. There was a small sink, but no shower or bathtub. On bath night, mom would heat up water on the stove, fill a washtub with the scalding water, mix it with cold water and sometimes a piece of ice from the ice box, and give Nancy and Erin a bath. Erin went first as she needed more assistance then Nancy. By the time Nancy bathed, the water was lukewarm. (As an adult, to this day she takes steaming hot showers and baths). Bath time was special. Mom would turn on the radio that sat on top of the ice box and tune it to "Sergeant Preston of the Yukon." Nancy envisioned herself riding the dogsled over the snowy trails of the Yukon along side the handsome man with the voice that always sounded like he had a cold. She would close her eyes as she waited for her turn in the tub and daydream that this man was her father, and they lived in a lovely house with flowers and a white picket fence…. only to be awakened from her trance with the cooling bath water Erin would flick her way.

The next room overlooked Main Street. With the windows opened you could hear so many different sounds. From the bar across the street garbled laughter of those that imbibed, the melancholy notes of the piano tinkling tunes about lost loves and passionate promises, the occasional brawl that had been taken outside--- all those sounds made their way into the apartment. Trains' forlorn whistles echoed in the night mixed with the loud blast of the horns on ships as they passed through the harbor bound for distant ports and exciting adventures. The bedroom had very little walking space, as it was filled with a double bed, a cedar chest piled high with clothes and blankets that didn't fit into the sole closet, a dresser and a crib.

The crib where Erin slept was both playpen and nest for the little one. That crib sat against a dresser with a dull mirror perched on top, leaning precariously against the water stained wall behind it. The double bed was crammed against the crib. You had to scoot the crib right up against the bed in order to get in any of the drawers of the dresser. Great planning had to occur in order to retrieve clothing from the dresser drawers, find a space to get dressed and to throw the covers on the bed in some fashion simulating bed making. All this had to be performed without waking anyone.

For several years, Erin had crying spells that would seemingly last for hours. Her "fits" would crescendo into breathless sobs, almost as though she would stop breathing at any moment. Often their father would stomp into the room and give the sobbing baby a "whack" on her little behind. She would gasp and whimper for a while, eventually falling asleep. Nancy would pretend to be asleep facing the wall so her father could not see her face, barely moving for fear his anger would turn toward her. Nancy would shake the crib during the fits hoping the shaking would shock her sister into silence. It only caused her to scream louder bringing the wrath sooner. There were times when Nancy would feel so sorry for her sister, especially when she would whimper in fear. She knew how that felt and would tiptoe quietly over the crib to lay her cool hand on her sister's damp curls and forehead. Where was mom? Why didn't she come in to soothe her child's pitiful tantrums? Why did she leave so often knowing he would turn his anger toward his children? Perhaps Erin sensed that her mother left when the beatings were too much for her, when her tolerance was spent. During the day Erin was a happy contented child. Nancy would make fun of the way she would crinkle up her pug nose and make bunny noises.

Nancy was often sick as a child. The pain of ear infections and tonsillitis was no stranger to her from about the age of three. The doctor advised Nancy's mother to bring her into his office to have her tonsils removed. Having worked some in health care, Ethelyn had seen some disasters evolve from office surgery so decided to take Nancy to the hospital near Long Branch. The hospital was located near enough to the amusement park that the music from the calliope on the merry-go-round could be heard in some of the rooms. Nancy loved carousels especially the ones with white horses all trimmed in gold and jewels. Her mother would hold her as she stretched her arm as far as she could to catch a brass ring, leaning dangerously far off the side of the horse in order to earn a free ride.

The hospital was white and clean. The nurses were white and clean. The doctors, the bed, the other patients were white and clean.

As if colors were an invite for bacteria, everything seemed to be white and clean. Miss Stark RN (Nancy thought it was "Miss Starch" as she crackled when she walked) must have liked sharing as she stated, "We will get ready for bed now. We will have our bath. We will drink all of our milk".

"We" had a hard time sleeping the night before the surgery. "Our" mother had gone home and "we" had been tucked in the clean white sheets for the night. Nancy crawled out of her clean white bed with the clean white sheets and moved cautiously toward the thin beam of light drawing a line on the floor from the nurses' station up her gown and outlining her inquisitive face. A nurse was bent over charts busily writing information about her patients. She wrote "sleeping" on Nancy's chart just as she heard a rustling sound coming from a short distance away from the desk. She stood up just in time to see a clean white starched gown disappear into the room across the way. The slap-slap of bare feet on the cool linoleum floor was also a dead give-away. Most of the nurses' patients on that unit couldn't run or even get out of bed if they had wanted to.

Nancy had dived into the bed and covered her head with the clean white sheet. The door made a creaking noise as it opened. Nancy was lifted out of bed wrapped in the sheets onto the lap of Nurse Starch.

"I know you are a little nervous about tomorrow and can't sleep. Does your mommy sing you to sleep? I always had a favorite song my mother would sing to me, especially when I was scared. Do you have a favorite? I may know it."

"Do you know the crocodile song? I love the crocodile song." Nancy whispered.

"I know that one! It's one of my favorites, too."

She sang the crocodile song softly, rocking Nancy back and forth as her eyes closed and she drifted off to sleep.

She sailed away on a happy summer's day
On the back of a crocodile
You see, said she, he's as tame as he can be
Go sailing down the Nile

As the lady waved good-bye
The crock winked his beady eye
And giving a sly little smile
At the end of the ride
The lady was inside
Of the smile on the crocodile!

Nancy fell asleep by the time the lady waved good-bye.

Everything sounded hollow and distant. She was flying on a magic carpet and stars twinkled around her as she was wheeled toward the operating room. Martians with their faces and heads covered in masks and hats lifted her onto a small table under a huge spotlight. She only heard a few of the words they said to her as a mask was placed over the lower part of her face. "Count backwards from ten," she heard several of the Martians say.

A sweet pungent odor filled her nostrils and lungs as the ether was dropped onto the mask.

10.....9......8.....6...no...7.....5....

Nancy awoke with a start. Her throat was aching, and she tried very hard not to swallow. Her lips were parched and she felt nauseated and dizzy. She saw her mother dozing in the chair across from her bed and wanted her in the worst way. When she tried to speak only a squeak came out.

I sound like those chicks in Nanny's coop, she said to herself. She dangled her legs over the bed and slowly rose on them, testing her ability to stand. She started to walk over to her mother when she caught a glimpse of herself in the small mirror on the wall over the sink.

She backtracked and looked straight into the mirror grasping the edges of the sink to steady herself.

Oh, my god! My hair is red! Carrot red! she screamed to herself. *Somebody dyed my hair when I was asleep in the operating room! It looks horrible! YUK!*

Ethelyn woke sensing someone moving about the room just in time to collect her daughter as she swooned and was about to crumple, new "hairdo" and all. Ethelyn got her back into bed and Nancy squeaked "My hair is red!" as Ethelyn attempted to fluff her pillow and ignore her daughter's pitiful squeaks.

"It goes really well with your freckles, Nan," Ethelyn tried to joke.

Nancy was having none of it. She wanted an answer and a solution right then and there. She didn't appreciate at all the smirk she noticed on her mom's face either. After her mother had left, reassured by the nurse that Nancy would probably sleep most of the day, Nancy had to get another look in the mirror hoping she would see her hair back to its normal strawberry blond. She was relieved that the door was closed to her room as she inched out of bed. It was a little better this time. Her legs didn't feel quite as wobbly. Grabbing hold of the sink once again to steady herself, she looked at the same image staring back at her as before. Carrot red hair stared back. Her lips were wrinkled and there was some dried blood in the corners. With her pale skin and dark circles under her eyes, she would have made a great character for the Halloween party at school.

Maybe I can wash it out, she thought as she bent down to wet a part of her long hair. Bending down pushed the acid in her empty stomach into her already burning throat and she let out a squeal as the burning acid attacked the operative site. Her nurse came running when she heard the screech. She found Nancy bent over the sink blood coming from her mouth and an awful hoarse retching sound. Her hair was wet and looked like it too was bleeding. The nurse rang the buzzer for assistance and soon Nancy found herself surrounded by nurses and aides moving her into the bed and ice packs wrapped around her aching throat. One of the nurses gave her an injection and she drifted off into a dream. She had a shiny new bicycle and everyone was happy. She and Erin and their mother had new, fashionable clothes, and her father was more than happy to give them anything they wanted without a moment of anger or violent rages.

A week after her first--- and she hoped, last-----trip to Memorial Hospital, she returned home. She was three pounds lighter, had carrot red hair, and a residual sore throat. She remembered the nurses in years to come. They were nice to her.

It's not easy being six years old. You have to go to school and sit at a desk, be quiet around adults, keep your dress down, and do more chores. If you are the oldest, you can't appear afraid of thunder or spiders, and you certainly should be able to walk across the street when the traffic light changes. That was six for most of us, but for Nancy there was more. Many of her nights were filled with screams, swearing and terrible fights. The thin walls of the apartment held demons that crawled out at night and sometimes even during the day. There always was that tension, that readiness for the scene to change from peaceful to a nightmare within seconds. Like a soldier awaiting the attack, the feeling becomes part of you if it occurs often enough. Anvils on your chest when you are any age are frightening but at six years old they are terrifying. It always seemed to be about money or "those damn kids". Nancy felt guilty and useless when she surmised she was the cause of all the bickering. Her mother felt guilty and useless and soon Erin would feel the same. The minutes ticking by on the clock can seem like hours. If you can't sleep you try to snuggle down under the covers and wrap the pillow around your head. You can fall into a world where life is sweet. A half dream, half real world of cozy bungalows, laughter, a playhouse with beautiful dolls, going to sleep at night feeling warm, secure and loved.

Something happens inside when you escape from the real world into an imaginary one. You never feel you belong to either world. You begin to punish yourself for your seeming inability to be fully responsible to the real world yet not able to fully escape to the imaginary one. A battle brews within you that may not be visible to those around you, even those closest to you. You can function, even do well, but the battle inside will win unless healthy ways to silence the siege are found. Compulsive disorders, drug and alcohol abuse, depression, aggression, withdrawal are responses both chemically and psychologically to this inner struggle.

It began when the seed was planted, a small defect in the balance of chemicals within the nervous system. The seed might never have germinated had it not been fertilized by constant fear and anxiety. Some seeds bear healthy fruit despite the lack of nourishment needed to grow. Others bear thorns and bristles daring anyone to come near or choose them for a bouquet. Then there are those who never get enough, the overachievers, the caretakers, the amoebic graspers for any morsel of recognition, love, applause they can obtain. Nancy chose the latter.

Chapter 5

Nanny

It was warmer than usual for July. One of those days when your clothes felt damp a few moments after you put them on and the bath you took did very little to ward off the sticky feeling on your skin from the humid, stuffy air. The bees lazily circled the forsythia bush, suckling the sweet nectar from the heart of the flowers. A skinny girl in plaid shorts and white T- shirt hastily detoured a fair distance from the bush rather than taking the path leading to the chicken coop overgrown with ivy and thistle branches at the back of her grandmother's lot. Freckles dotted the bridge of her slightly turned-up nose. Her hair was reddish gold and hung in loose curls around her slim shoulders. Her blue eyes squinted as the sun darted through the branches of the old oak tree that divided her grandmother's property from the Ashton's next door. A tire swing hung by a thick hemp rope from one of the huge tree branches, twisted ever so slightly whenever a brief breeze cut through the sweltering air. She was tempted by the creaking sound it made as it called her to jump on for a ride. She rubbed her nose nervously, warding off the urge to stray from her appointed destination.

Nanny (the only name she knew for her grandma) would surely notice her diversion from the chore she was assigned, so Nancy sighed, turned her eyes away from the swing, glanced toward the forsythia bush to make sure the bees had not spied her, then ran toward the old coop, lifted the latch from the door and tiptoed in to the darkness. Small rays of sunlight sifted through the spaces where the boards did not meet – just enough light to see the cubby holes that housed the fuzzy newborn chicks. The smell of the damp grass floor strewn with droppings, straw and left over feed combined with "hen sweat" was familiar and not particularly offensive to her. She loved the cooing and peeping sounds in the chicken coop. It seemed to calm the sadness and fear that welled up inside her. The fluffy chick down would only last for a few weeks and be shed to allow feathers to grow. She would be allowed to hold only the chicks that were not healthy enough to grow into chickens for the dinner table or hens to lay eggs for breakfast. Close to her chest she could feel their warm, soft bodies and sense their heartbeat tapping rapidly as if to say, "Save me, save me, save me."

She wanted to. Some part of her always wanted everything and everyone to be okay. The trouble was she already sensed in her limited seven years of experience that the world wasn't made that way.

There were two places where she felt safe to cry: the chicken coop and under the big credenza in Nanny's dining room. She would take this little plastic chicken she had gotten from her dad's store. You could blow on one end and its wings would flap out as it gave off the saddest whine, not at all like any chicken sound. She would listen expectedly for the creaking sound of the old front door and her parents' return. When they didn't come she would blow gently into the plastic chicken's behind. The bitter sweet whistle would bring tears to her eyes that Nanny would excuse (if she noticed Nancy scrunched under the credenza) prompted by the sadness in its sound. Nancy never cried while riding on the tire swing.

Nancy knew the rules. You didn't cry over spilled milk, you cleaned it up. You didn't cry over people that hurt your feelings, you smiled and moved on. You worked every day and kept a clean house, and you always said your prayers at night before climbing into bed. If you forgot, you must get out of bed, kneel down and tell God that you are sorry you forgot before asking his blessing. It always burned your eyes and dropped this lump in your throat when you held tears back. She wondered if you held them back too much if they would pour out of your ears.

It had been almost four months since her parents had walked away, suitcases in hand, from Nanny's immaculate little house. Nancy had stood halfway behind Nanny's housedress wanting so much to run up and grab her mother's warm hand and drag her back, or run away with her. She felt the butterflies racing around in her tummy and an awful urge to puke as she swallowed hard to gulp back the tears burning her eyes. It wasn't as though she hadn't awakened in the night many times to the sound of shouting and her mother's whimpering and cries for help. The past few nights were different as she sat, trying to be invisible, at the bottom of the attic stairs listening to the familiar battle. Words like "divorce", "leaving for good" and others that are too unkind to mention oozed up the stairs and pierced her racing heart.

Thus they had gone. No note scribbled in her mom's tiny script promising to return, No answer from Nanny when she would question where they had gone. No calls to see if she had died from a broken heart. Nothing was heard from them for those awful months. Nanny gave Erin and Nancy big wet kisses and made sure days were filled with chores and trips on a rusty bicycle over the hills to the grocery downtown. Erin was too young to do any long distance chores so she assisted with folding the laundry fresh off the clothesline and pushing the clothes through the wringer on the washing machine in Nanny's basement. Their treat was the sweet caramelized coffee mixed with carnation condensed milk that spilled over into the saucer from Nanny's strong Hungarian morning brew. Nancy and Erin learned that coffee wasn't coffee unless it was strong enough to chew. Nanny rarely was chosen over the years to make coffee for a group, as many would have palpitations and sleepless nights after drinking one of her staunch brews.

At least fifteen hours had passed, Nancy surmised in her analytic brain, before she was brave enough to peek out through a crack in the door of the coop to see if the bees had flown back to their hive. She acutely remembered being stung by one on the playground at school some weeks ago. The pain was much worse than the shots she got at the doctor's office. Sister Agnes had hiked up her habit, run over to Nancy, grabbed her arm and plopped a big blob of mud on the rapidly swelling wound. Nancy did not relish the thought of another attack. Anyway, there was no mud anywhere as it hadn't rained for weeks. Keeping one eye trained on the bush and the other on the hens clucking noisily around her ankles, she cautiously crept out of the coop, closing the door quickly and dropping the rusty metal latch into place so the hens wouldn't escape. She ran toward the back porch of

Nanny's house, stopping suddenly as the one eye that no longer had to watch her feathered friends spied three huge green apples lying on the ground near the tire swing.

Nanny won't miss me for a few minutes. Just enough time to scarf down those crunchy apples and swing a few times on that wonderful swing. She felt the smallest amount of guilt, as she was not totally following orders, but rationalization comes very early in life and she was sure that allowing the apples to rot on the ground would be worse than pure obedience.

Do you know how high you can go on a tire swing hanging from a giant oak tree? You start pumping your legs in the air if you don't have someone to push you from behind. You may have to pump for quite a while, leaning way back and letting your hair dangle in the air as you stare up at the blue sky between the branches. It takes work and coordination to get to the place where you feel your tummy tingle, the place where weightlessness occurs for a brief second. Past that point, if you can keep pumping, you could almost go over the branch----- almost except something called gravity causes the rope to snap you back. At that moment if you don't hold tight to the rope, you could fall. Trying to do this and eat a green apple while swinging and pumping your legs, hoping that Nanny won't notice your escapade, can wreak havoc later in the day. You may pay in more than one way for your transgressions. At times the tire will twirl you in several directions or never twirl at all. A phenomenon, she supposed.

Isn't it somewhat the way life is, riding on a tire swing?

"Nancy!! Nancy, where are you? Come in this house right now!!" Nanny hollered out the kitchen window that conveniently had an excellent view of the yard, the tire swing, the apple tree and one disobedient granddaughter.

Oh, dear ---I'm cooked! Just one more bite. Just one more pass on this swing. I'm in trouble, anyway, she mused as she allowed the swing to slow down just enough to be able to jump off. Of course, she landed on her hands and knees, scraping them against the arid ground and dead grass.

She tried brushing away the dirt from her hands, knees and blouse before facing her grandma's wrath.

Nanny had returned to stirring a gloriously delicious-smelling pot full of homemade chicken gumbo soup steaming on the old coal stove. Uncle Sid had remodeled the old kitchen with new cabinets, a Frigidaire to replace the ice box, a brand new gas stove, and even a new double porcelain sink. Despite the effort, Nanny had insisted she needed to keep her coal stove.

"Those new fangled stoves just don't turn things out right," she would complain. Nancy and Erin missed the ice box as they used to always get a ride around the block in the back of the ice delivery truck. The driver, Jimmie, would give them a big chunk of ice to lick. They would laugh as they peered through the clear ice as it melted down their arms. Everything looked distorted as they held it up to their eyes. People had tiny bean heads and long fat torsos similar to how people looked in those trick mirrors at the amusement park.

Nancy tiptoed into the kitchen stepping on every part of the floor that creaked. Nanny had eyes in back and on the sides of her head as well as in front, so it wouldn't have mattered if she was a mouse, she would have known someone was there. Nanny turned away from her pot. She was holding a big wooden ladle that dripped savory sauce back into the pot.

"You've been eating green apples again and swinging on that tree swing, haven't you?" Nanny's mouth puckered under her abundant nose. She didn't have any of her own teeth and only wore her dentures when she went out, so it appeared that she was scowling even when she wasn't.

Nancy's tummy rumbled as if to answer the question. "Yes, but......they were going to r..."

"I told you to go directly to the chicken house and take care of things, to come straight back here as I have some errands you need to run in town, didn't I?" Nanny scolded as she moved toward Nancy, who was shrinking into her dusty shoes. "You should always follow instructions, honey. It's for your own good."

"Yes, but the apples were going t-t-to...." Nancy stammered.

"No excuses! Go and wash up. I have a list of things I want you to get for me at the grocery store." Nanny ordered.

Nancy ran past her, but not fast enough to avoid the *whap* from the ladle on her dusty bottom as she exited.

"Make sure your sister is still in bed for her nap!"

Those apples would have rotted and, anyhow, I did my chores. What's wrong with playing after your work is done?! Phooey! Mom wouldn't care. She turned on the water really hot and washed off the dirt she had gathered. She had little scrapes on her knees so she washed them extra good. She looked in the medicine cabinet for the ointment Nanny always put on her hurts but couldn't find any. There was a jar of Vicks Vaporub that kind of looked like Vaseline she saw Nanny using on her hands when they were chapped. *That'll work*, she thought, the nurse was already brewing inside her. After smearing a small amount on both injured knees the full effect of the medicine caught fire in the tiny wounds and she almost screeched. Thank God she held it back except for a sharp intake of breath and watering of her mouth as the vapors reached her blue eyes and they began to tear. She would have wakened her sister and been in more trouble than she already was. She tried in vain to wipe it off with the wash rag, but it had slithered into the wounds. Forgetting that she had the ointment on her hands, she tried to wipe away the tears, getting some of the menthol goo in her eyes. That did it. She yelped like a new puppy. Erin began to cry, and Nanny came bounding up the stairs to see what had happened. Hardly able to see, Nancy stumbled over the little stool in front of the sink, landing spread eagle on the floor in front of her glaring grandma's seasoned slippers.

"For heaven's sake! What are you doing with the Vicks? Nan...are you okay?"

Nanny bent down and gathered the disheveled, tearing, vapor-ized child; soaked the washcloth in cold water and held it over her eyes. Sitting at the top of the stairs, she held her and gave her one of her wettest kisses. Erin came down the stairs from their bedroom in the attic and nestled in Nanny's lap. She made little smacking noises, sniffling occasionally. Nanny rocked back and forth with them. For those few moments they felt loved and protected. Nancy might have goofed up, but she knew Nanny loved her. Nancy touched her sister's damp curls, twirling them around her finger.

"You are good girls, Nanny's good girls. Mom and dad will be home soon. Don't you worry. Families stick together no matter what."

Nanny, Violet Akerly, knew about family hardships. Born the elder of three sisters in northern Hungary, she toiled on the hillsides planting and praying for good weather to nurture tiny seeds into the vegetables that could be sold in the markets of the towns and cities nearby. Her family was a part of a community of gypsies that moved with the seasons higher into the hills or deeper into the valleys depending on the weather and the condition of the soil. They carried their tools, sparse furnishings and brightly colored clothes and food in large wagons drawn by horses or oxen. They would sing, argue, laugh and pray loudly, wave their arms demonstratively when expounding on politics or, for that matter, any type of conversation. They worked from sunrise to sunset and made love flamboyantly. Their passion for life came from their appreciation of the land and the forces of nature. Violet came to America with her father when she was a teenager. Her two sisters arrived two years later accompanied by their Aunt. Their mother had died in her early fifties from a lung disorder.

Nancy was assigned the task of brushing both of Nanny's sisters' long, thick hair when they visited. Aunt Miranda and Aunt Isabel lived with Nanny for a few months a year and visited often. Nancy remembered their talking in a language very unlike the one she had learned and smelling lavender as she brushed carefully so that she would not hurt them when she encountered a tangle.

Nanny had married an Irishman named Rayner Fitzpatrick. Rayner was, from what the family can gather, a lover of the brew and the ladies. They managed to brew a son together and then Mr. Fitzpatrick enlisted in the service where he died without ever seeing their son. Nanny spoke very little about him. It's always amazing to think that families have ghosts that weave a thread of fabric into their lives, but are lost in the design of the patchwork quilt representing their time on this earth. Walter was Mr. Fitzpatrick's son and Nancy and Erin's father. Not only did he eliminate (not legally) the Fitzpatrick surname, but he never spoke of the man. Nanny married again to Mr. Ball (Nancy much preferred the last name Fitzpatrick!), an Englishman with whom she had a boy and a girl. Mr. Ball passed away when the three children were young and Violet did what she knew best ----worked. She was the housekeeper, cook, social administrator for a wealthy family living along the river in the town adjacent to Atlantic Highlands. Nancy remembered seeing their huge pantry – almost as big as her grandmother's entire kitchen and the crystal chandelier in the dining room that sparkled like the jewelry in the window of a store she once saw in New York.

Nanny worked until she died from a stroke one day as she was preparing one of her elaborate meals for a dinner party for her employers. While she lived she smoked long cigarettes, closing her eyes and tipping her head back as she inhaled the smoke encircling her. She had a cough medicine bottle in her apron pocket filled with a dark brown potion called "Tom Collins", and she swore by it to calm her smoker's cough. She cooked fabulous Hungarian dishes filled with butter and white sauce on her beloved coal stove. She went without her teeth a good share of the time and gave warm, wet, hard kisses on your cheek just when you needed them the most.

Garfield Avenue was a pleasant street lined with large oak trees pushing the sidewalk up with their hungry roots, causing them to be somewhat of a challenge to anyone riding a bicycle. The houses on the east side of the street were on a small hill that overlooked the houses on the west side of the street. Those houses on the hill were supported by a stone wall about six feet high. Ivy grew from the top of the wall and caressed the stone like a veil. Turning left from Nanny's house you could coast part of the way past the public school and then begin the long climb up to Mount Avenue, the steepest hill in town. There were less difficult, but less challenging, ways to get to town. To Nancy and many other children (and adults yearning to be children) the ride up was so very worth the thrill of coasting down Mount Avenue without having to pedal one little bit. By the time you reached Main Street you had caught your breath and this feeling of excitement and accomplishment made you want to hug everyone you encountered in town.

Nancy's skinny legs cramped about halfway up the hill. She stopped and allowed the pain to subside before attacking the rest of the climb. Looking down she could see the school playground and made a promise to herself to stop on her way back to see if any of her friends were there. Finally, a few more cramps later, she reached the top. Her mother's two aunts lived a few houses to her right. Her aunt Lizzie owned a cruller and custard shop in town and she decided that another stop on her trip would be at the Cruller Corner. If she swept the floor for Aunt Lizzie she would be rewarded with a warm sugary cruller and a small cone filled with icy lemon custard.

Just the thought of it brought memories of the scrumptious twisted crullers baking in the ovens as it called to passers-by, "You can't resist, you *must* come in and buy a dozen!"

One deep breath, one last check to make sure your brakes still worked. One little push, and suddenly you were a giant bird, free and beautiful. You were a princess on a magic carpet or the only passenger in the front seat of the roller coaster at Asbury Park. It took barely sixty seconds to realize you were at the bottom. Your legs felt like mush and you might have gathered a few pieces of gravel hitching a ride in your teeth on the way down, but it was the most amazing feeling! Nancy did not want that feeling to stop. In fact, she searched for it all her life.

She rode her bike to the grocery store, up and down the gentle hills of Atlantic Highlands. She stopped for one-half a minute to smell the popcorn as the aroma wafted from the movie house. She stood on tiptoes to try to peak at the screen through the open door. The screen was where wars were fought, where lovers kissed, and lovers parted, where ladies in colorful costumes danced on giant stages. She pedaled past the drugstore where she would often go alone during lunch hour at school to order a coca cola and a ham sandwich on white bread. In the window of the drugstore there were two large glass apothecary jars representing the pharmacist's profession. One jar held green colored water and the other held red. She could see the people moving past reflected in the colors, making the world around her seem distant and she was the center of that world.

The small town in New Jersey was quaint and peaceful, as many towns were along the bay. A mixture of tourists, commuters, and townspeople it draped itself from the highland bay hills down to the waterfront lined with yachts, sailboats and fishing cruisers. Many members of the Mafia and wealthy businessmen from New York City across the bay kept their yachts hidden in the harbor away from the scrutinizing eyes of the law and to avoid taxes. Nancy and Erin loved to tiptoe along the docks, peering into the cabins of the huge Chris-Crafts as the passengers and owners partied with sparkling champagne, the ladies decked in diamonds and wearing silk and satin gowns, the men with jeweled fingers and dapper tuxedos.

The hills above the town were dotted with mansions and middle class homes, some with pillars supporting elaborately decorated balconies, and others with glass porches allowing a view of the bay and, on a clear day, the outline of the big city. Two main streets contained most of the hustle and bustle in the town as one led to two bars near the waterfront and the other to the railway station. Trains journeyed to New York City and all the small towns in between several times a day. For fifty-five cents you could ride to the city or any town on the way and back to Atlantic Highlands.

Ethelyn loved to travel. She would plan entire day excursions to the "Big Apple" by train or by the Sandy Hook boat. There were often groups of men on the train with massive jeweled rings on their fingers, finely tailored suits and overcoats and hats pulled down to shade their eyes. Nancy had learned to play pinochle and poker from Nanny and these men often would be playing among themselves and murmuring obscenities as they slammed a losing hand on the table. One of the men who rode frequently on the train had dark brown piercing eyes and a black mustache that hid his mouth when he talked. He spied Nancy and Erin craning their necks as they peered around their seats to catch a glimpse of these mysterious gentlemen. Ethelyn would look up from her paper or back from staring at the scenery rushing by the train windows and motion the girls to stop spying. They were mesmerized by the jewelry and the card game. "Mr. Mustache" caught them spying and stood up from his seat, walking unsteadily toward them. The train moving on the track caused one to walk funny – like a robot, flat footed, and hanging on to seats as you tried to keep your balance. The only person who the motion of the train did not seem to bother was the conductor who walked just fine, didn't need to hold on to anything, and could balance tickets and a ticket punch in his hand as well.

"We're in trouble now!" Nancy whispered to her sister who continued to stare at the stranger approaching them.

They almost jumped out of their seats when he stood in front of them. "Hi young ladies, I'm Jimmy, Jimmy the...., Jimmy. Hello, ma'am" he said in the deepest voice either of them had ever heard. Ethelyn, all five foot one of her, stood between the stranger and the two girls who were melting into the scratchy wool seats.

" Ma'am, I have noticed you and your two sweet girls riding the trains. The girls seemed pretty interested in our card game and I know it is a boring ride for kids, so thought I would come over and introduce myself and invite the girls to come over and watch, if it is ok with you, ma'am." He smiled under his mustache and you could see one gold tooth amongst his pearly whites. He smelled like their grandfather's cherry cigar and mint aftershave cologne. His eyes were kind, and he looked right into theirs as they stared at his perfectly manicured hands bejeweled with diamonds, and sparkling gold.

"I'm not sure you want them in your way, sir. They are very inquisitive and are constantly asking questions," Ethelyn explained.

"That's good. Kids should ask questions. That's how you learn. I would be honored if you would let them watch for a little while. I have two girls about their ages...," he looked away, sadness running across his face for just a moment, "....and I don't get to see them very much."

Always a sap for a sad story Ethelyn gave in as the game was just two seats away from where they were sitting.

"Thanks," he put his hand to the brim of his hat and bowed his head slightly.

"Your mom says you can come and watch the card game for a while. Would you like that?" he bent over the girls while reaching into the pocket of his overcoat. "Do you like Life Savers?"

What kid doesn't like candy? Lynn thought.

"Yes!" the two girls chimed in together.

Every ride on the train after that Nancy and Erin would eat Life Savers from the handsome man with the mustache, watch the card game, and listen to the mutterings of the losers. Nancy even got to play a few hands and won once! They probably let her win, but she didn't care. She won enough to take several more rides on the train to the "Big Apple". The winnings also helped pay for one trip with their car on the Sandy Hook ferry that left from Atlantic Highlands to New York City.

Another adventure was to drive up the hill to Lookout Point. The drive would begin in town and weave through hairpin curves lined with moss and sassafras trees. Tiny rivulets of icy water trickled from hidden springs in the rocks along the way. The air would change during the climb from the fishy smell of the harbor to the perfume from wildflowers. Occasionally, a spooked skunk would fire a pungent retort at the disturbing parties.

A restaurant and small petting zoo with a goat, two ducks and a beaver greeted visitors at the top of the hill. Most came to look through the viewers for five cents at the panorama of the peaceful harbor to the outline of the ever growing metropolis that seemed close enough to touch. Nancy loved to go on these trips with her mother. She missed her so.

One trip in September, the men were not on the train. The seats were filled with other passengers. They never saw Jimmy the....again. The papers told a story about a shooting in a barber shop in Brooklyn. "Jimmy the Knife" was one of the victims. Nancy always wondered. She never saw a knife just life savers and a big grin with a gold tooth.

She missed him. She hated the feeling of loss. She had promised herself that if her mother would ever die she would die too. Her mother had a way of injecting happy moments into bad ones, taking the sting away from wounds. Nancy knew she would never be able to live without her. That was a promise she made often as she rode her bike through town, up and down the hills, to the harbor, running errands like a good little girl.

Nancy had to peddle really fast on the return trip, because the green apples had reached her intestines and were about to explode. Nature called----no, it yelled! She headed toward the bushes near the school playground, dropped her bike hastily on the ground, and relieved her tsunami in the greenery. Looking around to see if anyone had noticed her plight, she was relieved (literally!) to see there was no one in sight. The she looked toward her bicycle lying on its side. Next to It was the bag of freshly ground coffee and other items she had been directed to pick up from the grocery store. Her relief lasted a millisecond as she noticed the coffee bag had broken, and coffee was fertilizing the moisture-deprived ground.

I'm really in trouble this time. Wait till Nanny finds out the coffee is wasted. I'm such a jerk! I'll never eat green apples again, at least not three of them!

She had to face the music. Not the kind her mother played, either.

She knew her grandmother would say, "What! You what? You can't do a simple job! You are to go to your room and stay there every day after chores until school starts, young lady! Get upstairs now!"

Those were the kind and loving words she knew she would hear when she limped home to face her grandmother's hot Hungarian temper.

Grounded meant something very different back then. After breakfast and chores, unless she was sent on a mission to town, which Nancy doubted she'd be entrusted with any time soon, she was banned to the bedroom in the attic. There was one small window through which only hot air seemed to flow. The attic had at one time been converted into an apartment for Nanny's son, Alfred and his wife, Betty. Uncle Sid had put up drywall and wallpaper, separated an area for a small kitchenette, and put in plumbing. A window fan had been removed from the only window, as Nanny thought the girls would poke their fingers into the sharp blades.

While the neighborhood kids and her sister played outside in a sprinkler and an old tub of water to cool down, Nancy would lie on the linoleum floor to escape the sweltering heat of the attic, covering her ears so as not to hear their giggles. She didn't know which was worse----the heat, the self-reprimand, or the sound of every one having fun in these last days of summer right below her prison window.

Nancy had come to realize that feeling good----feeling free----always came with a price tag. Nanny was right when she said that life was just that way. You had to pay one way or the other, on earth or in the hereafter, for the good things in life. It was sometimes with money but more often with acts, hard work, doing penance---or with loss.

Chapter 6

A Little Bit About Ethelyn and Walter

When Irene died, Lynn was just nineteen years old. Lynn's father could not bring himself out of the loss and pulled away from life, burying himself even deeper in his work. Lynn packed up her few belongings, made sure the furniture was safe in storage, kissed her father on the top of his head and made her way to New York City. She had graduated from Julliard, gave piano lessons and played in a few concert halls including one fabulous evening at Carnegie Hall. She needed to earn a little more than the few dollars giving lessons brought her so she answered an ad for a governess for a wealthy Jewish family who lived in the top apartment at Central Park West, a very upscale predecessor of condos in a more lucrative part of the city adjacent to Central Park.

Rachael Filmore was twelve years old. She was at that age when you are never quite sure who you will be when you awaken each day. Sometimes a child, other times a young adult, always a surprise to those around you and to herself as well. The youngest of two daughters, she had become an albatross in her parents' very busy social and business lives. They loved her, but this late-in-life child did not fit well into the schedule filled with dinner parties, business trips, and other social events. Their older daughter, Melanie, had graduated from Harvard with a law degree and was climbing the rungs to partnership in one of her father's law firms. This left Rachael confused and lonely. In came Ethelyn, the white-knight governess from New Jersey to the rescue! But Rachael was determined to knock the white knight off her horse and show her just *who* was in charge.

When she wasn't pouring oatmeal into the window plants, frightening Ethelyn to death in the middle of the night standing over her with a mask of white cold cream and groggily eyes surrounded in black make up, pushing Ethelyn into the bathtub as she drew the water for Rachael's bath, hiding under the clothes racks in the department store, and emptying all the dishes from the cupboard and filling them with food and other amenities, Rachael was a wonderful child. Extremely bright, with a beautiful soprano voice, long auburn curls and soft chestnut eyes, she soon learned that it took way too much effort to rattle this lady from New Jersey. She pretended, at first, not to love the gentle touch of her governess's fingers on the keys of their grand piano, but gave in gradually to even sing along with the music that filled the immense living room of their suite. Rachael's desperate need for attention and love---- played out in raucous acts of mischief---- lessened during the year Ethelyn was with her. When Ethelyn's father became ill, though, the white-knight had to ride away.

Many years later, during a trip to New York, Lynn happened to run into Rachael and was praised for her perseverance during those years. Rachael was married and had chosen a career as a social worker (of all things!) She thanked Ethelyn for her patience and caring.

There are people who enter your life, sometimes for a lifetime, and sometimes for just a few moments. Somehow they change you. Somehow they change you. They may push you on your ride on that swing, they may join you as you move in all directions, they may take your place for a while, or they may encourage you to try to go over the branch, pick you up when you fall or snap you back on the path on which you started. All of them help to make you what you are. Good, bad, indifferent –they impact your life.

Walter, Nancy and Erin's father, was forced to leave high school in his junior year to go to work full-time to help his mother and her two other children.. He worked as an apprentice to Mr. Bond in his photography shop. He felt cheated as he wanted to attend college and leave this boring town for the "good life". The anger built up inside him but had to be buried as his responsibilities took precedence over feelings. One of his talents was a photographic memory. He could scan a page of print for a short period of time and remember every detail with complete recall. He took over the business and became the town photographer. He was the tall, handsome young man with a good head for figures and a talented eye for photography, especially figures on two shapely legs. At weddings, he became a familiar part of the festivities. His ability to capture expressions and emotions in the photographs he took was so unlike the man who colored his inner portrait with black emotions. Few saw the part of him he hid so well. He was the kind and helpful usher at church, the patient and tolerant photographer when the fretful child did not hold still for the snap of the camera, the fellow who could sweep his dance partner off her feet with grace and agility.

That's who Ethelyn saw when she left New York and came to live with her Aunts Lizzie and Laura on Mount Avenue. She worked at Aunt Lizzie's cruller shop, taught piano and played at weddings, funerals, bar mitzvah's, and birthdays. It was at one of these weddings she met Walter, and he swept her off her feet. They were married. They lived above the small photography store on Main Street in the small town they both knew they would leave someday. The apartment had a studio room that sort of doubled as a living room, a kitchen, a bathroom without a tub or shower, and one bedroom with one small closet. The back yard was on a small hill overgrown with weeds and debris from the businesses on either side. To enter, you had to go through the front entrance to the novelty portion of the store. Long counters in the middle aisles held yo-yo's, trinkets, doodads, small tools – sort of a retail garage sale. A long glass counter held samples of photographs her father had taken and some of the old portraits that the former owner had produced. There was a back entrance to the apartment but the stairs were outside and in need of repair.

Ethelyn could have been wearing a beautiful flowing gown awaiting her turn at the grand piano sitting in the middle of the great Carnegie Hall stage. She could have waited for the hush of the audience as she lifted her hands with perfectly manicured fingernails perched to caress the keys that brought concertos to life and tears to the listener.

Perhaps Walter could have discovered the torment in his soul that erupted into violent outbursts and uncontrollable rage and put it to rest. His talents were imprisoned by that anger – a sickness, an albatross. They never reached the heights they could have because of that terrible defect in his character, in his soul. There was a hint of softness there that was overshadowed by the storms. Not until several years before his death did the embers cease to burn leaving a quiet and petulant man.

Both Ethelyn and Walter had disappeared. Were they together? The store had been sold. Walter was working for the government as a photographer. Nancy knew a part of her missed him, too. Not the angry him, but the "him" that he showed the rest of the world. The "him" that came out on rare occasions at home. The "him" that gave them the small smattering of hope that he could change.

September came. Nancy and Erin had listened with anxious ears when Nanny read the letter that their parents were coming home soon. There was a crack in Nanny's voice when she read "soon". Not knowing what "soon" meant in the grand scheme of things caused a lump to develop in her throat, and she had to take a swig of cough medicine from the flask in her apron pocket.

Chapter 7

St. Agnes, Early School Years

Nancy was attending Catholic school with the first grade at age six. She continued to attend St. Agnes Catholic School when she was living with her grandmother until her parents returned and the family moved to Red Bank, New Jersey. The Catholic School was managed by Franciscan nuns. There habits were traditional and non-revealing. The only skin that dared to show itself was that on their hands and their faces. In summer, the habits were a glistening white with a gold rope tied around their waste and a rosary dangling from a tab on the belt. When Fall arrived, the black-trimmed-in-white habits came out of the cedar chests, were hung on the clothes line to air in an the crisp breeze. Glancing toward the convent, it looked like ghosts frolicking as the habits waved their capes and skirts in a dance with the wind.

Rigidly adherent to their vows, the nuns managed the students with the Ten Commandments and strict rules of conduct and obedience. Whenever the students stood, walked, knelt, or prayed it was done in straight, silent, line. A line to walk to the lunchroom, a line to receive your small carton of milk, a line to go to the church each morning for Mass, a line to go to the chalk board and practice your writing with your right hand only (those who had a tendency to be left handed were quickly reprimanded and taught to write, no matter how awkwardly, with their right hand. Nancy always wondered if that somehow confused those poor souls with a dominant right brain.) There were very strict rules on what behavior was tolerated and what wasn't. Mother Superior dealt out the punishments, which consisted of five whacks on the back of your hands with a ruler, or sitting in the corner of the room while the other classmates giggled. You didn't dare to look around, or the punishment would extend into the next day.

Lines can have their advantages. Standing behind Clarence Baker was not too shabby. He had blonde hair with three or four hairs that stood up at the top of his head, like Alfalfa's in a new movie she had seen. Nancy waited hopefully during every journey the "line" took each day for him to turn around and smile at her. Not that she thought he could be interested in a skinny, very shy classmate, but just the thought that he might be made her heart do funny little dances. One day on the walk from the school to the church it happened. The heat of the blood rushing to her face and turning her cheeks the deepest apple red made her feel like she actually stood out in the line of kids in front and behind her. The line halted for viewing, so that the sisters could make sure no one was talking or goofing around, and Clarence turned ever so slightly. When their eyes met, little prickly feelings ran up Nancy's back and her heart beat so loudly she could hear it pounding in her ears.

"Mr. Baker, Miss Ball ----step out of the line...... immediately!!" Sister Eva commanded as she marched toward them arms folded across the white starched bib covering her chest and her headdress billowing out like bat wings from her ruddy face.

Clarence Baker turned his head forward and Nancy folded her hands in front of her and cast her eyes downward in the most saintly pose she could imagine. They both stepped out of the line as ordered and proceeded to listen to the lecture on following orders in the name of the Lord that they had heard so often given to others in the line. They knew the rest of the kids in the line were enjoying the moment way too much, but stood as still as possible, praying for a rapid end to the scene rather than forgiveness for their transgression.

After school Clarence invited Nancy over to sit on the porch of his beautiful Tudor home. With the permission of her Nanny and his mother, they sat on the porch swing, drank Kool-Aid, and discussed their views on lines, nuns, and the trials of seven year.... almost eight year olds. You never forget that first love. Lines do have their advantages!

When Monsignor Perry passed away all the children in St. Agnes' school were marched (in lines of course) into the rectory parlor where he lay in a gold inlaid casket among an array of flowers, incense and rosaries donated in homage by parishioners and nuns. Nancy often fainted when incense reached her nostrils, so she tried to hold her breath or just breathe through her mouth so she wouldn't melt away on the parlor floor, especially in front of Clarence and her dead friend. Candles played with the shadows of the nuns standing along the walls of the parlor murmuring prayers as their fingers passed from one bead to another on their rosaries. Nancy and the other children were led to the side of a big mahogany box with gold angels and railings that sat in the middle of the room. Keeping her head bowed as Sister Agnew had instructed, Nancy lifted her eyes to peer between her bangs that had grown way too long. She caught her breath before a sound pushed its way forward. There was Monsignor Perry, the smiling, portly, kind man with a bull dog face and kitten eyes that would always cover Nancy's head with his massive hand as he gave the blessing every Wednesday to each of the children. His eyes were closed and there was the hint of a smile on his pale face. Dressed in the white garment used only for special holy days, his great hands folded over a glittering crystal rosary, he appeared to be sleeping. The hands were stone-like, chiseled from the rock of religious sanctity that called a man to priesthood. They did not move from bead to bead as they had done for so many years, praying for the lost, the dead and the end to the evils of this earth.

Is this what *dead* meant? Everyone comes in lines to look at you lying in a box with candles flickering and smell of incense and gladiolas all around? She wanted to close her eyes and pray like the other children seemed to be doing, but she couldn't. Nancy could only stare unblinkingly at the wooden hands that had so often comforted her and blessed her. She stared at his hands clasped over his big belly and at the twist of a smile on his face. Then she saw it. He was breathing. She knew he was! The white garment covering him and his hands moved up and down – ever so slightly, but they moved. She should tell them. She didn't know much about death, but she knew they would put the box in the ground, cover it with dirt, and put cement cross with his name on it to mark the grave. Her mouth was dry, like eating corn flakes without milk. She felt she would choke if she tried to swallow. She blinked her eyes as they began filling with tears. His belly was still moving and his face was grinning as if to say, "See, Nancy, I haven't left you. I am playing this trick, but I will get out of this box and come pat you on the head."

She wanted to shout to everyone that he was still there. Suddenly, before she could get enough courage to shout, hands were on her shoulders and she was turned to face Sister Agnew. Nancy looked around the incensed, flowered, candlelit parlor and found she was alone. The other sisters, her classmates, everyone had left. She grabbed Sister Agnew's hand and sputtered, "He's alive! I saw him breathe! Just watch, Sister, please. You've got to tell someone.....you have got to!"

Sister Agnew looked at Nancy blandly, "Now, Nancy, you know that is just your imagination. It is something you are wishing to be true. So much so you imagine it is true. Monsignor, bless him," she made the sign of the cross, "is with God at last. That is where we all hope to be in the end."

This psychology did not work at all.

"But, I saw him breathe! Oh, Sister, please, please tell someone before...."

"Nancy, we will have no more of that." She guided the shaking child out of the parlor.

No use. She just could pray that someone would see him breathing or he would give up the ruse and climb out of the box. She was too small and not brave enough to fight a battle she surely could not win alone. It was misting now, and the cool air cleared the remnants of incense and gladiola smell from her senses. It did not make her feel any less frightened and helpless. She walked slightly ahead of Sister Agnew and ran up the steps of the school.

The halls were dark and empty. There were no sounds of children reciting their prayers or giggles coming from the washrooms. Nancy's small footsteps echoed off the dark green cement walls. She almost turned and ran back outside to hide against Sister's woolen skirt, but she hesitated listening for "Eddie sounds" coming from the basement. A broom sweeping, "Peg of My Heart" whistled between crooked teeth, "goddamn" uttered when he dropped something---- any sign of

Eddie would be so welcome at this moment. He would listen. Eddie always listened. He always had called her Na-a-a-a-ncy from the day he first met her two years ago. She figured he was pretty old, as he shuffled when he walked and had wrinkles around his eyes. He smoked cigarettes, and his breath smelled like her mother's---- a combination of Pall Mall's and mints. Eddie had taught her that running away never solved anything.

"No matter what, Nancy, you plant your feet, take a deep breath and walk right into it----whatever it is. Runnin' away just makes you out of breath, and whatever you run from usually comes chasin' you," he would tell her while he held her on his knee.

When her neighbor had dropped her off in front of St. Agnes Catholic School that first day of school, she stood frozen outside the steps leading up to two massive doors. The other children, some hesitant, others barreling ahead, were being swallowed up as they went through the opening. Soon she was the only one standing there as the two massive doors closed and the bell rang announcing the start of classes.

I could have just run up the steps with the other kids----now I'm late. What a nerd! I guess I'll just run and hide in the park across the street until lunchtime and try to sneak in when the bell rings, she mused. She knew her father and Nanny would be mad if she walked home. Maybe she could pick up some coffee at the grocery to calm her, but there would be nothing she could buy to calm her father. That plan "B" wouldn't have worked, as she had no money and wasn't too sure which way to go to Nanny's house. She only knew the way home to the store on Main Street.

She turned to scope out the park but ran right into a red flannel shirt with tobacco stains on the front. Afraid that it might be the police, she closed her eyes and tried very hard to think of an excuse for being outside the school on a school day.

"It's ok, I'm not gonna hurt ya, little lady," a gravely voice said. "What's yer name, ma'am. You can open yer eyes. I'm ugly, but not *that* ugly!"

"N-n-n aaancy," she stammered as she looked into a weathered face with kind, deep set brown eyes framed by fuzzy black eyebrows.

"Naaaaancy---Naaaaancy-----Hmmm, sounds French to me," as he drawled her name several times. He had knelt down beside her and had not touched her. He blocked her view of the escape route to the park with a large muscular frame and long arms. An old railroad engineer's cap reigned in an uncontrolled mass of grey black curls sprouting from his quite large head.

Nancy decided not to try to run past the big man. There also was something in those eyes that made her trust him, even like him--- right off.

"I've missed the last bell to go into school and just cannot go in there late, or go home 'cause Nanny will be really mad ---even if I brought her coffee. I don't have any money, so that wouldn't do. I thought of maybe running to the park and hiding until the lunch bell rang and going into class then. They probably will notice though.... so I was just deciding what to do when you were here," she told him.

"Well, now, that is quite a plan comin' from a little squirt like you!" he chuckled. "My name is Eddie, n' I'm the janitor here at St. Agnes. It's a pleasure to be meetin you, Naaaaancy. How's about I take ya in to Sister Angela. She's the first grade teacher and is a real sweetheart. I'm sure she'll understand that you all were sort of skeered on yer first day."

"Oh, I wasn't "skeered," she mimicked "just confused ---a little" she retorted.

"Well then, Naaaaaancy, let's go in. Ya ain't missed too much 'cept mornin' prayers"

She took his large calloused hand and walked with liver legs up the steps through the massive doors and into the dimly lit hallway. They turned to the left down a small hallway toward a door with a picture of baby Jesus petting a lamb. Eddie squeezed her tiny hand as he explained her plight to Sister Angela.

Sister Angela was two heads shorter than Eddie, laughed often, and loved to play baseball with her habit skirt hiked up between her legs and tucked into her belt like trousers. She was strict, but in a gentle, fair way. She took Nancy and guided her to her seat in the front row, shushing the titters from the other members of the class.

"This is Nancy. She was a little late due to things she could not control. So we will catch her up on what we have missed so far. Anyone want to volunteer to tell Nancy about our class?"she asked, grinned slyly.

Nancy waved to Eddie as he exited the classroom, thanking Sister Angela and tipping his tattered railroad cap. Eddie became her best friend the short time she was a student in St. Agnes. She confided her fears and her pain, her joys and her hopes to him. He always listened and let her know that no matter what life threw your way you made the best of it.

She had to get help for the Monsignor and she knew she could count on Eddie.

Filtering up from his basement room, Nancy could hear Eddie humming his favorite tune. There was a dim light that crept up to the landing from the partially open doorway to the room where he slept and ate and read and dreamed. Nancy ran toward the light and almost knocked him over as she grabbed him and buried her head in his flannel shirt.

"Their going to put him in the dirt in that awful box and he is still *alive---I saw him breathing and he is not dead!"* she blubbered through her tears.

"Naaaaaancy! What in God's name 'r ya talkin' about! Who's alive …or daid…or what?" as he pealed her away from the stranglehold on his shirt.

"His hands, their like figure eights… they moved…his belly moved and he was smiling, I swear…not supposed to swear… I'm sure!" She looked up at him as he sat down on the bed to get on her level.

"Okay, okay 'r you talkin' about the priest…the monsignor?"

"Yes, yes. You have got to stop them, and he has just got to stop pretending he's dead!" she implored.

"I know all the kids were paraded in front of the casket today by the sisters. Didn't think that was such a good idea but ya gotta see dead people sometime, so I guess it was okay. Let's go see him now and make sure things are what ya say ya saw 'n I'll take care of it.

That ok with you little one?"

Nancy didn't really relish the thought of seeing Monsignor again, no matter what the state of his existence might be, but she dreaded the thought of leaving him to be put away if he was still alive. So they walked hand in hand from the school to the rectory and stepped ever so quietly into the parlor. The candles were burning and they had dripped rivers of white pearl wax along their sides and into the brass candle holders. The incense had retired and allowed the full fragrance of the flowers to fill the room.

At first, she could not see the priest, as the satin liner of the casket was level with his body. Their shadows crept along the wall ahead of them as the candles painted their ghostlike apparitions. He was breathing. She heard him breathing! She grabbed Eddie's hand as tightly as she could as they moved closer to the casket. Her heart pounded in her chest louder than it had ever pounded for Clarence Baker. Her legs were rubber, and she had a terrible urge to pee.

Eddie guided her so close to the casket she could touch the cold gold handles. Her hand left a print on the gold, a telltale sign she hoped would not get her into trouble she was sure she already was in.

"Let me hold yer hand and we will say good-bye to him the way he used to say hello to you all," Eddie whispered softly into Nancy's ear.

"I…I…I can hear breathing…his breathing," Nancy insisted.

"That is the fan in the corner of the room, silly," Eddie smiled. "C'mere, honey, let's say good-bye"

He took her wet, trembling hand in his big calloused one and laid it on the stone cold hands wrapped in the glittering crystal rosary. There was no movement, none at all. She glanced at Monsignor Perry's face with the tiniest hint of a smile, and she felt sad but not as frightened as before.

"Good-bye Father, thank you," she whispered as a tear fell onto his white holiday garment.

They walked to the door as the fan blew kisses of gladiolas, roses, and lavender after them.

As Eddie was taking her to her Nanny's house in his rickety green truck with faded letters spelling "Perzynski's Plumbing" on the side, she felt like she had grown older somehow during that long, long day.

"Ya know, it's alright to miss someone and cry fer them, donchya? I remember when my mama died, I wouldn't believe it. I kept tellin' myself she was away on a visit. For two months I did that 'til my daddy finally packed away the last of her things, and I knew she weren't comin' back. I cried all night 'til my pillow was soakin' wet." Eddie reminisced.

Eddie never did tell her who Perzynski was. Maybe it was his last name. She never did know his last name, but she never forgot him. Through all the years that followed, the memory of the kind janitor with the tobacco stained shirt, enormous hands, and tattered railroad cap was tucked in a corner of Nancy's heart.

Nancy and Erin were being molded in these first seven years by the rocky relationship of their parents, the stability of their grandmother and the fear of abandonment that haunted them. They began to take on roles to cope with the insecurity. Nancy became the caretaker, the performer who took on the role she felt she must play to be loved and valued. Her sister, Erin, quietly watched the world spin around her, people come and go in her life building the tolerant and patient, frugal and practical, apologetic and strong woman she would become.

Erin expressed the inner peace she sought in her paintings and drawings. She was able to see colors and shapes in her mind and transpose them onto a canvas with clarity and artistic magnificence. So different from her sisters, she decided to deal with life in an orderly, quiet fashion much different from the chaos of their lives growing up. Nancy always wished she could manage things as well as Erin, but Nancy seemed to be uncomfortable with calm seas. Erin always appeared "together" despite the tragic moments in her life. She calmly dealt with them and never seemed to spin out of control nor need crutches to lean on. All three sisters became caretakers, insatiable caretakers. There are several roles that people assume when they are abused or grow up in turmoil. Some become aggressive and defiant. Others become withdrawn so they are not noticed. They retreat from society and human contact for fear of injury, abandonment, or disappointment. Then there are the caretakers; the ones that put everyone else ahead of themselves either from feelings of undeserved self satisfaction or from a need to be loved and depended upon. The problems arise when the poor self image cannot be made whole and the need for recognition can never be satisfied.

Alice, the youngest sister, became pregnant in college from a fellow student who never acknowledged either she or the child existed. Ali and her baby moved in with her parents when they lived in Iowa. Shana, Alice's daughter, was a bright light in the lives of Ethelyn and Walter. Perhaps she was one of those angels God sends to squelch the demons and breathe happiness into a relationship. Though Walter's temper and rage continued, it was demonstrated less often and not with its usual vehemence. Both Nancy's sisters were blessed with intelligence and resourcefulness. They all had unimaginable tragedies in their lives. Somehow having to cope with fear, loss, pain and rejection, the crevices in their injured self image were filled with courage, kindness, and a willingness to face challenges and forgive.

Chapter 8

Surprises

Nancy rode back to her grandmother's house, up Mount Avenue to the top. Her calves cramped, and she had to stop for a moment before descending down Gregory Avenue to Garfield. The wind grabbed the scent of the damaged coffee in her bicycle basket as she rounded the corner. Nancy rehearsed the reasons she would give for taking so long and why the coffee was half gone. At first she thought she must be seeing things. There was her parent's car parked in front of Nanny's house. Her heart was already pounding from the ride and it grew loudly in her ears as she approached 53 Garfield Avenue. Leaping off the bike almost before it had completely stopped, she grabbed the injured bag of coffee and bolted through the front door into the living room. Her mother was sitting on the big overstuffed couch , Erin was sitting on her mother's lap curled up like a kitten. Dad was reading the newspaper, sitting in Nanny's favorite lounge chair with the flowered coverlet draped over it to protect the deep green velvet upholstery. Nancy attacked them both with ferocious hugs and kisses, almost knocking her mother off the couch.

"Mom, Dad, I'm so happy you are home. I missed you so much! I tried to be very good and run errands for Nanny …and not eat too many green apples….and I've seven new marbles…. Father Perry died. I thought he was still alive! I got stung by a bee…and there was a boy in my class named Clarence ……and….."

The half filled bag of coffee dropped to the floor and for a moment the comforting smell of coffee beans being ground at the A&P filled the room.

"Slow down Nancy. We missed you too. We are so sorry ---we went away to try to sort things out and make things better for you and Erin. " Her mom's voice cracked a little as she looked over at her husband who had placed the newspaper between his face and her glance.

Ethelyn watched him drop the paper on the floor and pull the handkerchief from his slightly frayed pocket. He blew his nose loudly, sounding much like a bull preparing for a charge, then pushed it back into the pocket, leaving a part of it protruding.

"Your mother thinks she needs more time away to herself so you and Erin will be staying here with Nanny for a while longer until *she* decides to come home." His *"she"* reference to her mother was sneering and impersonal. It could have been *"it"* for all the humanness it represented. They all seemed to be a nuisance... a piece of furniture to be easily discarded.

"It has nothing and everything to do with you girls." her mom pleaded. "I need to be able to sort things out, and I can't do it here."

"Don't go, please don't go, Mommy!" Nancy's eyes filled with tears as she looked from one parent to the other. "I will be good. I won't crab about anything. I can help more around the house. I'll clean the ice box and take out the garbage. Anything! Please, please don't leave again!!" Her nose was running and she wanted to run out to the chicken coop and hold a warm fuzzy chick to her aching chest and belly.

"Stop crying! It's just for a little while. I'll be here." Walter announced. "Nanny will be here. We can go down to the docks and peek in the boat windows. Mommy will hurry....won't you?"

Erin looked up at her mother with wide innocent brown eyes. Always the practical one, she seemed to stay neutral in the worst of moments even at age three and one-half.

Walter got up from the chair, allowing the flowered coverlet to fall onto the floor. He looked at the three of them with a mixture of sadness and scorn, picked up the newspaper and placed it on the end table near the chair. He stepped over the flowered coverlet leaving it in a heap on the floor, walked out the front door to the car, slammed the car door and screeched the tires as the old DeSoto sped down Garfield Avenue toward town.

"Your father has headaches and doesn't know what he is doing sometimes, but he loves you both," Unable to look either girl in the eye, Ethelyn coughed and lit a cigarette.

She walked over to the discarded coverlet, picked it up and tenderly draped it over the chair. Her hands gripped the arms of that chair, and her head bent for just a second. Ethelyn turned and smiled at her two little girls. She took a long drag on the cigarette and started to walk toward the kitchen. She took the sweeper out of the closet and swept up the spilled coffee.

Nanny came from the kitchen into the living room to see what the noise was about. She had been preparing a "welcome home" dinner on her faithful coal stove

"Was there another fight? Where did he go? Can't you two work things out? These poor kids are so confused." Nanny spouted. She grabbed for the cough medicine in her apron pocket while feigning a hacking that would have won an Academy award. "He'll be back for dinner. He loves paprikas." She turned and headed back toward the kitchen blowing her sizable Hungarian nose on the hanky in her apron pocket.

Walter returned for *paprikas*. Dinner was silent and strained. Nancy could hardly eat much of the creamy dumplings and tender chicken basted in real butter and peppered with real Hungarian ground paprika. She sat between her mother and father, a place she took much more often than she should have. She became the rescuer during the battles, the deterrent, and the decoy. Rage is blinding. Anyone in its path will fall prey, even if it's not the intended prey.

Ethelyn left a note on the kitchen table the next morning. She had gone to San Francisco to stay with her cousin. She promised to return soon.

Letters came from San Francisco. They consisted of Ethelyn's tiny script, using every bit of paper, the words circling round the edges. The pages were numbered one on the first page, three on the next page, number two on the third page, page four on the back of the first page, and so on. They were folded around pictures of an enormous bridge, fog lifting off the bay to reveal the hills dotted with buildings sculpted from the ashes of an earthquake, sailboats bowing their billowing sheets into the wind as they traversed the harbor, and restaurants covered with posters of succulent seafood, oriental cuisine, and thick rich coffee.

Days came, days went. There wasn't a day that the girls did not think of their mother.. They missed the adventures they had with their mother. They missed the smell of camphor and cigarettes, the warmth of her hand, her fingers caressing the white and black keys of the old upright piano. They had some good times with their father— visiting the Sea Scout captain in his old wooden boat; eating sardine and mayonnaise sandwiches on hot dog buns while he told stories of rescues and sea storms; standing very still in the darkroom with its orange light making everything look like an eerie movie while Walter dipped special photograph paper in several containers filled with solutions that smelled like vinegar. Each time he moved the paper from one tray to another, a picture would magically appear until just the correct blend of white, black and muted gray was present and finally hung on a clothesline in the room to dry. When tears made there way from her tummy to the corners of her eyes, Nancy would swallow them back and hide under Nanny's credenza, blowing softly on her plastic chicken. The wings would spread as the air lifted them, and the forlorn squawk would last just a second. Somehow, it allowed the warm tears to trickle down her freckled cheeks at the same time she giggled at the silly look on the chicken's face as its eyes crossed at the same time it squawked.

I'll bet no one knows you can laugh and cry at the same time, she mused.

That year was long and lonely. Summer was plucked away by an early frost that dragged the colors of fall from the trees in a matter of weeks. Nancy returned to school. The nun's prayed, she prayed, Eddie prayed. Her hair turned a dark reddish brown. Erin lost two teeth which made her look even more like a rabbit. Nanny cooked and cleaned for the Pillsburys and gave big wet kisses. Walter was rarely home. If not taking photographs, he was at the Fire Department or at the Sea Scouts. He never mentioned their mother nor did he seem too interested in Nancy or Erin except for the few occasions he allowed them to accompany him.

Winter blew in off the Bay with a foot of snow that year. It frosted the houses like cupcakes sprinkled with strings of colored lights and holly. The air filled with the aroma of turkeys roasting in the ovens, sweet cinnamon tea, and warm apple pies. Sledding down Mount Avenue far surpassed the trip on a bicycle. Dozens of children, teens, and even adults bundled up in snowsuits, mittens and scarves dragged their sleds up the hill on Sundays after church to brave the challenge of the slippery snow covered slalom. Most all the businesses closed on Sundays, so there was less traffic, pedestrian and otherwise, to impede the sleds that made it all the way to Main Street. A little Vaseline rubbed on the runners of a sled added a little more excitement to the ride. Like Olympic champions the brave hearts would lovingly prepare their equipment--- covering the runners with goo, testing the strength and agility of the steering rope, and smoothing the snow at the starting line so the take off would be pristine. Some of the boys would even attempt to stand on their sleds during the ride to show off for the giggling girls. Most would topple early in the decline, but someone would be this week's hero, hanging on till the very end.

A couple of deep, deep breaths, a tiny moment when she remembered the story about her Uncle whose steering rope had caught under the rail of his sled as he stood proudly racing down the ice-covered snow. The crowd at the top and others speeding alongside him drew a frightened breath as he flew off the sled crashing head first into one of the big oak trees lining the street. His lifeless body lay covered with uprooted snow at the bas of the tree, and blood trickled onto the white snow from somewhere near his head. He was alive, but not conscious. His nose and right eye had taken the worst of the blow leaving a face that looked like those she had seen on the fighters in the boxing ring. After several weeks of recuperation, begging for his mother's permission, he trudged up the hill with his newly painted sled as if to let the hill know it could not defeat him. He didn't stand up to show off this time, but the crowd cheered as he mounted his vehicle and swooped down Mount Avenue all the way to Main Street.

Spring bought more letters, more promises and lots of rain. The east coast, well known for hurricanes invading its shores, was preparing for a fierce storm brewing about thirty miles off the South Carolina coast. Eloise danced in frantic circles gaining momentum and force with each rotation. She moved in dervish like madness demonically dancing toward the shore. Sid and Walter pulled the storm shutters from their resting place beside the windows of Nanny's house. The entire town became a bustle of ritualistic preparations for the onslaught as it had done for many years. There was no panic in the exercise, just a calm camaraderie among folks that had weathered many storms, both personal and environmental. The children loved the storms. Schools were closed candles and fireplaces glowed in the darkness of the boarded houses. Pets, adults, and children huddled together on the first floor, bedded down wherever they could with fluffy comforters and warm blankets. Emergency supply bags were filled with canteens of water, juice, and coffee, fruit, candy bars, and non-perishables. Boats were secured to pilings and docks, and potential missiles such as signs, flagpoles, and mailboxes were removed or secured as best they could be. The daily routines continued but with a sense of readiness and expectation charging the air.

On Friday after school, Nancy was walking Bugsy, Uncle Sid's cocker spaniel and Nancy's best animal friend. Bugsy was more or less walking Nancy rounding the block a fair distance from Nanny's house in a determined path toward the home of that adorable girl poodle Bugsy had his eye on for this mating season. Nancy strained to hold on to the leash as the pooch tugged away anxiously toward his goal. She loved to stop near the big oak trees lining the streets, bending down to peer into the velvety moss carpet surrounding the trees, imagining tiny fairy princesses flitting about in the rich green forest. The sky eerily began to darken and there was a sudden stillness pierced by a musty odor as the air grew cool and damp. Bugsy began to whimper sounding a bit like Erin when she wanted something she couldn't have. In the distance there was a moaning sound that was all too familiar to even the smallest of residents. Nancy turned and started running alongside the dog that was panting beside her. As she turned the corner onto Garfield Ave. she could hear her grandmother yelling her name from the front of the house. The moan had grown closer accompanied by the town horn atop the firehouse blasting its warning message. The rain came in sheets mixed with a wind that started high in the treetops and worked its way down to the rooftops picking off shingles and siding along its journey. Just as the moan became a howl the drenched eight year old and dripping, glassy eyed cocker spaniel dove through the front door into the safety of the living room. The winds had reached one hundred miles per hour. A crackling message reported over the radio sitting in its prescribed position on the dining room table reported the storm's progress. Eloise had decided to waltz up the coast toward New York after ravaging the Carolinas leaving destroyed buildings, homes and bridges in her path. Moving at record speeds of seventy miles per hour she could attack with little warning gaining momentum as she plotted a course toward the "Big Apple". Skyscrapers are horrifically vulnerable and difficult to protect. Thousands of windows and their sheer height made them auspicious targets for storms and other attacks, both natural and man made.

Inside Nanny's house candles projected flickering shadows of the humans moving about the downstairs rooms. The adults played pinochle and poker drank rich Hungarian wine and beer, smoked cigarettes and cigars, laughed at old jokes, ignored the kids playing board games in their assigned post in the living room, and collapsed on couches, cots, or portions of the floor intermittently. No one ventured upstairs even if they heard limbs or other paraphernalia pounding the roof and even entering the rooms. The old house trembled and creaked, but held its own during the three days of pounding.

Uncle Sid was the first to brave opening the front door. He met with branches resting against the small porch that had been totally destroyed. Portions of some of the homes that were on the small hill across from Nanny's were missing. Electric wires ripped from poles snapped and sparked as they played hopscotch among the debris. The sun peeked through the parting clouds as if to enhance the visibility of the disaster. The air smelled of smoke and the pungent odor of ozone, reminders of the bigness of those things we cannot control at all.

"Guess I'll be doin' a little fixin' up again," Sid mumbled as he surveyed the damages. People began to peek out from whatever was left of their houses and silently sort through the debris for personal belongings, the injured and the dead. Thousands of people died or were injured all up and down the east coast. Tears were shed, funerals were attended, broken bones were mended, towns were rebuilt and life went on. Neighbors helped neighbors, strangers helped strangers to rebuild, repair, and move past the pain. The unspoken lesson that one could survive any storm as long as you had help in the aftermath became a part of Nancy's and Erin's being.

Hot humid days once again, the cricket sounds and bees humming about the forsythia. Watching the new yachts and fishing boats move lazily in and out of the harbor, eating sardines covered with mayonnaise on hot dog buns in the look out tower with a toothless, white bearded old sea captain, memories of trips in the old DeSoto up the hill to the overlook with their mother, running errands, savoring letters with Ethelyn's tiny handwriting. The tire swing stood idle more of the time as Nancy traded the excitement of nearly touching the branches of the old tree for the tingles in her shoulders whenever the handsome boy from her class asked to walk her home. She was finding boys to be difficult to understand and extremely fickle. Some days she despised them while other days she longed for the slightest bit of attention from them.

Back then one of the treasures kids flaunted was "cleary" marbles---the ones that you could see through with tiny air bubbles floating in a sea of blue, green, or no color at all. The giant ones, about the size of a jawbreaker were few and far between, cost far more than the bag of regulars, and were hidden in their own special place until that moment when a daredevil shooter was willing to risk one of his or hers to entice someone's prize possession out of its hiding place. After two months of fierce competition at summer playground camp, Nancy finally had won enough of the beautiful, clear bolsters to fill the felt bag Nanny gave her that had come with the new bottle of "cough medicine" she bought each month.

It had rained cats and dogs in the morning. Nancy always wondered when she would witness "raining cats and dogs." Deep in her psyche she knew that truly never really happened, but she liked to hold on to the magic, like Santa, the Easter Bunny, and fairy princesses in the moss grass. After the third trip to the grocery, pharmacy, and five-and-dime, a peek at the Tarzan movie through the slightly parted curtains of the movie theater, Nancy calculated she had about fifteen minutes extra time before Nanny would be pacing back and forth across her small, newly remodeled front porch puffing on her cigarette, stewing over the tardy errand girl. She turned her trusted old bicycle toward the muddy playground to see if anyone she knew was jumping puddles or shooting a few rounds of marbles (which would be really difficult in the wet sand). As she approached the school, she heard the dreaded growl of Johnny Blackwell spouting off his usual obscenities.

"Goddamn! That was my play! What the hell were you thinkin'?" he erupted.

Johnny's father had left home a year ago after beating his kids and their mother, leaving them destitute, angry and depressed. His mother worked at the town laundromat six days a week trying to feed her five children. Unable to make it on a measly two dollars an hour, she entertained the men folk of the town in the sleazy motel just off the highway leading to the Highlands. The church women of the town ignored her, the men pretended not to know her at all, and her kids were openly disrespectful. Nancy felt sad for her when she passed her or saw her in one of the stores. She had been pretty at one time with deep brown eyes that had sparkled with anticipation at the high school graduation but now mirrored the hopelessness inside her tiny frame. The product of his environment, Johnny was always in trouble, always angry or sarcastic, and always ready for a fight. When Nancy saw who it was she ran back toward her bicycle, her bag of precious bolsters knocking against her thin hips as she stumbled toward a fast escape.

"I aint got any more marbles because of you scum! But I see where I can get some" he snarled.

Billy Jackson and Terry Straight just sat there mesmerized by his evil stare spit spraying from his rotting teeth. They slowly turned to watch Nancy barreling across Mr.Gable's perfect lawn. All five-feet–ten and one-hundred-and-ten pounds of the ten-year- old monster had leaped up and was running after her. Billy and Terry were supposedly

Nancy's friends but the testosterone of the hunter took precedence over the friendship thing and they began rooting for their new found commander.

"Yeth, get 'er Johnny. I hear the has a bag of clearieth!" Billy lisped

"Hey, Nancy, want to play some games?" Terry sneered though his voice cracked a little.

Everything seemed to be happening in slow motion. Nancy's feet felt as though she was wearing lead boots. Her bladder was full, and she tightened her buttocks praying that the usual incontinence she experienced when she was frightened would back off –not here--- not now! Almost within reach of her bike, she suddenly felt a cold bricklike object hit the side of her head. Mud covered her eyes as she fell onto the ground. Hands grabbed her arms and legs and dragged her across the sidewalk, scraping her exposed back on the concrete. Her eyes burned and her heart was pounding in her chest and her ears. She felt wet grass grabbing at her arms and face and heard the hideous laughter of her attackers. Hands ripped at her blouse and she felt the bag of marbles sliding from her belt as that too was torn away from her waist.

"Hey, Johnny, let's get out of here…w..w..we got the marbles, leave her be!" one of the boys yelled.

"Oh, no we're not done here..ha..ha.. yer jest a hor like all girls. I know how to treat a hor!" His voice was deep and sinister. Nancy thought she was about to die. She really did. She tried to remember the Hail Mary, but her head was throbbing and the cruller she had eaten from Aunt Lizzie's mixed with stomach acid was rising up into her throat. Just as she felt she was going to hurl, a mouth covered hers and a slimy tongue slithered like a snake into her mouth. The smell was putrid and it made her retch. Hands grabbed at her chest and hair and pulled at her slacks, groping wildly. The weight of his body collapsed on top of her as the air was forced from her lungs. Vomit ejected from her mouth into his and he cursed her as he struck the side of her face with his muddy hand.

"Jesus!! You bit…!" Johnny never finished. She couldn't see or feel or think. She heard feet running and fading away from her.

She lay there trembling and retching. Tears burned through her mud caked eyes. Strong arms gently pulled her from the wet grass and mud and a handkerchief began to clear the mud, tears and spit from her face.

A soft, deep voice said, "It's going to be okay, they're gone. Don't be afraid."

She could not see who it was, but the voice sounded familiar and the handkerchief she held in her trembling hand smelled like....like incense.

"You will be all right. Just sit here and close your eyes for a minute." He was buttoning the two buttons left on her blouse and brushing some of the clogs of mud off her pants. He held her gently and stroked her disheveled hair.

"Who are you?" she stammered. "I know you, don't I? Thank you, oh thank you....I was so scared. He was going to kill me," she sobbed. A cool hand lay against her throbbing cheek.

He did not answer her. "I have to go now, little one. You get on that bicycle and peddle has hard as you can to your Nanny's house. Tell her and your dad what those boys did, and God will take care of you and them."

He was gone. A shadow of a man whisked past Nancy's mud and tear filled eyes. That was all. There was only one person who had ever called her "little one" and he was with the angels. Fear scattered the wondering. Fear that Johnny and his two puppets would return to finish her off. Every part of her ached and her head was a pounding drum as she stumbled to her bicycle, pointed it toward Garfield Avenue as the sun dipped through the clouds making sparkling patterns on the wet pavement.

Nancy went home. Her father was at work. Nanny was preparing a buffet for the weekend gala at the Pillsbury mansion. Nanny had taken Erin with her to work. Nancy felt like every step she took was in slow motion after she dismounted her bicycle and deposited it in its place next to the porch. She felt the same as she always felt after a beating.... numb, emotionless, and frozen. Bugsy greeted her with a wagging tail and a bath of wet kisses. Pets seem to sense when you need them the most or when there is something wrong with those who feed and nurture them. Nancy knelt down and buried her mud caked face into his soft fur. Tears would not come. Nothing inside her would rise to the surface of her consciousness. She knew the eruption of fear, pain, and nausea would eventually overcome the numbness. She knew she would have to push it down and cover it with other more acceptable responses. She took her muddy shoes and torn clothes and put them in a paper bag, climbed the stairs to the bathroom, turned on the water until steam rose and covered the mirror. She did not want to look at herself. She just wanted to take the brush used to scrub the tub and scour away that day. She wanted it to slither down the drain and be forgotten. She buried her clothes and shoes in a deep hole she dug with ferocity behind the chicken coop. When her father and grandmother arrived home she was sitting on the tire swing as it twirled ever so slightly in the evening breeze. Green apples lay on the ground around her untouched.

Johnny never returned to school. Nancy heard that the family had left town. Ther other boys acted as if nothing had happened. Nancy wondered how they could pass by her in the halls and sit in class with her knowing God knew what they had done.

Their mother came home, gave them both a restrained hug, thanked Nanny for caring for them, packed their few belongings and they all moved to a small rented apartment on the other side of town many blocks away. The house did not have an apple tree or a tire swing. . It was as if nothing had changed. The battles continued. The beatings happened less often, but with no less ferocity. Nancy and Erin would walk to their grandmother's house as often as they could. There was a breath of security and peace there. They rode double on the tire swing holding tightly to one another. They visited the chicken coop and held the tiny chicks close to their hearts humming softly in concert with their tiny peeps and the cooing of the doves who often rented a space in the coop.

Chapter 9

Red Bank

The little town was bordered by the serpentine Navasink River. They had moved again. One of the twelve moves their family had made in the years since Nancy was a baby and Erin had arrived. Nancy was eight and Erin was four when the family settled in Red Bank. The name Red Bank was well deserved because of the reddish-brown clay banks that rose gently from the river's edge. Most of the clay was covered with sod grass as though the townspeople had wanted to hide the virgin soil. Wealthy businessmen and even wealthier men in the "protection" business built beautiful homes overlooking the river and on the gentle hills surrounding the main business section of town.

Nancy and her family lived in an apartment (or two-family unit, as they are called today) right on the river. It was one of the nicest apartments or rented houses they'd occupied, and it seemed like it was a time of mostly good memories for them. The girls shared the huge dormer bedroom on the third floor at the end of a winding staircase that led to the main portion of their apartment. The living room was also large (at least in her eight year old memory) and there were windows all around. Her very best friend, Catherine, lived on a houseboat right next to their apartment.

Isn't a houseboat just about the most exciting place to live, except for the fairy princess house! Nancy had thought.

From their back yard (really, it was the owner's back yard) they could see Catherine's faded blue houseboat, the Molly Pitcher Hotel, the bend in the River and the docks where the rich kept their yachts. If you looked hard enough, you could see steeples of the churches and the top of the Bank of New Jersey peeking over the treetops. .

The girls' bedroom was so awesome! Erin and Nancy had room for their dolls, two single beds that didn't match, two dressers, that also didn't match, and the old cedar chest their mother had inherited from her mother. The floor was linoleum with designs of checker boards, chess boards, Parcheesi boards, racing tracks – all kinds of games impregnated in the linoleum squares. They had enormous fun in that room. Pretending that it was their private apartment, they shared many moments of childhood fun on the floor of their very own room.

They weren't sure to this day where Mom and Dad slept. Nancy recalled a room across from theirs that always seemed dark and spooky. She knew that many nights she would sit on the top stair with her book of the moment (she was voracious reader) with a flashlight reading as fast as she could while listening for her dad's footsteps at the bottom of the staircase. The staircase wound its way up to a landing and then turned toward their bedroom so she would have just enough time to dash into bed and feign sleeping when she would hear her dad yell, "Ball, you better be in bed up there – if I find you up you know what's going to happen!" Maybe now that she was older and looked back he was warning her and really knew that she was reading. He was as voracious a reader as she. He had a photographic memory – appropriate, since he was a photographer. She remembered him watching a ballgame on TV years later (when they had a TV) next to a stack of ten or more paperbacks that he had read in a very short period of time– westerns mostly, listening to a different ballgame on the radio and supposedly sleeping in the chair. If anyone dared to switch off either the radio or the TV he would be out of his chair in a shot. He knew every ball player's number, average, and the score of both games plus who had just gotten the last run or error. Did he fall short of his potential in such a way that he was angry with himself? How sad!

One of the girls' fondest memories was walking along the bank of the river up to the privacy gates that surrounded the Molly Pitcher Hotel like a fortress. The hotel was an elegant Virginia-plantation-style with immaculate white pillars adorning a massive porch and patio. They would creep along the old red brick walls and peer into the corners of windows just to get a glimpse of the ballroom that covered almost one-third of the front part of the hotel. Crystal chandeliers hung like tiers of diamonds from a ceiling with gold-trimmed panes.

The ballroom floor seemed to be a pool of green marble that mirrored the glitter from the electric candles on the chandelier. Hunter-green velvet draped the tall windows that surrounded the room. One could only imaging ladies in their flowing gowns floating about the room in the arms of handsome gentleman sporting their finest tuxedos and white gloves. It was more than once that they were chased by a caretaker, maid, or attendant from their stakeout on the porch.

Nancy's third grade class painted a picture of the Molly Pitcher Hotel on the back wall of Mrs. Dern's classroom. . Nancy would smile as she painted the windows looking into the ballroom as though she was the only eight-year-old who had stolen her way along the massive porch and starred into those windows in wonder.

She and Erin had received a doll house for Christmas the year of Nancy's ninth birthday. They would play for hours sitting on the living room floor with the family of plastic dolls that had come with the house. The father doll had black hair and wore blue suit coat, white shirt and tie, and brown pants. The mother doll was always smiling. She had blond hair and wore a rose colored dress that flared a little at the bottom as if she was always standing in a gentle breeze. The children could have been twins. They looked about ten or eleven years old and very much the same features as the mom and pop dolls. The boy wore a white tee shirt and blue pants and the girl wore a yellow shirt and blue skirt. There also was a little plastic baby sporting only a plastic diaper. She (or he) fit very well in the depression in the crib residing in the upstairs nursery. Erin and Nancy would make sure that all the plastic furniture - it even had patio furniture and a patio- was in its proper place. They would take the plastic baby in the plastic carriage for walks to the amusement park. It is amazing how very much like a Ferris wheel an overturned tricycle can look! The dolls would take turns riding on the pedals of the makeshift ride as they turned the wheel ever so slowly and screamed for the plastic passengers when the wheel would leave the pedal at the very top - rocking precariously (just to make it more like the real thing!) If the operator of the wheel got carried away the poor kids and parents would go flying. They never seemed to mind as they kept right on smiling and climbed aboard bravely for another ride. The small back wheels of the tricycle worked marvelously well as a merry-go round. Nancy loved merry-go-rounds. Next to the tire swing, that was her favorite ride. There is no beginning or end. Everyone finishes first or last (depending on how you look at it), and if you dare to stretch yourself and bend a little you might catch the brass ring for a free ride. If you make a decision quickly you can ride on the most beautiful ornate decorated horse - the one with fire in his eyes ready for the race, muscles tensed and firm or you can choose to sit in the throne-like chair and watch how each person rides his horse to the finish line. No matter what everyone on the carousel is riding you all enjoyed the same ride and will all get off when the ride is over. Every carousel Nancy has happened upon, she always took at least one ride.

The plastic family rode their carousel often, too, straddling the spokes of the small back wheels, riding around and around, looking for the brass ring. Imagination can be the vehicle that takes us beyond the norm to unbelievable places. It somehow softens life's barbs, opens doors to creativity and discovery, and distorts dreams into believable realities.

Their Red Bank living room was spacious and cheerful. There were tall windows all around the side facing the river, and you could see all the way to the first bend. There were boat docks resting in the blue-green water with sailboats, fishing boats, and even some yachts moored to their posts. The town could be seen just a mile from the Molly Pitcher Hotel, which was perched on a small rise a short distance from the main streets of Red Bank The riverbed and shoreline was spurned from reddish - brown clay which made the water seem even more blue in contrast.

One beautiful summer day Erin and a neighbor friend decided to crawl into the small rowboat moored at the dock in their backyard. They did not notice the boat was tied very loosely to the dock. The rocking of the boat as they got in it loosened the rope and the small boat was carried by the breeze out into the large river. The little girls were terrified as they saw the shore moving farther and farther away. Fortunately, one of the neighbors saw their plight and rowed out to the rescue. That put an end to playing alone in the back yard for quite some time.

A large tapestry rug from their great-grandmother covered the hardwood floors in the living room. Another of their great-grandmother's antique keepsakes was a round table inlayed with real marble and four lion paw legs that gripped the floor to steady their heavy marble load. The table made the most amazing skating rink for the Martin family. That was the name chosen for the dollhouse family. .

Their mother had managed to rescue one of great-grandmother's tiffany table lamps, which she guardedly placed on a crocheted doily on one of her mother's antique tables. The light from the lamp added a pleasant golden hue to the large room from its gold, tan and rose-colored stained glass panels. The girls always loved the feeling when dusk came and the lamp was turned on. It seemed to take command of the room and made the somewhat tattered furniture seem less tattered.

The "entertainment center" at that time was a brown radio with two big dials that starred at you like emotionless eyes in its plastic face. The family would huddle around the "beast", especially on Sunday night when "Jigs and Molly" would banter back and forth as they all laughed even when they didn't understand why they were laughing. It might have been the inflection in their voices and the thick Eastern brogue that made them laugh more than anything. When your speaking voice is the wand with which you paint pictures in the listener's imagination, that amazing talent has to be trained to perfection. If the girls were good, they could stay up until eight o'clock for the eerie tales of "The Shadow" and "Inner Sanctum". Chills would crawl up and down Nancy's and Erin's skinny arms as the creaking door of the inner world of terror slowly opened and invited you into its clutches.

Perhaps that is why Nancy would often have this horrible dream. It doesn't sound nearly as terrifying when told to someone, but to Nancy it was *horrible*! When it would sneak into her sleeping brain she would wake up trembling, in a damp sweat, her little heart racing and occasionally skipping a beat or two.

She was in a tunnel with slippery walls, running, running so fast! The walls echoed with her footsteps, her anxious breathing, and her thundering heartbeat. There was something chasing her...She could hear it closing in; no matter how hard she would try to run faster *it* ran just as fast or faster. When she would tell someone what this thing looked like, they would laugh, but in her dream it was so frightening. Its face was contorted and it had these huge bulging eyes and a mouth that was lined with gruesomely jagged teeth. It seemed really strange but… it was a *tuba*.....a big, huge, ugly, *tuba*! The walls kept closing in on her but didn't seem to stop the *thing* from chasing her. It was always the same dream, exactly. It always ended the same way. She would wake just as she was running out of room to run and the tuba was ready to devour her. Don't run to your psychiatry 101 books to see what kind of insane potential she had. ….there is nothing in any book that she has studied in future years that can explain this dream . Maybe the big saucer-like eyes were the radio's dials. But why a *tuba*?

She had to get into the light in the hallway but was so afraid that her dad would hear her. She crawled to the doorway of their room and down to the first landing where a light shone dimly over the curved stairway. She didn't want to breathe and tried holding her breath which only resulted in her heart pounding louder. "Stop!, Please stop!" she would whisper to herself. The fear of him finding her was less terrifying than going back to her dark bedroom where the *tuba* lay in wait. He heard her. He always did. As his pounding footsteps came closer and closer that wall would come down around her and she couldn't feel his big hands slapping at her head and arms. She couldn't smell his body or feel his spit as he hurled obscenities at her. She couldn't feel....anything. Her mother would come then and he would push her away. Once he pushed so hard her mother fell down the four steps that led up to the landing.

You don't have to get into this, Mom.... let him go....don't get hurt.... I can't feel it ... it will be over and I will gladly go back to my bed, cover up my head and let my heartbeat (skipping a little) drone me to sleep.

She was always exhausted after one of those encounters and she always forgot about the stupid *tuba*, at least for that night. She would just lay there praying he would leave her mother alone and that she wouldn't hear any cries or slaps....but the silence was worse because she was so afraid her mother was dead.

Chapter 10

Oreo Cookies

They had moved again to a small rented house (they never owned a home) at the end of Prichard Avenue, not too far from their Nanny's house. The street ended at a wooded area, and the trees would drop foliage onto their front porch. They had moved often before and after the year of their mother and father's separation. It always seemed they could not make the rent payment or the heat or phone was being turned off. Their mother taught piano to some local kids and their father worked at a government job that paid fairly well. It never seemed that they had enough money to pay the bills, and that led to more and more bickering and abuse. The girls longed to return to Red Bank where things seemed to be more normal and happier. Looking back it was a time where some reconciliation must have been attempted.

The girls would make frequent trips to their grandmother's house. The visits increased as the battles escalated. Nancy used to escape to the wooded area near their house and prided herself in the fact that she did not seem to be affected by the poison ivy that was prevalent on the ground surrounding the tiny path. Mary from school had a horrible case of the ailment. Her face bloated so grossly that her eyes became small swollen slits. Her lips were blistered and red. She could only eat puddings and oatmeal, some of which her mother would use as a poultice for the blistered areas.

One night, Ethelyn was giving piano lessons at someone's house, and their father was snoring, asleep in his chair. He would occasionally lift his lids to watch *Your Show of Shows* with Sid Ceasar and Imogene Coca on the black-and-white TV.

Nancy had gone into the kitchen to look for some scissors. She and Erin loved to create wardrobes for their paper dolls. Their favorites were Katy Keene and Betty Grable.

On the counter a package of Oreo cookies yelled to her "Open me…open me!" Because she was not one to ignore a plea she opened them and began to pull each chocolate cookie apart in order to lick the creamy white filling hiding inside. After about twelve cookies, she was lost in a hyperglycemic reverie until suddenly she heard her father rustle from his chair,dropping the newspaper on the floor. Panic took the place of the sweetness of the cream filling and she pushed the denuded cookies down in the waste basket as far as she could.

"What are you doing, Tootsabum?" He asked as he moved toward the cupboard.

He called Nancy and Erin "Tootsabum" when he was in a pretty good mood and many other not-so-nice names when he wasn't.

"I was looking for the scissors. Erin and I are making some gorgeous outfits for our paper dolls. Do you want to see them, Dad?"

"Maybe. I was looking for those Oreo cookies your mother just bought."

Oreo cookies range in her ears like a siren.

"Don't know ……don't like chocolate" she barely managed to whisper.

She knew her voice was trembling and, she was not winning any awards for her acting. Just then the scissors fell into the wastebasket. At the same time her heart fell into her shoes ….socks. She didn't have shoes on.

"I'll get them, Dad" she shrieked as she leaped toward the wastebasket.

Too late. He reached down and pulled out the scissors along with a couple of saliva moistened cookies.

I am dead! she shivered. Not only had he found the cookies, she had lied and he had a weapon in his hand.

"*What…who….did you eat all these insides?*" he yelled, his face glowing red in the dim kitchen light.

He raised the scissors pointing them so close to her head she almost felt them going through her. Her eyes were as wide as saucers, as she was sure his temper might allow him to strike her down.

"Don't you dare hurt me again!" Put those scissors down now!" It's just *cookies*, for God's sake….you're going to kill me for *cookies*?" It wasn't coming from her mouth; it was coming from her soul. Part of her wanted him to do it, get it over with. Then he would go to jail and leave her mother and sister alone. Another part of her felt painfully sorry for him. What demon haunted him so terribly that he could not control it?

He looked at Nancy with astonishment then at the hand that held the scissors. He dropped them to the floor and began to sob uncontrollably. She put her hand on his head. It was hot and moist. She turned and picked up the scissors. She washed them, dried them, and placed them in the drawer. She picked up the broken soggy cookies from the floor, removed the bag from the wastebasket and walked out of the kitchen into the little porch that housed their old upright piano. She walked into the yard and glanced at the stars twinkling above in the early evening sky. She sighed and placed the bag in the garbage can. She covered it quickly as the stench of maggots devouring the remains filled her nostrils. She walked around to the front of the house and into their bedroom. Erin was asleep, having given up waiting for the scissors, especially after she heard the commotion in the kitchen. Nancy wondered if this was her way of dealing with all this …going to sleep. Was she pretending? She stuffed the paperdolls and their attire under the bed. They had so much stuffed under the bed that it tilted to one side.

She didn't go back into the kitchen nor did she want to. She heard the front door close as he left, breathed a big sign and hid under the warm covers.

Chapter 11

California

She wrote it in pencil on a small envelope.

*Dear Walter (*she always started her notes formally with "dear"),

I am taking the girls to California to see my cousin Harriet. I don't think I

can take much more of this. I will call you to let you know we arrived

safely.

Love, Ethelyn

They had packed their small overnight bags obediently when their mom wakened them early Saturday morning.

"We're going to take a little trip to see my cousin. She sent tickets for us to ride on a big airplane all the way to California!" their mother whispered as she straightened their beds and herded them into the bathroom to brush their teeth and hair.

"An airplane! California! That's so exciting!" Nancy yelped as she almost knocked Erin into the bathtub with her jumping up and down.

"Shhhh--- it's really early and your father just left for work. Aunt Liz is coming to take us to the airport, so get dressed. I have most everything we need packed. You put the toys and paper dolls and any favorite clothes I may have missed in your overnight bags."

Nancy's overnight bag was blue with butterflies woven into the fabric. Erin's was green with flowers dotting the faded fabric. . Both were a little worn but still were serviceable.

"Dad isn't coming?" Nancy asked hesitantly, hoping the answer would be "no," yet feeling sad that she secretly wished it to be that way.

"No. He….he has to work. It's just us ladies!"

Erin did a little dance and proceeded to fill her bag with her stuffed cocker spaniel, a tee shirt with flowers on it and several books. Nancy brought her Tom Sawyer book and some paper to sketch new clothes, California style, for her shapely Katy Keene paper doll, her soft blue sweater for chilly nights and, of course, her chicken whistle.

Teeth brushed, hair combed, suitcases packed, tiny note on the kitchen table, they ran to Aunt Lizzie's shiny Buick waiting in the driveway.

The airport was buzzing with passengers, stewardesses, handsome pilots in their uniforms, soldiers in their dress uniforms, workers, clerks, wheelchairs, suit cases piled high on carts, lights, music, and speakers announcing gate assignments and flight schedules above the roar of the planes taking off and landing. Erin and Nancy clutched their mother's moist hand and their small bags, their eyes darting from one person to another. They had never been on a plane before and were so excited they just wanted to run through that huge airport and tell everyone they were going ----- flying to California, a million miles away!

Ethelyn kissed Aunt Lizzie on the cheek and handed her an envelope. Liz looked sad as she hugged the girls, turned abruptly, and ran out of the drop-off area to her Buick

Nancy caught the look between them. Grown ups hate to say good-bye. *I hope I don't look sad when people leave. I will fake a smile if I have to,* she vowed to herself.

After checking their bags at the service counter and sipping a soda from the fountain, TWA flight 307 was beginning to board. People in wheelchairs followed by families with children boarded first. The walk from the terminal to the stairs leading to the plane gave a full view of the awesome metal bird to those boarding. Nancy's and Erin's mouths hung open as they viewed the wings and lettering on the side of the plane. Their tiny hearts were beating loudly in their ears mixed with the whirr of the engine as it sat waiting for them to board.

The inside of the airplane smelled like the seats in the new cars they had imagined owning one day. Many of the passengers appeared quite laissez-faire about this amazing beast. They eased into their seats and adjusted the seatbelts, yawned, pulled a magazine from the pocket in the seat in front of them, or gazed out the tiny windows.

Ethelyn sat between the two girls, made sure their belts were secure, sighed and closed her eyes tightly. Nancy looked out her window, which was a few seats away from the wing of the plane. She could see the terminal with all its lights blazing and hundreds of people walking about. A man with a cart full of suitcases and boxes drove up to the back of the plane. Nancy strained to see if her overnight case with the butterflies was part of the pile, but the man and cart disappeared around the other side of the plane. She glanced back toward the terminal as the engines began to roar louder and a pretty stewardess was giving evacuation instructions over the speaker in the plane.

Then she saw him, standing just outside the glass doorway they had walked through a few moments ago. She squinted and blinked, thinking it was someone else, but it was him.

"Mom…Mom! Dad is out there. Look! Is he supposed to go with us?"

Ethelyn almost ripped the seatbelt from its holders as she leaned across Nancy to look out the window.

Her face was ashen and tears were brimming in her eyes. One small salty tear dropped onto Nancy's hand as her mother tried to see him and yet tried not to see him.

His shoulders were slumped under his raincoat, and his face was rigid and pale. He watched the plane taxi away from the terminal toward the runway as though he was watching a casket at a funeral. Ethelyn eased back into her seat and patted the girls' hands. Erin, oblivious to the scene, continued to fold the pages of a magazine into triangles and squares. Nancy looked at her mother and back out the window as lights from the runway raced by the plane.

Ethelyn had taken her handkerchief with lace all around the edges and was patting her face, which was wet with perspiration. Nancy felt suddenly so very sad. He looked so frightened and alone. Despite the fear and anger she felt toward him, there was a part of her that loved him. No matter what, he was her father. She wished that he could love her back.

The metal bird roared as it sped down the runway. The feeling of weightlessness and excitement was amazingly uplifting. It even surpassed that feeling when the parachute jump at Coney Island popped and floated its riders back to earth. She pushed the vision of her father standing alone outside the terminal back. *It was nice of him to leave work and try to see them off,* she mused. The other voice inside her knew better.

The hills, houses, and roads began to move away as the airplane soared toward white cotton- like clouds. Nancy imagined this to be like the world buried beneath the fairy grass surrounding her grandmother's huge oak tree. Houses with different colored roofs surrounded by lush green trees and lawns, roads winding their way through the Jersey hills with miniature vehicles moving about. From this distance everything looked magical. No imperfections, no potholes, no defects in the landscape. If you could get enough distance between yourself and the impurities of daily life the "big picture" is much lovelier.

I would love to fly a plane someday, Nancy mused. *What a great feeling!* She looked over at Erin and her mother to see if she could slither past without them questioning her. Her mother had closed her eyes and appeared to be napping though she wasn't making her usual snoring noises. Erin had curled up in her seat and leaned her curly blonde head on her mother's shoulder.

Now or never. Nancy thought she would explore the plane as she ever so quietly made herself as skinny as possible in order to move past the two.

Once safely in the aisle, she tiptoed past the other seats as though she was ordered forward to assist in flying the plane. Her throat was dry, and she was ready for any one of the passengers to halt her progress to ask "just where did she think she was going?" The two stewardesses were in the galley to the left of the nose of the plane and in front of the first class area. Nancy almost felt invisible and also quite confident as each step brought her closer to her goal. She was just about to knock on the cockpit door when the curtain closing off the galley made a screeching sound as the rings of the curtain scraped over the metal rod. Nancy jumped and spun around ready to run past the disinterested passengers and bury herself in her seat. The stewardess who had opened the curtain held a tray with soft drinks and cookies that went clattering to the floor. Some of the liquid splattered both the startled hostess and the intruder and dripped down the sides of the small space outside the cockpit.

Nancy leaned against the wall trying to disappear somehow. The stewardess who had dropped the tray had turned into the galley to extract some towels from one of the drawers. The second stewardess was standing over Nancy with a look that might have said, "I'm thinking of throwing you out of the plane but that might get me in trouble." Instead she knelt down so she looked Nancy right in her eyes and began to wipe off some of the cookie crumbs and sticky soda from her bright yellow dress. Nancy had chosen that one to wear in case the plane crashed or she got lost. Her mother had told her the story about the red balloon many times. Since they preferred not to have balloons in the cabins of the airplanes, she thought it wise to wear a color that could be easily spotted----and spotted it most surely was, with blotches of soda.

"Honey, are you lost? Were you looking for the bathroom? I'm so sorry about your pretty dress. I'm sure if you soak it when you arrive in California, the spots will come out." The stewardess's eyes were inspecting the damages and glancing occasionally at the sober face of the girl in the dress.

"I...I wanted to see the pilot and the instruments. I think it would be so wonderful to fly! I am so sorry I am such a klutz. If you give me a towel, I will wipe off the wall. I am really good at cleaning. Not really good at navigating....I mean walking. Please don't tell my mother. She is kind of sad, and I don't want to upset her anymore than she already is. My sister will think this is good that I am in trouble again. I am so....."

"Hmmmmm. Let me see if we can turn this into a better situation for you, dear," the stewardess said as she knocked on the cockpit door. A green light flashed above the door and Mary (Nancy had read the name on the pin attached to her uniform) entered the dark room filled with panels of gauges and dials all lit up in blues, whites, yellows and greens. Nancy bent forward just enough to see the cockpit through the opened door. Mary was talking to one of the pilots who glanced towards the truant pre-teen, trying to look as petulant as possible. She supposed he was going to scold her for leaving her seat and invading first class, causing an accidental spill, and for being bold enough to request an audience.

Mary smiled as she looked down at Nancy. "Come with me and we will ask your mother if you and your sister can visit Captain Regan and Co-pilot Ben in the cockpit. I will tell her you lost your way attempting to find the bathroom and wound up here. How does that sound? What is your name, dear?"

"Nancy, ma'am. Nancy Ball. I hate my last name." Nancy answered with a shaky voice as she was about to burst with excitement at the prospect of a visit to the cockpit.

Mary took Nancy's sticky hand and led her back to the coach section of the plane. Ethelyn and Erin were still napping. They had not noticed their missing relative.

"Miss....Mrs. Ball," Mary whispered gently next to Ethelyn's head. She stirred and Erin yawned as her mother straightened up in her seat.

"Yes? Is it time to land? Are we there already? Nancy, what are you doing out of your seat?" She had awakened enough to see her eldest peering out from behind the stewardess's starched blue uniform.

"Your daughter went the wrong way looking for the bathroom and we noticed her heading toward the galley. I was carrying a tray of refreshments and lost my grip on the tray. Some of the soda spilled on her lovely yellow dress. We blotted it with a damp towel but I am afraid it has left a few spots. If you soak it in St. Louis when we land to change planes I'm sure it will come out" Mary said as she crossed the fingers of one hand behind her.

Not totally a lie, just a little twist on the truth. Nancy was crossing her fingers too, but not for the fib--- in hopes her mother would allow she and Erin to visit the cockpit.

"Captain Regan has invited your girls to visit the cockpit for a few moments. Would that be all right? You definitely are welcome to come with them. Your daughter seems very interested in the mechanics of flying. She seems very bright."

Erin snickered at that comment.

"Oh, that would be wonderful! Would you girls like to go see where they fly the plane and meet the Captain?"

You don't have any idea how much I want to do that, Nancy thought.

"Yes, yes! Oh, can we? Please!" both girls squealed.

The three of them followed Mary, who by now was a dear friend. As they entered the small cockpit and gazed mesmerized at the instruments and the sun casting pink and yellow rays of light across the clouds below the airplane, they were greeted by the captain and his co-pilot as they watched and calculated the plane's airspeed, relationship to the horizon, fuel gauges and wind speed. Captain Regan explained the intricate calculations they needed to make in order to carry their passengers safely to their destinations.

Erin got to sit in the co-pilot's lap and hold the steering wheel as it moved back and forth steadying their flight. Nancy hung on every word the captain said as though she was to be tested on the information. Ethelyn stood in the doorway observing the scene. She was so pleased with her proper young ladies. They were so good despite the insecurities of their home life. She needed time to think. She needed to talk with her cousin who was also her dear friend. She needed to find the courage to make a radical change in all their lives if she had to.

Back in their seats Ethelyn closed her eyes and slipped into a dream of concert halls with dazzling crystal chandeliers and ladies in satin and velvet gowns peering at her on stage, her hands caressing the ivory keys of a baby grand piano. A hush falls over the audience as a poignant concerto from Mozart moved about the fabulous theater. Erin busily put together a balsawood model airplane the co-pilot had given her. Nancy gazed at the city of St. Louis as the TWA flight 307 began its descent.

The closer you get to the city the farther you get from heaven, she mused in her ten-year-old, almost eleven-year-old mind.

Ethelyn and her girls waved good-bye to the crew, thanking them over and over for their hospitality as they deplaned and walked across the tarmac to their second designated flight heading for Los Angeles. Nancy looked back at the plane to see if she could catch a glimpse of her overnight bag with the butterflies. She had become somewhat of a worrier in her ten years on this earth. She needed to make sure every detail was in place and that nothing in her list of duties had been left out. Never feeling that she had quite done enough, she became compulsive about making sure tasks were completed and she had contributed her fair share.

After devouring ham and cheese sandwiches on white bread and coca colas--- attempting to remove some of the soda stains on Nancy's yellow dress--- Ethelyn and the girls boarded TWA flight 459 for California. Nancy took on the demeanor of the frequent fliers attempting to look bored as the plane lifted into the air, though her insides were screaming with excitement.

Nothing could have been more beautiful than flying over the Grand Canyon with the rapids of the Colorado River slicing its way through mile high red, rust, and deep brown rocks or the majestic Rocky Mountains dotted with sparkling white snow. Nancy wished they could stay longer, flying above the clouds and dipping below every so often to make sure the earth was still there should they ever wish to land.

She thought about her father standing alone at the airport searching in vain for faces in the smoky windows of the planes. She would write a letter to him. That's what she would do. She pulled out some paper with the emblem and title of the plane at the top or the page.

Dear Dad,

I saw you.......

She couldn't think of the right words. After all, she was only ten.

Maybe another time, she thought.

She closed her eyes as the empty papers fell to the floor.

The announcement to fasten their seat belts woke them as the plane began its decent. The airport was bustling with activity. There were people embracing, some staring dazedly into nowhere, others sipping coffee and reading newspapers and magazines. There were dark skinned princes in turbans and jewels. The people were from everywhere---- Chinese, blond haired folks from the Netherlands, Germans, folks from India in their turbans with deep dark eyes and sullen faces, actors and actresses, businessmen and vacationers. Ethelyn saw Charles Laughton and courageously asked for his autograph. Mom had tied a red balloon to Erin's belt for some reason. Nancy supposed she was much too mature to have a silly red balloon tied to *her* belt. They took a cab from the airport to the Fontaine Hotel near Hollywood. Palatial homes with exquisitely manicured lawns and gardens, theaters and hills, endless traffic and people with every kind of outfit you could imagine passed them by as the cab weaved its careful way through the traffic.

The hotel Cousin Harriet had recommended was built in the late 1800s and had been renovated several times since, keeping the original style of those early days intact. Dark red velvet draperies hung from shiny brass rods covering floor to ceiling windows. The carpet was a mixture of red, gold and green woven into ornate patterns and dotted with winged cherubs sprinkling flowers amidst the weave. Their rooms were elegantly decorated with ornate furnishings and four-poster beds covered with thick flowered down bedspreads. Nancy wondered for just a moment how they could afford all this since lack of funds always was a topic of loud discussion in her home----- but the thought lingered only for that moment as the excitement of the whole experience pushed it away.

The Pig 'N Whistle was a restaurant adjacent to the hotel and highly recommended by the concierge at the front desk. They awoke early the next morning anxious to tour the city and take in all the sights they could in the next two days before they were to travel to Cousin Harriet's in San Francisco. They ordered the "special of the day," fluffy golden brown waffles topped with strawberries and whipped cream. The girls giggled with delight as they dove into the delectable, juicy, sweet stack in front of them.

A far cry from dry old Wheaties or lumpy Cream of Wheat! Nancy thought

The next two days were amazing. They toured Groaman's Chinese Theater, stepped into the imprints of star's feet imbedded in the cement walk, stood breathless in front of Michelangelo's painting of the Last Supper. As the lights dimmed in the huge auditorium housing the canvas, the face of Jesus continued to glow. The pain and sadness in his eyes touched the hearts of awe struck audiences. Even non-believers were amazed at the scene and the mystery of the face of Jesus that glowed in the dark. Several theories were developed about the ingredients used in the paints Michelangelo used to place the face of the Master on the canvas. His eyes depicted the pain and suffering he was about to experience mixed with the hope and knowledge that his Father would save His flock from their transgressions by that very act.

Cousin Harriet looked crisp and chic, even in her house dress and flowered apron. She was attractive in a "confident" way with shining honey colored hair, a wisp of which always fell just above her right eye as if to let the sculpted appearance of her hairdo know there might be some impishness left. She had a smile that hugged the girls when she greeted them that warm Sunday afternoon. One could feel the love between her and Ethelyn by the way their eyes empathetically communicated amidst cheery greetings and muffled kisses.

People from the East Coast love to give big wet kisses and very demonstrative hugs. Greetings, especially those occurring after any length of time, are more like a folk dance, with arms flailing about and everyone talking between *ooohs* and *aaaahs*.

Harriet's home was so much like her. The long curved drive was adorned with mums and irises. Bushes neatly coifed and luminously green encircled the white two-story Tudor house.

The windows were sparkling and dressed with fresh white shears. One of the windows was a massive bay with soft blue drapes skirted with shear lace curtains. Two large oak trees cast soft shadows over the front of the gabled roof, and the vestibule all but called out "Welcome!" with its azure-and- white tiled floor. A mirror encased in delicate gold and blue leaves greeted the smiling visitors and was poised above an ornate mahogany table with a marble top. Fresh flowers, artistically arranged, set in a blue Dresden vase with a two-dimensional cream sculpture of a Greek goddess gave off a fragrance of sweetened lemons as they entered.

The living room was spacious and comfortably furnished. Just the right touches of end tables, coffee table and curio cabinets (all mahogany and matching, even!) gave an inviting and serene first impression. Of course, these were not foremost in the thoughts of a ten year old at that time. Nancy was perhaps more interested in the beautiful glass figurines in the cabinets. There were three hutches filled with glittering spun glass unicorns, teddy bears, ships, dolls-every figure imaginable. Nancy's eyes went quickly to them as the sunlight caught them in rainbows of color. She yearned to touch them from the start. Two large shelves held china figures dressed in eighteenth century regalia. The work was so detailed, one of the figures held a lace hanky which looked so much like the delicate fabric, you had to touch it to convince yourself it was china. Harriet had lovingly collected these treasures for years. Each had a special meaning and place in her heart. Many of them had been gifts from her late husband, William. All that the girls knew of him was that he was a very successful gentleman with a smile like an Irish salesman, a prolific sense of humor, and love of life. This had changed when the stock market did not fair well for him. A depression so dark and encompassing took this fine man to a ledge of his fourteen story office building in New York and a leap in desperation to the sidewalk below.

Harriet and Peter, her very young son, had moved as far away from that city as they could to start a life together that would have made William proud of their steadfastness.

They say that time heals all wounds but not all scars. Harriet had never married again.

Nancy saw her one day while she was gingerly dusting her treasures, reaching behind the figures on the second shelf of one of the hutches and holding something gold in her hand. She stood for a moment lost in time with a wistful look of a child on her face. Her fingers stroked the top of the object as gently as you would brush a tear away from a child's face. A tiny tear rested in the corner of her eye and fell on her fingers. She trembled slightly and looked around the room, as if embarrassed by her secret. Tenderly, she placed the object in a purple velvet cloth and placed at the back of the shelf, behind the glass figures. Nancy vividly recalled the memory of Cousin Harriet standing there, and though only a child, somehow knew how special that moment was to her. Nancy had hidden in the foyer behind a table almost reverently, not wishing to disturb her Aunt.

That week with Harriett and Peter was full of exciting visits to sites held in their hearts forever. Lost in the excitement of each day's adventure, the vision of their father walking away from the plane with his head bowed, looking so small and alone; that memory, like her cousin's figurine, had been pushed back into a safe place. That place in our minds never quite lets go completely; no matter how hard we try to erase them, the pictures are there, sometimes less vivid, but still etched in our memory.

Peter was thirteen years old. Taller than most boys his age, he seemed to be much older than his years. His room was a reflection of who Peter was and who he would become. Bookshelves almost sagged with the weight of books on energy, science, outer space, mathematical theories, wilderness expeditions and mystery. Model airplanes, carefully formed, tiny piece by tiny piece, hung from wires attached to metal plant hangers in the ceiling. A draftsman's table was cluttered with penciled drawings, amazingly detailed, and pencils with teeth marks in them. The only hints that this room did not belong to a twenty-one-year old engineer were a pair of blue-jeans and "surfs –up" T shirts thrown on the floor near the bed. The bed was made of old car parts. There were dust covered trophies for anything from football to science fair championships perched on the headboard, which was really a car bumper.

Can you fall in love at ten years old well before your hormones have surged? Well before the curves of adolescent women-hood have started to show? Well before you know the meaning of "love" if you ever *do* know the meaning? Nancy thought you could. Even if that person you feel that tingle in your tummy for----that person who causes your cheeks to flush whenever he glances your way, that person who you always seem to say stupid things around, when you are trying so very hard to be *cool* and *cosmopolitan*--- hardly notices you.

Oh, he knew Nancy was there, dropping things, bumping into him, sneaking peaks into his "cave", and trying so hard to be noticed, yet not noticed! A paradoxical pest is what she had become. She really did not know why; she just knew there was no one she had ever met in her short little life that made her feel so good.

Well, she managed to get noticed, emphatically! Two days before this wonderful vacation was to end, she became brave enough to go near the figurine cases------near enough to see the eyes of the unicorn and the kittens chasing a ball of yarn all in spun glass, catching the sunlight and projecting little fairy-like lights on the wall and ceiling. They were so beautiful! The colors of light broken apart into soft pinks, blues and yellows by the hundreds of glass facets were mesmerizing. She and Erin were dusting the tables when she ventured into *no man's land! off limits! no touching zone!*. In her trance, she dropped the dust rag, and when she came to her senses, she bent down to pick it up and slither out of there. When she stood up her head hit the corner of the shelf with the figurines and it came loose from the wall. Down they came ----it seemed like an avalanche of icicles in slow motion as they crashed into millions of glittering fragments on the floor. The kittens lost their ball of yarn---as well as their tails, ears, and bodies. The unicorn was nowhere to be found among the debris, and in the middle, the velvet cloth lay gaping open with a small glass heart broken in two.

Peter was the first to enter the living room --- the scene of the crime. He gasped when he saw Nancy in the "forbidden zone", and his face paled when he put together what had happened. There she stood, surrounded by the evidence, feeling like she had just committed murder , with that awful, familiar ache in the pit of her stomach that she had not noticed during this vacation,.

"Oh my God ----w-w-w-what have you done!" he said with a shriek that would have been great on Halloween night.

"I-I-I-It was an accident, I was dusting and---and I wanted to look at the figures....they are so beau--- they were so beautif---I am soooo sorry---I didn't mean to hurt them." Nancy stammered.

"You are such a *klutz*! Always dropping things and bumping into something. Just wait until Mom sees this. You are in *big* trouble!"

Her hero suddenly had turned into a thirteen year old brat! Falling out of love at that moment was very easy. Then it started—that feeling of helplessness. It was so awful! She just wanted to disappear, melt away like the bad witch in *The Wizard of Oz.* . " I never do anything right" – that voice inside her screamed. "Never.....never... *never!*"

Her mother and Cousin Harriett walked in as she stood frozen in the midst of the debris. She had seen a movie once about a man who could make himself invisible at any time. *This surely would be a great time to have that talent,* she thought to herself. They were giggling like school girls, carrying packages that rustled as they walked. It was so good to hear Mom laugh like that. Her cheeks were rosy from the California sun. She had not seen her look so beautiful in a long time. And there she was, ruining the moment. As the disaster scene became apparent to them, a hush pierced the room. It was so loud you wanted to break it with some kind of sound.

"I –I – I –I'm so sor—"

Erin sat demurely on the couch with the innocence of a nun covering her face.

"Oh, h-h-honey, what happened, ----are you hurt?" That was Mom, of course!

"The ...... the figurines!! Oh, my goodness, where is my heart?" That, of course, was Harriett!

" You're having a heart attack! Oh, my God, get a chair!" That was her "hero," Peter

" No, Peter, I'm not having a heart attack, I'm just---just a little in shock!"

"Shock! Shock!" Peter cried out. "Aunt Ethelyn, call an ambulance, call the fire department, call someone!" .

"Honey, she means she is just, ------well ---surprised.," Ethelyn said hesitantly.

"*You---you*" Peter yelled, pointing his finger at his dejected former lover. "*You klutz!*"

"No, *dumb klutz!*" She finished for him. Then she felt them, those hot, stinging tears! *Blink them back, you fool. Blink them back!*

"I'll clean it up! I am sooooo *sorry----*I *am* a *klutz----*I *never* do *anything* right! I will buy you new ones, I promise – I am so *stupid*! I was trying to see the little heart, Aunt Harriett, the one that makes your eyes all misty. Oh--- here it is! Oh, my God, it......it....it's broken! I just want to die! I broke your heart.......I broke your...."

Suddenly Harriet was holding her tightly, perfumed breast warm against her cheek, tears still stinging as she let them pour out on to Aunt Harriet's pretty pink blouse. Harriet kissed her hair and whispered, "You are *not* a klutz and far from stupid! Don't you ever say bad things about yourself. They are only figurines. They can be replaced. *You* never can be replaced!" That was Aunt Harriet...sweet Aunt Harriett.

In 1954, Harriet died of cancer. Nancy never saw her after that vacation. Mom let her read Harriet's letters. They always smelled like the perfume on her pink blouse. Sometimes, when Nancy needed a hug and to remember to love herself, no matter what, she would feel Aunt Harriet's warm arms around her and her heart beating next to her tears.

Before they packed their things to return home Ethelyn, Nancy, and Erin shopped for a whole day looking for figurines that looked like the ones Aunt Harriett had treasured so. They only found four: a kitten playing with a ball of yarn, a tiny basket with colored glass flowers, a unicorn and a heart. Harriett was thrilled. Nancy was sure that was really good acting on her part. Harriet placed the new heart next to the broken one on a piece of blue velvet near the back of the case, and her eyes looked far away and misty as the sunlight played music with the figurine's rainbows.

Armed with two huge dolls with boxes in their tummies that talked and sang five actual phrases when you pushed the button, extra "barf" bags, books, and some snacks, they pushed their way through the crowd at the busy Los Angeles airport. Faces of every color and shape; short dresses, and long flowing gowns that looked like whipped cream wound around deeply tanned skin and swirled around deep, round eyes that peered out from masked faces; poodles with diamond collars, perfectly groomed and looking very much like their owners; beautiful ladies with hopeful faces, in various poses, waiting to be "discovered" and praying for that one breathless moment on the "silver screen" that leads to stardom; sleepy- eyed security guards, midgets, giants, famous people, people in love, lonely people, the thinkers, the flashers, the "suits", the sailors, the bums and the barons, the world in a teapot – they passed Ethelyn and the girls by without a glance.

The sounds of the paging system, calling flight numbers....243 to India, 486 to New York, 1137 to Chicago.... Paging Mr. John Hudson, please report to the Pan American ticket desk.....Flight 447 to St Louis with connections to New Jersey has been cancelled... all passengers please report to ticket desk in Aisle A 41.... Flight 447 to St. L...

"Oh... my goodness!" Ethelyn screeched. It jolted the girls out of the magic of this amazing collage. Nancy grabbed Erin's' sticky hand. She always held the lollipop at the sticky end. They ran behind their mom, trying not to trip over the dolls with the talking boxes that kept slipping from their skinny arms. At the flight desk people surrounded the attendant like flies swarm to a popsicle. The passengers were all asking questions at once, red faced, irritable, and impatient, some with babies, some with brief cases, letting everyone know that they were most important and could not wait. Mom waited patiently in line, always the lady. She lit a cigarette and closed her eyes as she inhaled the essence of whatever made her enjoy them so much.

"Erin, stop fidgeting! Do you have to go to the ladies room?"

Erin pouted, "No... I mean, yes".

"Stay right here, Nan. Don't loose our place in line. Do *not* talk to *anyone*. Don't worry... we will be right back!" Mom and Erin (smiling as though she had set Nancy up to be kidnapped) ran toward the ladies room several feet away. They were out of sight before Nancy realized what a huge place this was when you are left alone, in line, with all these *big* people, and with strict orders to keep your place! She already felt invisible to those people scurrying to their "wherevers," and she certainly was invisible in that line of anxious, late, and grizzly ex- passengers of flight 447. In less time than you can say "lost your place" she had lost her place. A huge man with a cigar and drool coming out of the side of his mouth where he held the stogie pushed her off to the side like a pesky gnat! She was so shy she was afraid to say anything, as if it would have made a crumb of difference to him. He barely noticed her face turning pale and the panic in her eyes, as one after another, the people kept filing past. She turned to see the look on her mother's face as she and Erin exited the restroom. Not the look of relief you would expect a mom to have knowing her daughter had not been kidnapped or something while she was attending to her sister's bodily needs. No, it was a look of trepidation. Yes, trepidation! Nancy did not know what it meant but it seemed to fit here.

"What happened, honey... I thought I told you to keep our place! Now we won't get a flight. Oh, my goodness, you need to be more responsible. What will we do now... Don't cry... I'm not angry with you, just disappointed!'

Maybe that is what trepidation meant... disappointed!

Most of the crowd had been taken care of by the haggard attendant by the time the three of them got to the desk.

"We have tickets for Flight 447 from St. L..." Ethelyn started to explain.

" Lady, where have I heard that before?" the attendant swaggered. " We have no more seats on other flights until Friday."

"Th.....That's two days from now! Don't you have anything? We are supposed to be home by next Monday! Don't you have anything sooner?" Ethelyn looked really worried.

"Ma'am, I have a seat on a bus leaving from the terminal in one hour. It is a seven day trip, but half the price of the flight. The only other thing we have is first class by way of Texas, then to Chicago and another flight to New York. That will take about the same amount of time as the bus."

The attendant must have noticed that they did not have a poodle with a diamond necklace, or a real leather briefcase, and that Ethelyn was smoking Pall Malls instead of those new, thin expensive cigarettes, and that Erin had scuffed the cloth off her sneaker so that her toe peaked through.... That was it! Erin's sneaker... He knew they were poor just looking at her shoes.

They could in no way afford first class so their mom decided it would be an adventure to ride across the United States on a bus with two darling girls, two talking dolls with speakers in their stomachs, and two pretty worn suitcases. Ethelyn loved adventure and if there wasn't one available, she would make one! She always made the best out of any situation, no matter how drab, or scary, or depressing. She had the courage to accept change as a challenge and to weave dreams out of nightmares. .

The bus station was a drab contrast to the hustle, bustle, and excitement of the airport. Dull green and gray cement walls with half –torn posters of long forgotten plays and movie stars, restaurants that had closed, and Uncle Sam pointing a worn finger "Uncle Sam Wants Y..." was all that was left. A single yellow, low watt light bulb hung over the head of the ticket master in a small cage at the end of the station. The benches were occupied by drunks, some weary soldiers, a little old lady in a felt hat with one daisy and an old sweater, clutching her carpetbag as though she was holding the Mona Lisa in there, and a man who needed a shave.. It was almost midnight, and Erin was blinking hard to keep awake. Nancy rarely needed much sleep, especially now, that she had to keep her mother and her sister safe in this dingy place. Ethelyn stepped up to the window and set the two bags down next to her.

"Could I have three tickets to New Jersey, please – one adult and two children?"

"Yeah, New Jersey... that's a seven day trip, partly through the desert... two kids and one adult... how many bags?"

"Only two, Sir"

" Here you go... that will be two hundred ten dollars for the trip"

That was half of the price for the airplane trip and twice the amount of time.

" Does that include rooms overnight on the way?"

"There are only two overnights ...one in Arizona and one in St. Louis. Those are included. The hotels are no Taj Mahals but they'll pass. Bus leaves at one a.m."

"Thank you." Ethelyn looked really weary all of a sudden. She perked up quickly and asked if the girls would like some hot chocolate from a machine nearby. They curled up on the hard chairs with their dolls and rolled up their jackets into makeshift pillows. Ethelyn brought over two cups of hot chocolate which tasted wonderful to two gurgling tummies. The warm thick chocolate made little beads of sweat on their foreheads. Erin dozed off after just a few sips so Nancy helped by finishing hers. Such a good big sis!

The lights from the buses cast eerie shadows on the green and gray dingy walls and the faces in the posters seemed to be staring at the waiting passengers. Nancy looked away and nuzzled close to Ethelyn, who smelled like Chantilly and cigarettes, camphor and a little hint of moth balls. The palms of her mother's hands were always very warm. Her mother was invariably cold and wore sweaters and gloves even in the summer to keep warm.

The bus for New Jersey pulled into the depot. The driver was short and pot-bellied. He laughed as he welcomed the few weary travelers on the bus.

"Glad to have you aboard! We will be good friends after seven days on this old Bessie!"

Busses back in the forties were not the coaches of the twenty-first century, by any stretch of the imagination. They were just busses. This "old Bessie" had Juicy Fruit gum Signs in every holder above the seats. There was a face with no nose, a smile with lots of teeth and a picture of a pack of gum next to the teeth. Juicy Fruit gum is way too sweet when bus gas makes you nauseated anyhow.

Chapter 12

The Bus Ride Home

The bus sputtered and spouted gases that filled their nostrils and throat even if they tried to hold their breath. People from other destinations filled a few of the seats. There was a bald man two seats behind them with large lips that flapped as he snored rhythmically despite the jerking movements of the bus as it exited the bus station. A lady wearing an oversized cowboy hat and studded sweater with braids of colored leather hanging from the studs gazed out the window into the darkness. The streetlights flashed an eerie light across her face, mimicking a silent movie's staccato film technique. She seemed to be lost in a place far away.

There was a soldier in his full dress uniform straining to read a magazine in the dim overhead light. He looked not too much older than Nancy, though it was difficult to tell in the darkness and occasional flashes of light how anyone really looked.

There was someone else in the back seat of the bus that stretched the width of the interior, but Nancy could only catch a brief glimpse of a figure lying on the seat. The figure did not move. She kept looking back, wondering if the person was breathing. She certainly didn't have the courage to check herself!

Ethelyn and Erin were curled up in the stiff seats, sound asleep. As usual, Nancy was not ready in any way to go to sleep, although there was really very little to do. The thought crossed her mind to slip over to the seat next to the "cow lady" but her mother's warning not to talk to strangers slithered over that fleeting thought. Nancy had not developed what most people would consider a normal sleeping pattern. She rarely needed more than two to three hours sleep each night. She thought she must be related to a bat or some other nocturnal rodent ---well, maybe not a rodent, some sort of a night wanderer. No matter how hard she tried, she spent an awful lot of time awake. Did that mean that she had lived longer than most folks?

I would really make a great lookout for the army. Maybe that is what I'll be when I grow up. But I am grown up! I am almost eleven years old and I even drove my mom's car out in the country one day. I weaved a little and had quite a time seeing over the steering wheel, but I did it for about fifty miles! Well, maybe not fifty, but a long way! she mused.

She closed her eyes and saw the "spider lights" flashing on the inside of her lids. She decided that she would do what she usually did at home, until her father would catch her. She would read a book. She devoured anything she could get her hands on to read. If not a book or magazine she would read every sign they passed, make up poems in her head, sing, hum, make faces...most anything.

Nancy didn't want to wake up her mother or her sister so she turned the reading light as far as it would go away from their seats. Of course, when she turned the light on, it shown on the outer armrest instead of the book. She leaned way out over the armrest which was really uncomfortable. The armrest poked her in the ribs and she could barely make out the words, but did she give it up? Oh no, not that kid. Whether it was stubbornness or the beginnings of some sort of insanity, she seemed to be more comfortable in stressful situations. She may have begun to subconsciously create them.

The big Greyhound had to stop often. They stopped at cities and tiny towns skirting the awesome mountains that nudged their way into valleys illuminated with lights from office buildings, homes, and street lights. Mountains were all around them. The mountains always seemed to warm Nancy's heart in the way sitting on someone's lap and having them hold you would. It made her feel nothing was so big that it could hurt her while she was protected by them. The moon wandered in and out of the shadows of huge snow covered peaks glistening like diamonds in the moonlight. Each time they stopped, the bus let out a tremendous belch of gas, like a satisfied guest after stuffing themselves with Nanny's *paprikas*. Nancy, Erin and Ethelyn dozed on and off between belches. Nancy dropped her book several times on the sticky floor. She noticed that the "cow lady" didn't sleep much either. She kept rummaging through her oversized purse, frantically looking for something she never seemed to find. When the passing lights outlined her face, she looked sad and almost frightened. Her eyes looked apprehensively from the door of the bus to the windows each time the bus paused in the towns. Nancy wanted to console her, if that is what she needed, or to let her know that the mountains would protect her from whatever demons appeared to be haunting her. Her curiosity surpassed her mother's warnings. About four a.m. she quietly slipped past her mother and sister, and then hesitantly moved toward the empty seat next to the "cow lady".

"May I sit here in this empty seat…I…I can see the outline of the mountains better from this side of the bus."

The lady nodded and moved her jacket from the seat. Nancy noticed some initials embroidered on the collar and the jacket smelled like old cigarettes as she moved it to her lap.

A very pregnant pause settled between them until finally the "cow lady" spoke in a half whisper leaning close to Nancy's ear.

"Shouldn't you be sleeping, little girl? I noticed you have been awake most of the way. Did you finish your book? What is it you are reading so intently?"

Not knowing which question to answer first Nancy tried to sum it up in a few whispered words.

"I don't need a lot of sleep. I'm reading Nancy Drew mystery number eight – it's really good, but I dozed off a couple of times and the floor is sticky, so I put it away, because I don't want to get it sticky, and I noticed you looked sad and maybe frightened, and I thought you might want some company. Since I'm the only one awake, I guess that would be me. We are going home from a visit with my mother's cousin. I broke her very most favorite glass figurines. I'm such a *klutz*! But we bought some more for her and I guess she's okay. She was very nice about it – she's a very nice lady. I thought I was in love with Peter, her son, but he turned out to be a *snitch* and wasn't very nice to me… but I guess you couldn't expect him to be. I liked the captain of the plane we arrived on much better… he was really handsome and let us come up into the cockpit. We couldn't get a plane back. I goofed that up too by not keeping our place in line while mom took my sister to the bathroom at the airport, so we had to take this bus back and it really is going to be a long ride, so I thought I'd come see if you wanted to talk, because you are awake too!'

"My goodness! That is quite a story! I don't think I've heard an introduction quite so complete!" The lady whispered as she laughed.

A few people around them stirred but the hum of the bus motor lulled them back to sleep.

"I'm sorry. I get my motor going and it's hard to stop it!" Nancy said sheepishly.

"That's okay, honey" The woman drawled just like Chuck at the supermarket in Atlantic Highlands. He was from Tennessee and never lost his accent. "I tend to ramble on even when nobody is listnen'! How old are you?"

"I'm almost eleven. I really act much older than I am, mom says. I think it's because I read so much. I feel a lot older sometimes."

"Honey, you don't want to grow up too fast. Life can be hard when you have to be an adult." She sighed.

"I can see some adults make it hard. They argue too much about things that really never get settled and then they argue about the same things again!" She volunteered wisely.

"My, aren't you the philosophical one! I think life could be much simpler than it is but we tend to complicate it somehow."

"What are the initials for on your jacket? I'm sorry... that's none of my business," Nancy stammered, kicking herself for asking something she shouldn't.

The "cow lady" paused and tenderly picked up the jacket that smelled like cigarettes. She held it lovingly to her chest.

"They are the initials of someone I knew a long time ago. He gave me the jacket on a chilly night at a concert in Texas. I kept it ....to remember him." She looked out the window wistfully.

"I went to a concert once at the marina in Red Bank. It was so wonderful! A band played marches ... Mom knows the names of all the songs... she plays piano and teaches piano, but I want to learn on my own. She gets upset with me. I don't know why I don't let her teach me. She plays beautiful! Do you play something?"

"Why, I sure do darlin'! I play guitar and banjo and sing country music. That's what I do for a living…when I can get a gig."

"Wow!! A real country star! That is just so cool! Can I have your autograph? Do you have your guitar? Can you play something for me?!"

Shhhhh!! The fat lady in the seat in front of them peered around the seat and glared.

"I'm sorry. We'll be quiet. She's a country star! She can sing and play the guitar and everything!"

The rather large lady grunted, seeming less than interested in Nancy's discovery.

The "cow lady" was having a difficult time trying to keep from laughing out loud.

She leaned over to Nancy "Child, you sure do get excited! I'm no *star*… I haven't even sold many records. I just keep tryin' and singin' and… maybe someday I'll be discovered."

"You made a record! Do you have one? I'll pay you for one. Then you will have sold more! I don't have a lot of money, but I have four dollars in my purse left from ten dollars mom gave me to spend while we were in California… but, I didn't spend it all, so I have four dollars left… if you have a record, I'll give you all of it! Don't tell mom, though. She might get upset… but she doesn't get as upset as Dad does!"

"Honey, I do have one record left and you can have it for free. Just because you made me forget some sad things I was dwellin' on that I can't do anything about!"

"You mean you will give it to me? Oh, I would have to pay you something… that wouldn't be right!" Nancy said excitedly.

"Okay…Let's see. How about one dollar? That would be just about what it cost to make the record. Fair?"

"Deal!" As the "cow-lady" handed her the forty-five record with Sherrie Lange on the label Nancy couldn't keep quiet and shouted "Yippee!" Right out loud, not only waking up the rather large lady in front of them but also her mother and Erin as well as several other dazed travelers!

Ethelyn wasn't sure who had belted out the rebel yell so she looked around the bus curiously. Nancy had hunched down in her seat while her new friend, Sherrie Lange, the "cow lady", covered her mouth with the brown jacket to stifle the giggles. How Nancy expected her mother not to realize she was not in her seat was ludicrous but Nancy remembered the cartoon from Mighty Mouse where a character wants to go unnoticed and says the "magic words"---- "Puff puff piffles. Make me just as small as sniffles," Unfortunately, that doesn't work outside of the comic books. Ethelyn stood up from her seat when she realized her eldest daughter was gone and quickly spotted her.

"What do you think you are doing, young lady? I told you never to talk to strangers! I am so sorry, ma'am, if she is bothering you. She has a difficult time sleeping... really doesn't need too much sleep, so she always has to be busy! I hope she hasn't disturbed you. Get back in your seat, Nancy Lynne!"

Nancy glanced at her new friend and smiled sheepishly as she leaped back to her seat. Erin was grinning triumphantly as she counted up the points she had just earned by not being Nancy! Once back in her seat next to the window she curled up with her prize. Erin sat next to her and continued to let her know what a pest she was. Nancy looked at the purple label and could see as the daylight began to arrive, "Love you, Sherrie" written on it. The title was "In No-One's Shadow".

The title meant little to her then, but the autograph meant lots. It was just for her... special, personal, one of a kind. Over time, the record was lost during the many moves to follow but the title and the short friendship with a stranger still remained important to her. There are moments, perhaps fleeting... there are people who you meet and bond with ...there are lessons that are worth so much more than those you purchase, that stay with you all your life. Somehow, "just keep trying, walk in no-one's shadow, and treasure small moments in your life" kept Nancy going in the difficult times and excited her in the good times.

The sun began to wink at the windows of the bus as it slowly peered over the majestic mountain range that separated California from Nevada, Arizona, and New Mexico. None of the pictures in geography books did justice to the enormity and power that the Rocky Mountain range elicited even if seen through a smudged and smoke- tarnished bus window. The feeling of awe ran from her stomach to her throat and mixed with that odd sensation that she was protected somehow by their visual embrace. The sun uncovered shadows, folding back the blanket of night to reveal splendid shades of brown, orange, copper, and sand, dotted with an occasional hunter green forest intermittently at the base.

They passed through small villages, some with only a vacant building or two, full of cowboy spirits, deafened gunshots and the dust of the cattle drive toward a long forgotten valley. One of the towns on the border of Arizona was their destination – almost six hours across the desert – "Abecrombie" or "Albecory" or something like that. They had to cross the desert during the hottest part of the day, which seemed like really poor planning. The temperature was already eighty-two degrees and rising. A young girl at the back of the bus with her tiny baby was already perspiring and looking frail. She seemed too young to be in charge of a whole helpless human being.

The bus stopped to fill up before its launch into "no mans land" and the bus driver recommended that the passengers grab some bottles of soda or juice and some salt crackers or peanuts to take with them on the expedition. The passengers stretched and mopped their brows with hankies, sleeves, jackets, as they all filed off the bus into the tiny diner next to the gas station. Erin and Nancy munched on sandwiches and gulped down milk while Ethelyn gathered all her change to try and call their dad to let him know where they were. She came back looking as though someone had performed an exorcism. She was flushed and sweat was making lines down either side of her face. She wiped a drop of sweat from her nose as it was just about to drop on her dress. The armpits of her dress were wet and she was shaking as she attempted to light her Pall Mall cigarette. As she inhaled deeply, waiting for the aphrodisiac effect she seemed to get from those things, she began to cough forcefully, in spasms that hardly gave her time to breathe. The trouble was that when their mom began to cough like that ---it happened often--- she continued to attempt to talk, and smile, and sputter. The girls rarely could understand what she was saying when this happened, so they usually guessed.

"Erin, Mom says we should go outside and see if the bus is ready to leave, but I have to go to the bathroom—so you go, okay? Mom would be so proud of you if you do that for her"

Nancy really just wanted to get her sister out of her hair for a few minutes so that she could run over and say something to the "cow lady". She had seen her taking her suitcase off the bus and just had to see her and thank her again for the record and especially for the autograph. Mom had gone into the bathroom and Erin had gone outside. Nancy moved between the sweaty passengers, some looking at magazines and waiting in line to pay for the recommended rations for the desert trip.

Nancy's new friend was on the phone, hunched over her overstuffed tan suitcase with worn decals pasted over its body like tattoos. Tattoos of places Nancy had never been and probably would never see. She waited a respectful distance from her just starring at the decals and envisioning her in sparkling costumes on stages in those places, belting out her country songs to huge crowds of fans. She couldn't help but hear, though muffled, her voice rising and falling, almost angrily and then pitifully. She banged the receiver into its cradle so loud that Nancy jumped and could feel the color rising to her cheeks as Sherrie turned and saw her standing there. Sherrie's eyes were puffy and red and her make-up streaked like roads on a map. Nancy thought it probably was the heat, but the look in her eyes, smudged with the black soot of her mascara, was filled with pain, anger, and sadness all in one. She stared at the ten- year-old for a few seconds, smiled ever so slightly, and picked up her bag and guitar. Another bus had arrived and was filling its bowels from the gas pump. The "cow lady" shuffled to that bus and was talking with the bus driver, who was shaking his head negatively. She seemed to be pleading with him as she rooted through her purse, which had a big bull embroidered on the front and fringe all over the bottom. She handed him a crumpled wad of bills and he waived her toward the door of the bus, taking her suitcase and pushing into the storage bin. Nancy had followed out the door, wanting so much to ask her what was wrong, but her friend disappeared into the bus. The bus driver climbed in behind her and shut the door. Nancy looked desperately into each window, kicking up dust clouds as she ran around to the other side of the bus. She saw her and as the greyhound sputtered its goodbye, Sherrie smiled through the smudged, smoky window. Nancy mouthed "thank you" and the "cow-lady" did the same as the bus pulled away.

What had hurt her? What had someone said on the phone to make her so sad? Nancy's heart felt like it fell into her stomach as she slowly walked toward the diner wondering why sad things have to happen to good people.

"There you are!" Ethelyn cried. "Nancy, I was frightened to death! I couldn't find you or Erin. I'm so glad you are okay. I thought someone had kidnapped you two!

Don't ever leave were I put you, especially in a place with strangers and in the middle of nowhere! I about had a heart attack! Where is Erin hiding…. we have to catch the bus … the driver was kind enough to wait while I tracked you down. Well, where is she?…. Nan!"

"I..I ..I told her to see if the bus was still here a little while ago… she should be right where the bus is…. I… I only wanted to say good-bye to the cow- lady and thank her again for the record…"

"Nanceeee…..where is Erin?" Oh, my God! The bus moved over by the diner… she probably thought the bus at the gas pump was our b…b….Oh …. *Help*! *Help*! My baby is on the other bus! She is on the wrong bus! Where was that bus going? Call someone!!" She moaned and tears streamed down her face.

There… you did it again. You messed up. My little sister. Oh, gosh. I would never hurt her, Nancy thought to herself.

Their bus driver heard Ethelyn's pleadings and came out of the diner to see what was going on.

By now several of the passengers from their bus had wandered out into dusty sunlight. Ethelyn was near hysteria not sure whether to spank Nancy, shake her, or just collapse. She had managed to shakily light a cigarette and was taking long drags in between her sobbing. As the bus driver shuffled over to her, she managed to collect her bearings enough to sputter out the story about Nancy not watching out for her little sister and how she was sure that Erin had gotten on the bus that had left fifteen minutes ago and that she was frightened to death (long drag on the cigarette, ashes falling to the hot dusty ground) that Erin was on the bus in the clutches of some crazy person that sold children into slavery!

Hmmmm. Just for the tiniest portion of a second Nancy thought that wouldn't be too bad. The thought whisked through her brain just for a breath of a moment – she really was not that mean a sister. The thought barely had time to register before she was getting that terrible ache in her stomach realizing that there was a possibility that she might not see her little sister again. The bond between them was delicate and dynamic because of the fears they shared and because Nancy felt she needed to protect Erin. Erin looked to Nancy to fill the void when their mother left them alone with their father.

Back in 1951, there were no cellular phones or personal computers to try to contact the other bus driver. Their driver seemed really concerned, which was very nice since they were making him late for his intended route. The driver rustled through a cubbyhole on his bus for a handful of coffee stained maps. He spread them out on the counter of the diner which had suddenly been converted to a "search and rescue" station. Some of the other passengers were bringing Ethelyn lemonade, more cigarettes, and cool paper towels. Mom looked so tiny sitting in an old rocker in the corner of the diner next to a pot-bellied stove.

Nancy wondered why anyone would need a stove in this heat but it really didn't matter much as she was not about to ask any questions or attempt to be noticed in any way. She just really wished she could disappear. The thought of two daughters disappearing, though, would have pushed her mother over the edge. Nancy really wanted to hug her mother and have her hug back but that was really a rare happening in their little family. Her grandmother loved giving big hugs and wet kisses, but as loving as her mother was, she rarely hugged the girls until later in her life. Even then it was not a natural thing for her to do. She always stiffened a little when the girls hugged her. Her way of showing affection was with words and strength and general kindness. As for their father, the physical contact Nancy remembered was far from a hug.

She knew that bad memories should not overshadow good ones, but his anger and violent attacks sadly pushed aside lots of the good moments. There had to have been good moments or why would Mom have stayed with him?

She made herself very small and looked out the diner windows praying for even a mirage of the other bus to appear over the horizon.

Their kind bus driver had found what he thought to be the next stop for the "kidnapper bus." The pages of a phone book were being turned frantically to locate the probable destination.

The young girl with the baby who had been sitting in the back of the bus had glanced Nancy's way as she hid behind a counter of dusty magazines and newspapers trying to make very little noise. The young lady handed her little sleeping bundle to the young man who was traveling with her and walked over to where Nancy was hiding.

"Honey, are you okay?" she whispered in the sweetest voice. "I know you feel this is your fault, but sometimes we loose sight of our responsibilities and make mistakes. We're only human----God knows I know that! C'mon out from behind there. I'll let you see my baby --- do you want to see her--- she's sleeping finally, so you'll have to be real quiet."

"O-okay," Nancy said hesitantly "I love babies—I love my sister, too …a - and, even though we fight sometimes, I want her back! I am such a dummy! I shouldn't…"

The lady placed her finger over Nancy's lips with a gentle "shhh" and took her hand leading her over to where the young man held the baby.

"Her name is Amanda. She is only two months old"

Nancy peaked over the fold in the blanket that covered the tiniest baby she had ever seen except when her mother had brought Erin home from the hospital. Amanda was sleeping, and her tiny pink lips were making sucking sounds. Her skin was like cream and looked peaceful and safe lying in the young man's arms.

The young man (Nancy assumed he was Amanda's father) had dark hair and deep set almond eyes. His skin was tan and he had a red neckerchief wrapped around his head.

"This is my brother, Tim. He's helping me bring Amanda to my mother's in Kansas City. She had offered to take care of Amanda while I......" She looked at her brother, Tim.... " I ...go back to s- s-school." Her eyes began to fill with tears and she turned away, rummaging in her cotton dress pocket for some tissues.

She blew her nose and said "You go over there and give your Mom a hug and tell her you are sorry. She needs you...even if you don't think she wants you!"

The young lady and her brother walked over to an empty booth with Amanda. Tim looked almost as sad as she did. He sat next to her and put his arm around her as she held her face in her hands.

Nancy wondered where Amanda's father was, why the lady and Tim were so sad. She knew going to school sometimes made her sad but really didn't think that was why she was crying.

People you meet, even for a moment, etch a picture in your mind that stays frozen in time. In her mind later in life she could still see the young lady's face as clearly as if she were still here. The sadness, the love for the little baby, and behind all that the fear that people try very hard not to show. If she was at all good as an artist she would have painted her face right then to capture a look she didn't understand until her adult years. She had seen it on the face of Jesus painted in the garden of Gethsemane—anguish, love, pleading, courage, failure, and resolve – all in one face.

Nancy did go haltingly over to Ethelyn, who was slumped in the rocker, looking weary and very frightened. Nancy didn't care whether her mom wanted her to or not---- she just hugged her. Ethelyn's sweaty skin was cool and left a wet mark on Nancy's cheek. She didn't hug her mother really hard----just enough. Ethelyn patted her daughter's back with a conciliatory hug in return. She smiled and patted Nancy on the hand and put her head on her daughter's arm. Nancy whispered to her "I am so sorry, Mom… Erin is really smart… she will be back… they will find her, I know"

"I know, dear… I know it was my job to take care of you. I always think of you as a lot older. You are a good girl. I am so worried. You keep looking out the window and praying."

Nancy had read a book when she was about five years old called *Nancy Nurse and Doctor Dan.* She knew after reading it that she wanted to be a doctor or nurse, for sure. She never changed her mind except for a daydream now and then of being a famous actress, ballerina, or concert pianist. She confined the latter three to her musings just before falling asleep. Heaven knows that with a little more practice and self- confidence, they might have been more than a dream.

That feeling of caring for someone—how could she describe it? It's like the warm, sweet smelling, touch of your cheek on an infant's head, the absolute knowledge that something perfect had happened, the joyous ache in your throat and tears welling in your eyes because you want to shout with joy-----the touch of aged, icy, fingers pulling you near – eyes pleading you to stay one more moment. The sun pouring like liquid gold and pink lemonade over a foggy morning on a summer's day---so very difficult to describe!

She felt it even before she had learned words to describe things. She felt "caring" for someone—helping them in the smallest or the grandest way. It was to be the pinnacle around which she centered her existence. It also was temptress that scattered reason to the wind. It would define her—it would drown her---it would be her salvation and her demise, all in one.

Mom needed her, depended on her, and trusted her. To process it and be able to be sure of it… of her self- worth was not natural. She could see the rainbow but couldn't capture it. The image lasted just about a nanosecond.

If, as a child, the "inner self balloon" is not fully inflated by three or four years old, it sits inside the person with wrinkles in it that must be filled with something. Many of us fill it with good fluffy cotton that is easily plucked away. Some over-inflate it artificially with pompousness and arrogance. Others hammer in steely armor that no one can penetrate. Some fill it with drugs, alcohol, and sex, others with gambling, overeating, overindulging, overspending. Whatever personifies the "inner self, the "outer self" rarely sees it for what it is. To truly "fill the inner self" something spiritual or unnatural must happen deep within the hollows of that being.

In that "nanosecond" that came after she heard her mother's words, the shrunken "inner self" began to push the awesome feeling aside with self reprimands and apologies.

"Mom, I should have been a better sister, a better babysitter. I always seem to do the wrong thing....I should be the one who is lost not Erin," she pleaded.

Before her mother had a chance to agree or refute her confession, their bus driver came running through the diner door flushed and grinning.

"Ma'am, your little girl is on her way. I just got a call from the next town where the other bus had been stopped by a lady passenger who was on our bus and must have recognized your daughter, who was sleeping curled up on one of the seats in the back of the bus. She insisted on the other bus turning around and bringing---uh, what was your little girl's name, again?...uh Everell... Oh, yeh...Erin. She's fine and the lady even bought her something to eat. They should be back here within an hour. Sorry, folks that you are delayed, but thanks for all your help! We should be taking off as soon as Everell... oops ----Erin gets back." He bustled out the door with Mom right behind him.

"How very sweet of that lady...I am so relieved! I wonder who that is? I didn't know anyone on our bus. Thank you, everyone, for searching and being so patient.

I am so sorry we delayed you. God bless you!"

The passengers were gathering their snacks, purses, bags of trinkets, wiping their brows in the heat – and nodding to Ethelyn. One older gentleman that smelled like Nancy's grandpa's pipe smoke gave her mom a hug. He bent over a little more than he was bending already and patted Nancy on the head.

"I'll bet you're glad your sister was found."

She was. . But she sure wasn't going to show it---- too much.

"Yes, sir." she said sheepishly "I am sorry that everyone had to wait for us."

"You don't worry your pretty little head about that! I've had to wait for a lot of things in my life that weren't nearly as important as finding a lost little girl." He picked up a cup of coffee from the counter, gave her the kindest smile, and walked hesitantly toward the bus.

Just then the bus that had kidnapped Erin pulled up near the gas pumps. It stopped jerkily as if to say "Well, here I am again – what a pain!" The way the bumper grimaced below the headlight "eyes", it almost looked like it was scowling at her.

Erin jumped off the step before the bus had barely stopped. She ran through the cloud of dust caused by the tires up to Ethelyn, who was running toward her. Big wet kisses all around and a few tears. Nancy's heart pounded a little harder seeing her sister safe though she was hoping that no-one would notice. Nancy ran over to the small crowd of passengers who had gathered around the two of them. It was then that she saw the cow lady stepping out of the grumbling bus. Erin ran to her, dragging her mother and the small crowd with her as though she had magnets in her hands.

"This is the lady that made the bus driver come back with me. Boy! Was he mad! She said that he'd better if he knew what was good for him. I was asleep! I didn't even know I was gone until she woke me up and asked me where you guys were."

Nancy ran up to her friend and gave her a giant hug. "Thank you, thank you… you are such a good lady…. Thank you for making the bus driver come back…. I wasn't watching Erin and she got on the bus while I was waving good-bye to you or when you were on the phone…. I will watch her like a hawk… I -- I…"

"Honey, you talk so fast!" she said in that slow drawl of hers. "I'm just glad you have her back and that I was on the bus and recognized her"

Mom was shaking her hand like a pump handle. "God bless you … bless you!

"Can I give you a little something for your trouble? I don't have much but I am so thankful to you…" Mom was rummaging around in her purse when the cow lady put her hand on Mom's to stop her.

"Please, darlin', I don't need anything just the hugs from your girls. Anyhow, it helped me in a way to remember what is important. I was running away from someone but I decided after meeting your girls and seeing your love for them that nothing should stand in the way of a mother's love for her kids. Even if it means you might loose someone you think you love. I guess he isn't worth it if he can't see that."

Maybe that was why she had tears in her eyes when she was on the phone earlier. Nancy was a little too young to understand but she knew that something more had happened than just the rescue of her sister that day. Maybe the "cow lady" was rescued that day too.

You never know when someone is going to make a vital difference in your life. It can be during a brief encounter or a long and close relationship that your path can change in such a way that it determines your fate from that moment on.

Back on the bus, they snuggled down in their seats once again. The air was still stifling, but the feeling inside was different. The passengers talked quietly and little hints of laughter wandered about. The bus driver was commenting on a story the old gentleman with the kind smile was relating to him with boisterous hand gestures. There was a bond that hadn't been there before. You see it often when people go through tragedies together. Perfect strangers seem like your best friend during those times. Though it passes and life returns to what we call "normal" it is a type of magic between humans that may be as primitive as wolves gathering in packs for one purpose, or it may be that "inner spirit" that someone much greater than humans or wolves---some one who made humans and wolves---- gives to us during those painful times.

It was newly constructed, this rainbow made of steel and brass, dressing the St. Louis skyline in glimmering adornment. "The Arch" would carry sight seers from all over the world high above the city. .

They had survived the desert, the stale sandwiches and salty chips, an overnight stay in a hotel in downtown Albuquerque, decorated in the ornate theme of its Spanish descendents, and stale taco's, and arrived in St. Louis at noon, four days into the trip home. Halfway----- that was what Mom said. Nancy didn't know why the old knot in her stomach kept coming and going. The trip had been an adventure. As the bus passengers arrived at their various destinations, they all blew kisses, gave hugs and seemed a little sad to be leaving the old Greyhound. Even the bus driver seemed a tad melancholy as he turned the keys over to his relief driver. He lived in St. Louis, and was anxious to get home to his family. That must be a really hard job, driving back and forth across the States every week. Nancy didn't for a moment think that was something she would like to be! A doctor doesn't usually have to travel too much. She comforted herself with that thought.

Erin had slept most of the time while they were traveling so she was raring to go when the bus made its stop.

They had about three hours before they would begin their journey again. Ethelyn asked the girls if they would like to go to a movie nearby the bus garage. Laurel and Hardy, Charlie Chaplin, and several other old time comedians were showing at the seedy- looking theater. Mom loved the old silent films---she loved movies, period, but especially those. Whenever she would take the girls over to New York City on the Sandy Hook Ferry (twenty-five cents for passengers and a car) they would stay at the old Waldorf Hotel, not the new fancy one but the less expensive one, and go to the theater next door to watch the comics perform their crazy antics in the "silents" and in some early "talkies".

Nancy remembered them like yesterday and still mimics some of the looks, gestures, and stunts when she became a ham on an amateur stage. Their ability to "speak" with their facial expressions and body language always intrigued her. Mom was mesmerized from the moment the shadowy light from the projector appeared on the screen. It didn't matter that you could see through the floor boards or that debris was rarely picked up from that floor, so you always had something sticking to your shoes, or that there were bums and "ladies of the night" lurking in seats around them. It didn't matter that the film sometimes broke and you could see it burning on the screen. No, none of that mattered. .

Charlie Chaplin swung his cane and walked his famous "duck waddle" across the screen. Laurel argued with Hardy and Hardy argued with Laurel and Ethelyn and her daughters giggled at their overt acts and expressions. The Victrola played piano music fitting for the mood of each scene, and the three hours passed quickly.

Soon they were back on the bus, with different passengers and a different driver, ready to face the next three days' journey until they reached the Greyhound station in Red Bank. Dad was to meet them there to take them home. Nancy's mind wished that a different person would meet them. One who rarely showed anger treated mom and both of them with respect and love every day… a new person who kept his belt in the loops on his pants. Her insides told her otherwise – that nothing would have changed. It made her sad not so much for herself but for Mom and her sister, for Nanny, and also for her father. Why would you choose to be angry and hurt those who love you the most? Would she grow up and do the same things? If it stayed the way it was when they left for California she would have to run away. But who would protect Mom and Erin?

She just couldn't think about it. So she read her books, slept on her mom's soft belly and sometimes Erin's shoulder, watched the towns go by through the smudged window of the bus and day dreamed of owning a dollhouse with all the very finest furniture, carved to scale, with every detail artistically reproduced. A mansion where the "fairy grass" princess, a tiny imaginary Lilliputian (very much like Tinker Bell from Peter Pan lore) she had concocted one day playing near the huge oak tree in front of Nanny's house. The fairy grass (grown-ups call it moss, or something) is as deep green as the seaweed clinging to the boats in the harbor and as soft as the velvet dress she had fondled in the department store. Staring at it as it hugged the trunk and wound its way through knobby roots pushing up the sidewalk in jealous competition for the sun, she imagined herself a fairy princess so small that she could fly among the velvet fibers of the grass to a beautiful mansion. There she had everything any one could want or even dare to wish for. The sun glistened every day through enormous windows, birds and butterflies swooped through trees with fragrant blossoms, friends came to visit and laugh and all was peaceful – no fighting, no sadness, no pain. She would fly about making sure everyone had all they needed to make them smile. She had managed to rid myself of every freckle. Her hair was golden once again and hung like Repunzel's mane in thick curls over her shoulders.

That was her daydream… perfection in a very "imperfect" world, the freedom and resources to help anyone, the great feeling that comes with a reprieve from anxiety and "just not fitting in". That was her fairy princess.

She stayed with her for many years. The fairy grass disappeared when the tree was toppled in one of those gruesome hurricanes. The mansion melted in the daunting snows of New Jersey winters. She looked for her one sunny afternoon, but she had faded with her daydreams as she lost the magic of being a child.

The bus arrived in Red Bank early in the evening. Walter was waiting for them. He was standing on the platform with his hands in his pockets. He always wore a suit when he was going out in public, unless he was helping with the Boy Scouts or coaching baseball. The baseball teams were all boy teams in the late forties and early fifties. It was very rare to have women's team sports even in high school until later in the fifties.

He seemed really happy to see them as he loaded their suitcases in the trunk of the old car. He gave them all kisses and unusually warm hugs.

Nancy thought, *Maybe we should go away more often and everything will be okay.*

The bus pulled away and they climbed into the car. Mom was enthusiastically expounding on their adventures, the sites they had visited, and how good it was to spend time with her cousin. Thankfully, she omitted the disaster with the figurines. Their father said very little. He nodded appropriately and kept his eyes on the road ahead during the trip back to Atlantic Highlands. Nancy pushed away the feeling he was a tiger patiently waiting for the right moment to pounce. She wanted so to have a normal life where they all got along.

Nothing had really changed. As soon as the doors closed and they had emptied their suitcases he had begun to rant and rave about the cost of their trip, the insanity of spending so much money. Their mother received the usual pounding and he had threatened to do the same to the girls, but Ethelyn threatened to call the police and he had left cursing them all the way to the car.

He called them all to the kitchen several weeks after their return. The kitchen meeting seemed odd since very little was discussed at the kitchen table. *This must be pretty serious,* the girls thought to themselves.

"The government is moving us in a few weeks. We have a choice to move to Japan or Toledo in Ohio." Walter announced.

"It will be an adventure----lots of new friends and places to see." Ethelyn said in her most convincing voice.

"What is Toledo? Where is Toledo? Do they have hills? Is Japan where peoples' eyes are slanted? That's not in America! I want to stay in America!" Nancy frowned and looked at her mother for support.

"I want my Nanny" Erin said holding tightly to her favorite stuffed animal.

"Yes…..Nanny. She would miss us all so much. Can we take her with us?" the girls almost chimed in together.

Walter stood up from the table. "We can't take Nanny. This is her home. If we move to Toledo, Ohio it isn't that far away that we couldn't visit her. We need to get packing since we only have a couple of weeks left on the rent. I'll ask Uncle Al and Aunt Betty if they would take care of you girls while your mother and I find something in Toledo that we can afford."

Nancy and Erin were happy that they wouldn't have to get slanted eyes and bind their feet, especially Erin who already wore a size six shoe.

Chapter 13

Finding Something

Their aunt and uncle lived in a small town just northeast of Cleveland with their daughter and some very spoiled German Shepherds. Al was Dad's half-brother and delighted in teasing their mom unmercifully.

Ethelyn was so trusting and shy that she fell into his practical-joke traps like a professional "straight man" in a comedy act. There was one time she received a call from a "collection agency" demanding payment for a diamond bracelet their Dad had supposedly purchased. Ethelyn was beside herself not only because of the cost (the voice on the other end quoted $1500), but more so because she rarely received gifts from Dad, let alone a diamond bracelet!

After about ten minutes of negotiations Nancy got a little worried when her mom looked like she was sizing her up to use as collateral and Uncle Al couldn't contain himself any longer. You could hear his voracious crowing as Mom scolded him affectionately.

Aunt Betty was definitely the alpha dog in the family, second only to the two German Shepherds, Schatzie, and Sheldon. Uncle Al had learned long ago that a passive resistance was the best way to keep the peace. Aunt Betty always reminded the girls of an army sergeant lining up her troops and waiting for one of them to step out of line so she could pounce. She was an attractive woman despite her tough demeanor and Uncle Al seemed to love her cautiously. His nose and a portion of his upper jaw was bent to the side and a scar over his right eye narrowed the space between his brow and eyelid in such a way that he always looked like he was winking. The scars were a result of the terrible accident while sledding down Mount Avenue during his tenth winter. He had looked back to see if any of the other guys who were screaming down the hill behind him were catching up. It was in that brief moment that his sled rope caught under the rung and the sled steered toward a huge Oak tree in Sam Turner's front yard. He tried to veer away from it but slammed smack into it, face first. His sense of humor and his kind eyes distracted from the distortion caused by the accident. He always seemed handsome to his nieces.

Betty and Al's daughter, Gay, was one year younger than Nancy and was very tiny. Nancy envied her "littleness." Eleven-year-old Nan had started to display that pre-teen chubbiness that always precedes the appearance of hips and a bustline. Compared to Gay she felt she looked like a schmoo. That was before she found out why Gay was so skinny.

Their father had been in Toledo for a week now and called Ethelyn after they had arrived at Uncle Al and Aunt Betty's house and asked her to come up to see some apartments he had found. Betty grudgingly agreed to take care of the girls for a few days. Nothing like being loved by your relatives! Their mom drove off in the old DeSoto toward Toledo.

Nancy and Erin were to sleep in Gay's room. There was a bed with a simple army blanket covering it, a small table and chair and a closet with two shirts, one dress, and a skirt hanging by their lonely selves. That was it! Even Nancy's and Erin's humble bedroom had a dresser and a few more clothes, plus the memorabilia that you collect as a kid. But in Gay's room there was nothing that would tell you a young skinny pre-teen was here --- nothing.

In the morning, the girls were all directed to sit at a card table in the living room and were given toast, jelly, and butter for breakfast while their aunt and uncle and the two very spoiled German Shepherds ate eggs, bacon, toast and hot coffee in the kitchen.

They were told to go outside after breakfast, and the door was locked behind them for the entire day. They were not allowed in the house until four pm, not even to go to the bathroom. Nancy had learned to hold it very soon after starting school as she was too shy to raise her hand and walk in front of everyone, especially when they all knew where she was going. Erin, however, was unable to contain herself so she went behind some bushes and relieved the pressure. Gay seemed fine with all this. Perhaps she was conditioned to the daily routine. She never so much as looked as if she felt neglected or put aside. Many years later, many lives later, she contacted Nancy and they correspond to this day. Gay had moved quite often throughout the western states and had finally purchased a piece of land in Northern California where she intends to build a small house with a porch, raise sheep, and grow Lavender. She has a daughter who has traveled with her to achieve this final goal. Some women find strength and resourcefulness within themselves when denied the external niceties and outward expressions of love. When Aunt Betty was in a nursing home and close to leaving this earth, Gay was there with tender loving care she had never received herself, lovingly caring for her mother without resentment or blame.

Three weeks later, Mom rescued them. Looking back on that time, it really wasn't that terribly bad. Nancy guessed Aunt Betty, as many did back then, thought that children should be seen and not heard. The girls did not starve nor did they feel neglected. Since they were "banished" to the yard after breakfast, they made up the most elaborate circus with a clothesline and the old swing set. The clothesline was ideal for the world's most famous tightrope artist, and the swing set had open ends at the top metal bar that they used to announce the fat lady, the elephants, and the brave lion tamer from Russia. When all you have is hours of time and a young fruitful imagination, the sky is the limit.

Chapter 14

Toledo and the "Greasy Spoon"

Nancy remembered the ride in the old De-Soto and the few nights they spent at the old Commodore Perry Hotel, or their first tour through Tiedtkes during the family's introduction to Toledo, Ohio. Most vividly, she remembered a place called the "Greasy Spoon" somewhere near Madison Ave. She, her sister and ther mom sat at the counter waiting for their slimy hot dogs covered with chili and dripping with grease. They were famished from their four hour ride and wanted to eat anything that didn't taste like toast and strawberry jelly. Their mother seemed unusually quiet and pale. Nancy worried that the past weeks alone with Dad, without her protection, had been just awful. They never talked about the state of thing, as though the silence somehow made it all a bad dream. Nancy sometimes wanted to scream at her mother and let her know how angry and frightened she and Erin felt all the time, but one look at her in one of her few old house dresses, shoes that didn't fit her so she would walk pigeon toed to try and keep blisters from forming, and her treasured cameo holding a lost button's place on her dress, the kindness in her eyes, and none of those feelings would form into words - they just stuck in her throat like a piece of gum you shouldn't have tried to swallow.

In the circle of the tire swing, she is number one.
The swing that takes you through the ups and downs of life
Until we're done
The warmth of it surrounds you, representing the amazing ones
Women who, in simple and astonishing ways succumb
To pain, loss, and tempests, yet hold on for the ride
Their bravery and resilience make a difference in our lives.
They hold you on that tire swing and keep your strength renewed

This ride speaks of many
Who brought out the best in you

Their mother was an amazing woman. In fact, this book is about several amazing women. Or maybe it is just about that indescribable "thing" that women have that allows them to keep going through the excruciating pain of labor over and over in order to keep this human race going; the special type of strength that carries on even though your heart is burning through your chest when "he" says he needs to leave you; the endless caring for, working for, keeping your place for, doing for, taking a back seat for, enduring harassment for, saving for, yearning for that life hands you. The physical strength to lift many times your weight off of someone that is injured; the courage to manage a household, raise kids, work fifty hours a week, put up with a boss who takes great pains to intimidate and embarrass you, and go to school with young people who are sure they know more than you (and your sure they do too!). The ability to run the vacuum, cook dinner, fix "owies", wipe runny noses, feed and change a crying infant, listen to a friends troubles, wipe up spilled milk, wipe up "piddle" from the orphaned puppy the kids found, read the paper so you keep some brain cells intact, pay the bills with less than what you make, and run a comb through your hair, put on a little lipstick before he comes home. Women who deal with enormous losses – their children, partners, parents, health, jobs, finances, homes, self esteem, self worth, and find the time and kindness to help others... That *is* the tire swing! It has extreme highs and stomach wrenching lows. It sometimes hangs by a strong vibrant rope or by a threadbare strand. It often is so hot it burns your skin or so cold you hardly want to sit on it. It encircles you so you feel safe, but if you go too far or too high you will be snapped back or fall. Yet you go back to it each time expecting that this will be the very best ride yet.

Life... That is simply what it is... a ride on the tire swing.

Chapter 15

Settling In

The brownstone duplexes were separated by a small easement of grass and a few scruffy bushes. There were two bedrooms, one bathroom, a kitchen and a living room. Their furniture was worn and dingy. The couch and chair had burn holes from Mom falling asleep with her lighted cigarette and Dad's chair had a grease stain right where the back of his head rested from the hair cream he used in his hair. Picking his nose was an unpleasant habit and the girls were sure that the contents that he removed was somewhere on that chair. Mom had managed to convince Dad that the old upright piano, rarely in tune that it was, should join us in Toledo so that she could teach piano for a little extra cash. A cot off to the side of the living room was where Dad slept. A big old double bed and chest of drawers Mom had managed to confiscate from her grandmother's estate and a cedar chest occupied one bedroom where Ethelyn and Ali slept. Nancy was sure that her second sister, Alice, was some type of immaculate conception. Yes, Ethelyn had managed to get pregnant, unbelievable as it may sound. That is probably why she was so quiet and pale when she brought them here. Nancy knew enough about getting pregnant after reading *Girls Grow Up*, and she knew her mom and dad never slept together .... so where did this one come from?

After Ali was born, Nancy was sure she was an alien. Not only did Nancy have to babysit her all the time---- in between babysitting for the people upstairs and several others--- but Alice would only stop crying and go to sleep if she was rocked in her basinette and someone sang "Happy Birthday" and "Smile, Smile, Smile" eight thousand times. The "change of life" baby was called" poochie", "Ali-Baba", "Ali-Max" and several other names. Those three years in the brown duplex seemed to disappear from memory except for a few harrowing moments. Ethelyn's notes saying she had to get away became more frequent. Nancy entered the teen era terrified of moving on to high school, quite shy and embarrassed about how her home and her clothes looked -- not unlike other teens. Moments with Erin and Ali seemed to pale with the enormity of Nancy's entry into this restless phase of life.

These were the years when she decided that she had to become much more than she felt she was on the inside. She knew she could put on many faces despite what face she saw in the mirror. Whatever person she needed to be to survive any situation, she could pretend to be. Was she a good actress? Her only formal acting lessons were those she had to give herslef to make friends without letting anyone know who she really was, or thought she really was. This resolve carried her through many phases of life, relationships, her career, and her obsessions

Often Ethelyn would not have enough money to pay all the bills. Walter made a pretty good salary working for the government, but he loved the ladies. The stipend that Ethelyn received and the little she could gather from teaching piano barely made ends meet. (Nancy always wondered which ends----- and if they met, would it have made any real difference?). Dad was still quite handsome and loved swingimg a lady around the dance floor.

He could definitely turn on the charm with other females. The four females who were closest to him, however, seemed to just be in the way. Nancy was a definite irritant to the dark side of his character; she saw the bright side occasionally, but it was most generally displayed to others outside of the family. To his credit, he was also sending money home to Nanny in New Jersey. There was so much incongruity in what they saw him to be. Nancy wondered if they ever really knew him at all.

Erin found out years later that some of his earnings were spent supporting another life with one, or possibly more, of those ladies. Many humans stray and are unfaithful to their partners. It seemed even more of an affront to his family because they were the ones to struggle through his rages and punishments. The girls were blessed to be able to forgive their father and care for him several years before he passed away.

Because of this shortfall in cash, the telephone was often turned off for weeks at a time. Now, the heat being turned off and the landlord hounding them for the rent paled in contrast to the loss of that amazing invention, the telephone - especially to a teen-ager! This was much worse in Nancy and Erin's case, as they rarely took the chance of bringing friends to the apartment. They certainly couldn't express their frustration to their dad. It was expressed vehemently to their mother. Nancy could be lethal at times. All the frustration, fear, and anger could be triggered by something like loosing face with her friends. Because she thought she did such a great job of covering all those embarrassments and feelings of not belonging, how could she explain not being able to talk on the phone?

After she had screamed and stomped around the living room one of the times the phone was shut off, she felt loathsome and empty. She had even raised her hand to her mother in anger. What could she have done? Somehow, Ethelyn came up with the money, and the phone was available again to the selfish child. Ethelyn would do anything to make things better for them. She had visited the pawnshop once again, and there was a space in the closet that was filled with a clothes basket where Dad usually kept the movie projector. She begged the pawnshop owner to keep the projector hidden at least for a week, until she could somehow manage to recoup it. The girls didn't know how she did it but she did, despite the consequences.

One warm night in October, Walter went to the closet to get out the projector just as the phone rang. That moment seemed to suspend in time as he put two and two together - the clothes basket substitution and the phone ringing when it hadn't for a week.

"How did that damned thing get turned on? Where is my projector?" his face flushing and one hand reaching for his belt.

"I...I... don't know, Dad" Nancy managed to squeak out as she retreated down the hallway.

"I think Mom had it turned back on because Nancy was scream....." Erin announced innocently.

Nancy gave her the *shush* sign, but it was too late.

"How did you get the money?" he bellowed at Ethelyn as she came cautiously from the kitchen. She seemed so small and helpless. Nancy just wanted to grow like Goliath and stand in front of her and watch him cower.

"I said, where did you get the money to turn the *damned thing on?*" His voice seemed to echo through the living room, and his face grew crimson as little beads of sweat formed on his forehead and around his nose. He turned toward the girls with his hand tearing at the worn leather of his belt.

Nancy's feet felt like cement, and her heart began to pound. The familiarity of the feeling at that moment strangely made everything seem like it was moving in slow motion. She could hear the "thud", thud" of her heart beating in her ears, and everything from that moment on happened like watching slides or a replay of a great hit at a baseball game in slow motion.

"I know that damned brat nagged at you until you finally gave in!" Saliva sprayed from his mouth, and a small excess ran down one side of his face as he landed the first blow against Nancy's right arm. "Goddamn you!! And you..." He turned to Mom and slapped her across her back as she tried to turn and protect herself.

Nancy tried very hard to wish herself invisible, but 105 pounds doesn't melt easily.

"Leave mom alone! Leave her alone!" she heard herself shout. It didn't seem like she was really part of the scene. It seemed like she was watching it. She felt nothing.

Nancy knew full well that he had somehow been hiding somewhere when she had begged Mom to turn the phone back on.

"My friends will think we are so poor...What will I tell them? I can't... I *hate* this life... I Hate...!" Her fists were clenched in a rage that burned violently inside, fueled by much more than a phone service's absence. *"I almost hit her.. my sweet Mom....I almost hit her...just like him! Oh, God I...I'm just like him!*

The scene flashed through her mind as she was slapped and pushed past the telltale clothes basket and into the bedroom. When Nancy had almost hit her mother, Ethelyn had looked at her with tears in her eyes, put on her coat, lifted the heavy projector from its place in the closet, brought it out to the car, and pulled away. Nancy had wanted to run after her to beg her forgiveness, hold her, wipe away her tears, and tell her she wasn't like him...she just couldn't be. But she sat in a chair with the stuffing coming out and a blanket with cigarette burns covering its broken springs and burn holes. She sat there seething and nauseated. Ali was crying in her crib. She walked into Mom's darkened room, lifted the baby out of her crib and rocked her, holding her close and burying her face in her baby soft hair, sobbing and singing "Happy B..birth...day....to you", in between the sobs and spasms of breath. "Hap...py..Birth..d......"

She had wakened with a panicky feeling that she had just done something awful. Ali was sound asleep on her belly with her thumb pushed gently against her perfect baby lips.

Oh, my God, What did I do?? What did I do?

The leather made a dull whisper as it made its way through the air and fell against her back. She heard the sound and knew it had connected but felt nothing.

He was sputtering obscenities, and part of her wondered why no one came to see what was happening. Surely the cheap walls of the duplex and the few feet between the other duplex next door were poor insulators for the shouts and cries.

"You did it again, didn't you? Where is that projector?"

He ran toward Ethelyn who was trying to comfort Erin and Ali. Nancy heard them crying and her mom sobbing between cries of, "Oh...ouch....please, Walter... the little ones... I...I'll turn it off "

Something unusual happened. Most times, Nancy would just go to bed after the onslaught had subsided, check mechanically with the others, make sure he was asleep on his cot as she listened to his snoring and wished it would stop. But this time, she found herself in the driveway.

What am I doing here? He'll find me and drag me back into the house! I need to be in there to make sure it is over and everyone is okay! I need to get back in there!

She couldn't. She just ran into the open garage. The smell of gasoline and rotting grass stuck to the mower acted like an ammonia capsule under her nose, and she felt the sting of pain in her shoulders and back as the wall lifted. Her heart began to race faster, faster, skipping a beat now and then as if to catch up with itself. She heard the crickets and the sound of her shoes. She heard everything so acutely. It was like the abrasiveness of sounds when you've just had the waxed flushed from your ears by the Dr. Her pupils dilated, accommodating to the darkness in the garage. She felt along the side of the car to the trunk area. The metal was cool and she leaned her throbbing shoulder against it to try to ease the pain for a brief moment. She climbed onto the trunk and then laid face-down on the roof of the car, clinging to the curved sides while trying to hold her breath so her heart would slow down. Her chest against metal made her heartbeat resonate like a tribal drum. Her mouth was so dry her lips stuck together. Her mind was racing in a million directions, it seemed.

She strained to hear anything coming from our apartment. She could barely see anything because of the overhang of the garage-door frame. A small ray of light slid past the tree outside the bedroom and trickled eerily onto the driveway at the edge of the garage opening.

Nothing… nothing but the sounds of the night.

I should go back. What if mom and Erin and Ali are...you need to go back in there! I'll just wait here until I know he is asleep... then I'll go in and check on everyone ..... they are okay... I'll go to bed and get up real early before he gets up and he'll think I got kidnapped or killed or something... and he'll be sorry...he'll be sorry. Maybe I can find the keys to this car. It's not our car. Our car doesn't fit in the garage so it's usually outside in the street. Maybe I can find a way to start this car and drive away and change my name or go back to Jersey and live with Nanny...

But I would make Mom and maybe even Erin so sad and worried and she has enough to worry about! She probably is so worried now... if she is okay. I should have stayed. I never run... why did I run?" Her thoughts raced by each other. Racing and racing.

It was about nine p.m. when the telltale call signaled the beginning of "Round on, prizefight #1001, no prize...the winner is....the winner....no winner, sorry!"

The door creaked open and slammed shut like a trap around a frightened animal. The shadow grew larger as its owner moved into the driveway.

"Where are you, Ball? You'd better get in this damn house if you know what's good for you! You are in *big* trouble...*big* trouble. Get the hell in here...now!"

His voice was so ominous, she melted into the roof of the car, begging God to do something... anything.

"Walt, what's the matter? Did you loose something? I heard shouts and wondered if something terrible happened down here. Is there anything we can do?"

Someone, perhaps the neighbor two houses away, was moving toward the shadow that had stopped moving toward the garage.

"No, it's okay. Just a little accident with water in the kitchen overflowing, and we all got a little carried away!" Her father's voice had changed completely... softer, almost jovial.

Okay....okay? She wanted to leap from the roof of the car and run to the neighbor and show him the slide show of the prize fight, all the slides, the hideous, frightening, slides of their real life. She was so tired, she decided that remaining hidden would do for now.

The neighbor waved, "Okay, I'm sorry to be so nosey but my wife thought I should come down and see if you all were all right . Do you need to borrow our water extractor?"

"No, it's fine now. Lots of towels to clean up the mess, but it spared the carpet. Thanks so much for your concern. We're all settled down now." Walter chirped cheerily.

Clean up the mess! What if he went too far and killed everyone! Oh, God, please let them be okay. I've got to get in there, no matter what, she whispered to herself, her mouth so close to the car roof metal that she could smell her breath. That was not very pleasant.

Her father had gone back in the house. She could see the entrance door was open slightly.

Maybe he's waiting for me with a club or a knife or something. Maybe I should take something from the garage to use as a weapon.

She slowly oozed off the car roof and onto the trunk lid. She had been prespiring so heavily her skin made a squeaking sound as it slid across the metal. Her legs were like rubber bands as she tried to get her footing when she landed. The darkness was broken occasionally by a car's headlights passing on the street. She peered into the darkness but could see nothing. She knew where some tools were hung on the back wall, and she felt her way along the wall until her hand fell upon something with long sharp metal spikes and a smooth wooden handle. The spikes were curved and felt rusted.

I'll just take it with me, just in case.. I won't use it unless he hits me or tries to kill me. I'll hold it by the prongs and use this handle just to knock him out so I can call the police. If he killed them... what will I do.... Oh, God, what will I do?

Any plan that entered her head had consequences. Consequences that were neither very palatable nor offered any real way out of the situation.

Just shut down like you always do. Then you can move back into the house and check things out. It couldn't be any worse than if I had stayed and gotten the battle over.

The crickets chirped rhythmically and a little breeze cooled the moisture on her face as I slid to the cool garage floor.

Maybe he went to bed and won't hear me.

The three-quarter moon looked like an eerie smile in the dark sky, laughing at her as she tried to make herself one with the wall at the side of the garage. The back of her shirt caught on the small rake hanging from the hooks. As she tried to inch its talons out of her shirt, it fell to the floor with a loud clank. Her feet and legs became cement as she froze, barely breathing. She stared at the door to the apartment without blinking until her eyes filled with burning tears *One, hippopotamus...two hippopotamus... three hippo...* her heart drummed along with the chant in her brain. She dared to take a long deep breath, begging God not to let her sneeze or cough. Her head felt like feathers were floating in it, and she had to hold on to the wall to keep from falling. Her legs now were like mush as she bent down and put her head between them.

It was lying beside her foot, its metal spikes molded into a claw.

Still lightheaded and beginning to feel the walls close down around her she picked up the small rake and held it close to the front of her shirt as she slowly stood up and began to walk toward the door. The crickets seemed to scream "go back... go back" louder and louder. The screams seemed like the music that is so terrifying in horror movies.

The moon was low in the sky. It must have been sometime in the early morning, as her shadow preceded her and plastered itself against the door as though it was blocking her way. The hand that held the rake was prespiring so much it was difficult to hold on. Her fingers were numb from squeezing. The other hand that reached for the doorknob seemed to belong to someone else. It moved independently. She felt nothing. She stepped into the dark hallway and noticed the smell of old cigarettes and leftover macaroni and cheese and the camphor mom rubbed on her aching hands to relieve the early discomfort of arthritis.

No one stopped her. She walked cautiously toward the cot at the other side of the living room. . The dim light from the kitchen outlined a figure lying on his side with an old army blanket thrown partially over him. She heard the snoring sounds bouncing off the wall. It sounded more like a growl than a snore. The arm rose up with the rake and perched in the air like an eagle preparing to pounce on its unsuspecting prey. She saw it perching there and wondered what it was doing. There seemed to be no connection between Nancy, her arm, and the rake. No thought of what could happen if it fell into that body lying there. No thought at all.

Suddenly, a tiny cry muffled by a closed door brought the hand with the claw down to her side. She jumped back as if she had just wakened from a horrible dream. The realization that she was awake and standing near his cot made her step back behind the kitchen doorway. A sickening acid churned up from her stomach to her throat and burned so violently she couldn't breathe in or out. The figure on the cot groaned and rolled away from facing the wall. She wondered what she was doing with that garden tool in the house when Ali began to cry pitifully.

"Mmmmmmmmammma. Mmmmmmmmammma".

Nancy forgot about where she was and what she was doing and

tiptoed into Ali's room.

Ali's tears mixed with the stuff running from her little pug nose, her hair standing out in all directions, and her arms stretched out, made Nancy's heart ache. She slowly picked Ali up from her crib and felt a little hand on her face, a moist warm head, and that wonderful baby smell (a mixture of a urine-sopped diaper and baby lotion), and she vowed she would never run again, no matter what. She wouldn't run away.

After a very subdued rendition of "Happy Birthday" and a fresh diaper, Ali fell asleep, her tiny bowed lips making chewing movements.

"Mom?" Nancy whispered. "Mom?" as I opened the door to their room expecting to see the comforting glow of Ethelyn's cigarette. Ethelyn would often sit in the girl's room and smoke so she wouldn't awaken Ali.

There was no glow, no one in the bed. Erin was deep in sleep, one pajama covered leg hanging out of the covers. The morning light was peeking through the window and winked patterns on the bed as it gradually filtered through the trees.

Mom's bed was made… undisturbed. There was a note written in her tiny handwriting lying against the pillow.

I need to get away for a while. You take care of Ali and Ethel. Be good. Remember I love you. I'll be back. Love Mom

Panic reached up from Nancy's empty, sore stomach and grabbed at her throat.

How could you leave us!? With him! How could you do that? The tears came then, buckets of them. She didn't want to wake up the other two, so she ran to the bathroom and locked the door, covering her mouth with a towel and sobbing, just sobbing.

"Mom… I'm sorry I left you… please come back… I can't make it without you. Remember I'm going to die when you die… please come back.. I'm so sorry I made you turn on the phone… I should have stayed!" The tap on the door stopped her outpouring.

It isn't dad. He would be shouting, she said to herself

She unlocked the door and opened it slightly. There was Erin with the note in her hand and tears running down her cute little face.

"Mommy…I want Mommy!" she sputtered between sniffles.

Nancy held her tightly "Mom will be back. She had to go back to New Jersey to make sure Aunt Laura is okay. She had something wrong with her... she... broke her hip and Mom had to help her. She will be back soon. Now wash your face, brush your teeth, and get ready for school. I'll make some cereal. I have to see if Mrs.Green will watch Ali until I get home from school. We'll be fine. We're big girls, aren't we?"

"B-b-but, Dad was mad. He hit Mom again. Where were you? You made her turn on the phone and...."

"That's all over now. I'll baby sit and get the projector back and Dad won't be mad anymore," she lied.

"Promise!"

"I promise, now get those big feet in those shoes. Get dressed, and I'll change Ali".

Nancy splashed cold water on her face, brushed back her frizzy hair (Mom had made her get a permanent and her hair had turned out like a Brillo pad), and pinned the bangs back to one side. She didn't look much like the fairy princess that morning, for sure!

One blessing was Nancy's amazing ability to carry on with very little sleep. She had been afflicted with the ability since birth her mom said. She was a good baby but very rarely slept more than four hours at any one time. She never seemed to need to sleep. Perhaps she was always in a state of readiness.

She picked out a blue sweater that mom had bought for her, a plaid skirt, socks, and her scuffed up saddle shoes.

It will be okay - just hang in there. Mom will be home...maybe even Wednesday...it's bank night at the Colony... she loves that...she'll be home Wednesday. I'll cook beef stew...she loves that!

He was gone. She didn't remember seeing him get ready for work, but somehow he did; every day, faithfully at five a.m., magically he would disappear. She didn't even know if he knew Mom was gone until he got home and found her note.

They saved the notes, lots of them, all the same few lines. Ethelyn came home on Wednesday. It was bank night at the Colony.

Erin and Nancy loved to go down to the Colony Theater and watch "Superman" movies for ten cents and walk through Ottawa Park on the way home to the duplex on Kershaw. The park was several blocks from the theater, but it was usually daylight when they went, even in the winter. They were allowed to go that way home as long as they got home by four p.m. Sometimes Mom would go with them. Ethelyn loved movies. The girls believed she lived vicariously in the romances and musicals so prevalent in the forties and fifties. The acting made those classics the works of art that they were. No special effects or computerized overlays, just pure passion for the art of impersonations and ability to portray every emotion on a single face.

They would treat themselves to sandwiches stacked with warm corned beef and melted cheese at Brauer's Delicatessen. Each sandwich was garnished with a huge kosher dill pickle and a scoop of coleslaw. Mom loved the adventure of an outing or traveling.

The paradox of their lives was so confusing that it was amazing that they felt comfortable in either world.

One scorching hot summer day, Erin and one of her friends squinted as they came out of the dark theater after and exciting two hours with "Superman" and several silly "Tom and Jerry" cartoons. It was Sunday, and they had gone to church early so they could make the twelve-noon matinee. Nancy had walked home with some friends who lived near to her on Kershaw leaving instructions with Erin and her friend to stay only a short time at the park.

Calculating the amount of time it would take them to walk to Ottawa Park across from Toledo Hospital, swing on the swing set, slide down the hot slide, and play a little hide and seek in the woods before heading home, Erin figured they had about two hours.

Erin glanced up at the hospital and recalled Mom lifting up a little bundle with a few hairs sticking up from the swaddling blankets in the third floor window of the hospital so they could see their new sister. Kids weren't allowed to visit the maternity wards back then; they had way too many germs and a potential to make noise and touch things they shouldn't.

Normally, after drinking ice cold water from the fountain, peeking into the brownstone building in the park where it was said the drunks would hold meetings, turning all the seesaws the same way up, swinging on the old creaky swings, they would have just enough time to hide behind the big trees in the woods adjacent to the playground area before they would run home about fifteen blocks to the west.

That particular day was so hot that they ventured a little farther into the woods, heading for the cool little brook they knew ran along a path that wound deep into a very thick and dark area of the park. Erin figured if they could find the brook they could take off their tennis shoes and socks and refresh their feet in the icy water before walking home. The woods gradually dipped down into a small valley that harbored their destination. Huge oak and sassafras trees allowed small streams of the blazing sunlight to filter through like spears cutting through the darkness.

They didn't see him standing there until he was less than ten feet from them. He shouted to them in a gravelly voice, "C'mere girlies!"

They were already quickly turning away from not only him, but what they saw he was holding in his hand. They probably set a record as they scurried up the hill on the other side of the brook. They ran through the woods and across the playground, streaking across Kenwood Boulevard, through the Colony, past the theater, past Brauer's, past the grocery store, past their neighbors' houses. They glanced back a couple of times just enough to see the man walking briskly about a block behind them. A lady and her son came out of one of the houses along the way when they heard the girls' screams.

Between gasps Erin and Lisa reported the horrifying tale. The lady's son walked up the street toward the Colony where the man had last been seen pursuing them, but he was nowhere in sight.

"You girls are only a couple of blocks from home. We will call the police and you run as fast as you can to your houses," the lady cautioned.

It took barely ten minutes to run down the two blocks to Erin's and Lisa's homes. Erin entered like a raging wind and slammed the door of the duplex behind her. Lisa ran into her house waving a limp hand toward her friend. Mom sat Erin's breathless body on the piano bench and tried to make sense of her sputtering tale between sobs.

Erin was trembling and was nauseated just remembering the vision of the grizzly old man with hollow eyes holding his privates and stepping towards them. Mom called the police station and, within an hour there was a lady knocking at their door asking to speak to the two little girls that had been in the park.

The lady detective was very nice. She held Erin's hands and asked lots of questions.

"Where in the woods did you see him first?" "How old do you think he was?" "What did he look like?" "Was he short, tall, or medium?" "Was he old?" "Did he have a beard?"

Poor Erin was so exhausted. Ethelyn gave her a cold fresh squeezed lemonade and tucked her in bed after the detective left. She held Erin's hand until she fell asleep.

Of course, they never went to Ottawa Park alone again, rarely venturing beyond the playground. Somehow, the woods had lost its appeal and magic. They never found out whether the man had been caught. It seemed really sad that he had to do that to get attention. They didn't remember Dad saying anything. Perhaps Mom never told him.

The spring and summer of Nancy's thirteenth birthday was full of interesting times and lots of new feelings. Her preteen chubbiness started to smooth into a few feminine curves and her hair was tinted with reddish blonde streaks. The awful frizzy permanent had grown out below her shoulders, and when she had dance class every third Monday in gym, it wasn't so awful to have Jim Galsgow's hands around her waist. Especially now that she had a waist, and he didn't step on her feet as often.

She thought there must be a sign somewhere that said "teenager for hire". Mom and Dad decided it would be safer for her to be residing in other homes for a while. Walter had asked his superior officer, General Forrester, if he and his wife could use some help around the house.

The general and his wife-- General and Mrs. Forrester--- had a beautiful early American home on the corner of a perfectly manicured and landscaped lot in Perrysburg, Ohio. It was a unique community southwest of Toledo proper that was a mixture of old Civil War mansions winding along River Road, overlooking the Maumee River as it curved its way to Lake Erie and newer homes of the growing upper middle class. To Nancy their home was like something she had seen in *Better Homes and Gardens*. Of course, she only glanced at that type of magazine while she was waiting her turn at the dentist's office. Every piece of furniture was "early American," from the four poster beds to the tiniest figurine. There were scads of those. Nancy was so nervous when her father dropped her off to spend her first two weeks of the summer cleaning their house and behaving like a lady. She really never knew how that arrangement had come about, but it was so pleasant staying with them and realizing that she was a good child - and a very hard worker.

With the haunting memory of the time she destroyed mom's cousin's glass figurines ever present, every one of Mrs. Forrester's treasures were dusted with tender, loving care, and placed back in the exact location from whence they came. She found a wonderful cleanser for the linoleum floor that had a wax in it as well. She scrubbed and polished the kitchen and bathroom floors until they glistened.

The general taught her how to make a bed so that you could bounce a quarter on it and by the end of the two weeks her mitered corners could pass any military inspection.

She was allowed full access to the library, which had floor-to-ceiling shelves of books. She began reading from Mark Twain's collection and also read four volumes of the history of World War I , various classical novels, and even old poetry books by Chaucer, Shakespeare, Wordsworth, and Browning. Each book made her feel as if she was taking a journey with the author, who painted the pictures so well she could see them as clearly as if she was an actor in the play.

On Sundays, she would put on her one best dress and tiny pair of high heels to attend church with the general and his wife. The last Sunday before she was to be picked up to go home, she had to pin her underwear together because the elastic waistband had broken. She prayed that the little pin she had forced to hold the band together would last until the service was over, and she could say her good-byes and run to Mom's car before it gave way.

No such luck! The pin held out throughout the service and until they were shaking hands with the preacher in the entrance to the church. People were nodding politely smiling at their fellow church members. It seemed like there were a lot more people this Sunday than the last and they were milling around a lot longer. As she went to walk down the steps slightly behind the General and Mrs. Forrester it popped! She could feel the panties sliding down her legs to her ankles.

Without missing a step, she kept walking right out of those horrid old panties and hopped into the car without looking back. What a memoir to leave from her visit to this elite community! She never told her mom or dad or anyone. She used the heat of the day as an excuse for her red face when her mom asked if she had a fever.

Chapter 16

Spin the Bottle

Mark Bernbaum had thick black hair that carelessly fell across his forehead and framed a superbly handsome face. Dark brown eyes flirted with Nancy's hesitantly as they attended the service in the synagogue. Rabbi Katz was enchanted to have a guest from the gentile world to show off his chanting of ancient Hebrew hymns and to demonstrate that there was only one God and not three Gods in one to this poorly informed Christian. It was a paradox that she was spending the summer before her entrance into high school with an Orthodox Jewish family, seeing how demanding her father was about observing the Catholic faith. But their life was a paradox, so she did as she was told and packed her few pairs of shorts, two blouses, panties with intact waistbands, and her only brassiere.

She had purchased her first brassiere at Tiedtkes a few months before. It had been quite embarrassing when the saleslady brought in the thirty-two AAA as a last resort after trying on several other bras with "real" cups and commented, "Honey , you should keep wearing undershirts for a while." She bought a thirty-two AA just to show her that she wasn't pulling in her underarm pudge properly and departed red-faced and completely mortified. Ethelyn had tried to comfort her with a strawberry soda at Walgreen's but she still felt even more "out of sync" than she already did.

She haltingly remembered one day at Scott pool earlier that summer. The pool was two bus trips away over on the south end of Toledo- a place where very few white kids went, but that never seemed odd to her. One thing their folks had taught them or had displayed to them was not to discriminate. We were all just "people" regardless of our color, station, wealth, or impediments. She thanked them for that, as it would open many interesting worlds to her that she may not have even thought to explore had she not been given that gift. The pool was so packed on that sweltering day, the kids had only enough room to bob up and down in the water. They looked like that muskrat game where they pop out of holes intermittently and you use a mallet to hit which ever one pops up. Being skinny, bustless, and awfully critical of herself, she had stuffed a blue neckerchief in one cup of her bathing suit and green one in the other to attempt to have some type of female shape. Suddenly, during a particularly energetic bobbing session, the group of African American kids nearest to her were laughing and pointing – at her—at her bathing-suit top----at the blue and green "floaties" sneaking out of their hiding place. When she realized what was happening, she quickly turned and pushed her way through the crowd, slithered up the ladder, trying very hard to be invisible and ran for the bathhouse. That was her last visit to Scott Park Pool and the last alternative use of neckerchiefs in her entire life. To this day, she does not wear neckerchiefs!

So she packed her one and only brassiere, some hair ties and her diary. She couldn't take any toiletries as they only had one bottle of shampoo and one bar of soap. She was off to the Warneke's home about eight blocks from their duplex. She was to clean their home, keep to herself, be polite, work hard, and not expect pay – this is a favor to Mr. Warneke, and mind her p's and q's.

She had recently read *The Source* two times through, so felt quite enlightened as she sat on the bench in the Synagogue between Ilah, the Warneke's teenage daughter, and Mrs. Warneke. Both were lost in the chanting and the demagogueries of the rabbi. Nancy noticed how very buxom both ladies were, though she tried not to stare. She could barely see Mark around the mountain like profile of Mrs. W.

Ilah barely acknowledged her existence the first few weeks after she entered their lovely home. Every part of the two story bungalow was neat and uncluttered. Two tastefully flowered couches faced each other in front of a fireplace with a mantle adorned with a vase of fresh cut flowers, geometrically placed pictures of Mr. and Mrs. Warneke in their finest, and a picture of Ilah coyly grinning at the camera as though she had the most delicious secret. A large coffee table with a lightly tinted glass top and simple but ornate wooden frame and legs was positioned exactly between the two couches. Two lamps with milk glass bases were positioned on matching wooden end tables at each end of the couch. A large easy chair with an ottoman sat in the corner between two windows with an end table and lamp to match the others in the room. A small area next to the stairway leading to the bedrooms and bath had two matching chairs and a small antique table with an antique lamp set between them to form a conversation area. Across from the staircase, majestically standing against the wall was an ornate grandfather clock that chimed deep lonesome sounds each hour. When she was dusting carefully, fearful of pulling another booboo like the one in California, she would sit in one of the chairs just to listen to the tick-tock of that clock. It was sedating and often carried the beat of her heart. She would do her work thoroughly and go to her small room, a sewing room with a futon and a small mirror on a desk, or take a walk around the block. The houses were built in the twenties or thirties. There were different designs, some brick, some wood, with manicured lawns and bushes.

Nancy ate food brought to her on a tray that first week, then was asked to eat meals in the kitchen. By the third week she was invited to sit in the formal dining room with the family at dinner time. Everyone ate at the table. Mrs. Warneke would not sit down until all were served and satisfied. In this household, satisfaction for the meal was demonstrated by a loud belch after the dishes were cleared away. Nancy had stifled so many belches over the years that it was embarrassingly difficult to bring one up, let alone forcefully. Ilah, up to that time, had barely spoken to her other than to ask if she had seen something or to sneer at her when she was being hoisted from piano to dance to Yiddish language class by her parents or those parents of her compatriots. Around the third night of Nancy making gestures like a flamingo in heat attempting to produce a real belch (she had faked them the past two nights), Ilah burst into laughter.

"She looks like a bird that ate a fish whole and is trying to swallow it!" she giggled. "Just give it up, Nan. You are going to erupt!" The adult Warneke's were trying very hard not to laugh with their daughter at the poor gentile child but soon they were all laughing.

Things changed from that moment, and Nancy was treated more like a guest than a servant for the rest of her stay.

One day as Nancy was coming down the stairs from putting the laundry away, she encountered Ilah sitting on the stairs with her head in her hands. Her shoulders were moving up and down and Nancy could hear sniffling and tiny little muffled sobs. Nancy sat down on the step next to her and cautiously put her arm around Ilah's shoulder. She wasn't sure if she was being too bold, but Ilah didn't move away.

"What is wrong, Ilah. Did you get in some trouble?" Nancy asked softly

"N-n-noooo.........it's.........it's ..... boys! Men! They are so mean!"

"Is it Mark?" Nancy asked hesitantly. Mark and Ilah were an item. They had grown up together, and their families were very close. In the Jewish culture, Jewish boys and girls, men and women rarely fraternized with, dated, married out side of there own. Despite what Nancy envisioned as Mark's interest in her, it would never be allowed. So the occasional "look" at the synagogue or grunt "Hi, kid" was all she could ever hope for. Nancy wanted to hear Ilah say that Mark had left his Jewish faith, was turning Catholic, and was head over heals in love with the Catholic servant, and Ilah was at that moment just mourning the loss.

Instead she heard, "Of course it's Mark... I was on my way to classes at the Center and I saw him with Jessica Lonewitz, holding hands and....and..... kissing!" A humungous wail followed by blowing of noses and sniveling followed, both of the girls doing in a half box of Kleenex. After several dramatic moments, they looked at each other and started to laugh, between blows.

"It's great you feel so bad for me" Ilah chirped. "You are really a nice person, even if you are gentile and can't belch!"

"Forget boys, at least for a little while! They are such boobs some time!" Nancy expounded.

They decided to put a new forty five record on the Victrola and practice their "chicken" to the tune of Bill Haley and the Comets' new one "Rock Around the Clock" They moved the precisely placed coffee table to the side and shook the milk glass lamps with their wild gyrations.

The door opened, and there stood Mrs. Warneke. The matriarch, the silent woman behind the very successful man, the orderly commander of the household, and the keeper of the traditions was home. There she stood with her massive breasts heaving and there they stood with their..... well, Ilah's massive breasts heaving, and Nancy's shriveled self trying to be invisible again.

"What is this?" You know you are not to dance in the living room! It is a living room, not a dance hall! Ilah Joanna Warneke – you help Nancy put things in order, and then both of you go to your rooms until dinner!"

For some reason, Nancy moved in front of the trembling Ilah and said," It was my idea, Mrs.Warneke, don't blame Ilah. I was trying to make her feel better, she has an earache".

Ilah tried to shrink behind Nancy and let her go on.

"See all the Kleenex over by the stairs. I think she is not feeling too well and probably needs some of your marvelous chicken soup," Nancy said, pleading Ilah's case.

"Oh, my darling....you shouldn't get all sweaty. Come and lay down here on the couch and I will warm you some soup," Mrs. Warneke lamented as she walked Ilah--- who was growing limper by the minute---- to the couch, covered her with an afghan from the hall closet, and planted a big wet red, lipsticky kiss on her forehead.

Nancy guessed that was a turning point in their relationship. The "serf" was transformed into the "friend," and the next three weeks were filled with trips on Warneke's beautiful sailboat to Put-in Bay, sharing raisinettes at the Colony movie (Superman was the special on Saturday matinees and he was so handsome and muscular), even shopping trips to stores Nancy had never even dared to enter. They laughed at each other, gossiped indiscriminately, and shared the roller coaster feelings of that time between childhood and womanhood. Nancy felt she had most certainly arrived when Ilah included her as a guest (not a waitress, as was usually the case) at one of her Saturday night parties. These, of course, were well chaperoned by the Mrs., while Mr. W. frisked the boys as they entered the front door. Nancy was sure background checks and fingerprints preceded any invitations. Yes, boys were allowed to come to these events but all snacks and drinks were provided by the parents, any games played were screened and approved, and the party ended promptly at ten p.m.

This particular party would end up a little differently than the others because of a twist of fate, or just pure luck: the Warneke's were summoned to Mr. Warneke's place of business, a clothing outlet, because of a possible burglary. Thank heavens there was not actual crime, but the three boys and six girls at the party were thanking their deity of choice when the chaperones departed with hasty instructions to call their parents and have them picked up early.

They figured they only had about one half hour to play an "unapproved" game before the Warneke's or the other parents came to retrieve the guests. Mark (*sigh*!) pulled out an empty Coca Cola bottle from his jacket pocket. There was only one size Coca Cola bottle in the fifties, and it could easily fit into a jacket pocket. He held it up to the overhead light in the basement where the no-longer-carefully-monitored party was being held. The light shone through the green-tinted glass like beacon from a lighthouse.

To the nine teen-agers sitting around on the couches and the big fluffy area rug, you could equate it to a person having their first drink of cold water after being on a desert for days without one. The girls giggled and looked shyly at the boys who were oozing testosterone and visions of being kissed, perhaps for the very first time.

The bottle was laid on the basement linoleum, and the guests arranged themselves circling it as though it was the Holy Grail. Everyone arranged themselves in a position that they felt would be most apt to be across from the neck of the bottle when it stopped spinning. The "spinner" would be the one to offer a kiss to the lucky winner. Each person would get two spins which guaranteed two kisses. In addition to Ilah, Nancy, and Mark, there was Freddy Spetka--- a blond-haired Arian fourteen-year-old who was six feet tall and was the pick of the crop from their grade school to play first-string basketball at DeVilbiss High in the Fall. No one knew much about Freddy, except he could run like a panther, had springs in his tennis shoes, and always made at least sixteen points a game. He was extremely shy off court and made sure he was surrounded by several of his team (guards, she supposed), as if he needed protection from the rest of the kids. No one never saw him with a girl, and rarely heard him offer much in classes. His smile was mesmerizing, and he was a mystery to most of the kids. The girls were very anxious to be the "one" to whom Freddie chose to bare his soul.

Then there was Marvin – poor Marvin. He was the resident "geek" of the group. Ilah somehow felt sorry for the way he was treated by the other kids and even some of the teachers and always included him in the social events she commanded. Marvin had some sort of a deformity of the bones in his spine, which made him look like the Hunchback of Notre Dame. In fact, that was one of the cruel names he was called, especially by the boys at school. "Hey, Quasimodo, bring us some slime from your dungeon!" they would shout at him. He never seemed to notice, nor did he react to their jeers in any way, which made them holler even louder and with more intense insults. Ilah stomped over to them, one day, as they were lambasting Marvin with all kinds of name-calling. Her fists were clenched, and she had tears ready to plunge down her reddened cheeks.

As she approached Tim Renshaw, the biggest and least scholarly of the group, she shouted, "Stop it right now! Suppose you were in his shoes, how would you feel if you heard the things you say to him every day? You are just a bunch of big, ugly, lugs!!"

Tim countered as he puffed up his big two-hundred plus pound body, looking very much like a blowfish, "Well, well, well...is this puny little Marvin's new girlfriend? Hey, Hunchie, come get your sweetie." He grabbed Ilah's arm and pulled her into his portly belly, then wrapped his arms around her waist and lifted her up about two feet off the ground. "Do you want to me to throw her to you, you bent up piece of *sh*-----! Come and rescue your baby, twerp!!"

Ilah tried hard to wrestle her way out of Tim's clutches, pounded her fists on his muscle bound arms and attempted to connect with his muscle bound head.

Marvin's face changed into something akin to a tiger that had just lost his last meal to a lion. As much as he could with his wrinkled back, he straightened from four feet six inches to almost five feet, an awesome feat. He headed straight for the backs of Tim's legs like a charging bull and sank his teeth into Tim's right calf. With a yelp that sounded like a dog in heat, Tim released his hold on Ilah and grabbed his injured leg. Snot ran from his nose and tears began to flow as he fell to the ground whimpering. Ilah ran to Marvin----- who had shrunk into a frozen four-foot-six-inch statue with eyes bulging out of his head----grabbed him by the hand, and they both began to run up Sylvania Avenue toward the corner drug store.

Tim's gang was laughing at him as he hobbled off toward his house. They probably would regret doing that, but they had never seen Tim look so small and vulnerable. Needless to say, they stayed out of Marvin's way for the rest of the year.

Marvin was guest number five.

Two of the girls invited were Sally and Susie Andrezach. They were identical twins and very best friends with Ilah. Their mother and father were Jewish Orthodox, and the Warnekes vacationed and socialized with them since the girls first year in DeVeaux School. The Andrezach's were very wealthy from some sort of airline-parts business and "good solid investments," as Mr. Warneke put it. They lived in Ottawa Hills in a splendid home with gardens tended by gardeners, dinners prepared by a chef, and even a butler. This affluence was never flaunted in any way. Mr. and Mrs. A were quiet, kind, and unassuming as were their beautiful twin daughters. The only way you could tell Sally and Susie apart was be the gap in Susie's two front teeth and her dimples when she smiled. They dressed alike, ate alike, and talked "twin talk" when they wanted to share secrets.

Maria Benaneche was number eight. Her dark Italian eyes and coal black hair set off her olive skin mysteriously and drove the boys insane. She had a deep, throaty quality to her voice, which gave her the opportunity to sing many solos with the glee club at school. She had six brothers who taught her everything she needed to know to be a class-act tomboy. She loved climbing trees, playing football with anyone who would dare to play with her, and chewing huge wads of gum as she slammed the tennis ball toward any willing opponent. Even with her boyish demeanor, there was this feminine aura that made her very attractive and needy. Nancy was sure all the boys in that basement wished the Coke bottle was magnetized toward her.

Number nine was Rhonda Markowicz. Her red hair set her apart from other Jewish girls and the fact that her father had married a gentile woman he had met when he was stationed in Ireland caused a difficult situation for them and their daughter in the community, as well as in their religious traditions. Yes, Rhonda's mother was Catholic and remained so while attending services at the temple on the Sabbath. Mr. Markowicz performed the same accommodation by attending temple on Saturday and Mass on Sunday at St. Andrew's Catholic Church with his wife. You have to remember this was the fifties, before the renaissance and the abandon of the sixties. Neither the Jewish nor the Catholic community accepted this arrangement, even though it did not seem that the Markowicz's needed or cared about their approval. Rhonda, in the middle, worried about everything. She asked every day if she looked okay, had she done all that was expected of her, what could she do for you to make you like her, was the light going to suddenly turn red without warning (even though it had just turned green). She worried that she had surely flunked every test, although she never missed even one question on anything. She was a bundle of nerves and bit her nails until they bled. She was pretty sure this spin-the-bottle business was a bad idea.

They dimmed the lights and looked at the clock on the basement wall cautiously. Ilah was the first to spin. The coke bottle turned into a green circle sparkling with the light from the one lamp next to the couch they left burning. It seemed to take forever to slow as everyone held their breath. It stopped, pointing its skinny mouth toward Freddie. He sat with his long legs bent pretzel-style and his size thirteen tennis shoes lying on his knees. If he could have untangled himself, he probably would have run up the stairs and all the way home, judging by the look of terror on his face.

They were sure they heard a squeak come from his throat similar to a dying mouse. Ilah, in contrast, was on her hands and knees in a matter of seconds after the bottle pointed toward its prey. She moved toward Freddie, who tried his darndest to melt into the file cabinet he was leaning on. Like a lioness coming in for the kill of a terrified zebra, she slithered closer and closer, wetting her lips in preparation for the attack. As Freddie closed his eyes and turned ruby red, Ilah planted one smack-dab on his lips. What Freddie did next was really out of character. His arms came away from their rigid position on the basement floor and he grabbed hold of Ilah and returned her kiss with amazing fervor. The other kids had to pry them apart and were sure they were in some kind of trance for the next five minutes. They just stared at each other without blinking.

Nancy wondered if they should call someone to make sure the two kissers didn't have a stroke or something, but she was overruled. Considering they were strapped for time, the guests allowed the pair to recover and continued with the game.

Mark was next – be still Nancy's beating heart! He even looked more handsome in the dim light with a lock of dark hair falling down over one eye and his full lips calling to be caressed by some girl's. *Please, Mr. Coke bottle, just once, let me win this game.* She knew she shouldn't pray for something as lame as a kiss, but she did. She even started to say the "Hail Mary" when the bottle stopped and pointed right at Rhonda, who was trying her hardest to move out of its range. They thought she fainted or faked fainting as Marvin jumped to his feet and ran to her side, fanning her with a magazine. Oblivious to the Rhonda and Marvin scenario, Nancy stared at Mark as he moved the bottle to point right at her. Everyone else except Ilah and Freddie, who were still in a trance, had jumped up to attend to Rhonda, so they did not see the subtle repositioning of the bottle.

Mark moved slowly toward Nancy, and she toward him. They say that you might see fireworks or hear music with a kiss that is magical, but Nancy heard nothing, just his breathing and hers as their lips touched ever so gently, then with more pressure. She felt his tongue push her lips apart and her body tingled and heat rose from her toes into her chest. She was dizzy and weak when they pulled apart. Every sound was acutely loud but seemed far away. Her heart pounded in her chest, and she had to run to the bathroom to see if she had been incontinent.

Wow! Wow! That was unbelievable! It was better than any kiss she had seen in the movies, better than Ilah's and Freddie's, better than cheesecake with whipped cream and strawberries, better than Mom coming home after an emergency absence. Nancy felt lightheaded and woozy. She ran back to the basement, hoping that Mark felt the same way too. There he was, planting one on Sally Andrezach! Marvin had his arm around Rhonda who had her head lying on his shoulder. Ilah and Freddie were no where to be seen and Susie and Maria were giggling uncontrollably.

All the sensations she had felt a few minutes ago drained into the basement floor. Mark glanced over at her as she stood frozen in the doorway, but did not grovel or beg for forgiveness. Nothing – nothingness – showed in his eyes, and he didn't move. Nancy did, though. She ran up the basement stairs, out the front door and into the darkness. Some one grabbed her arm as her heart was breaking into little glass pieces. Someone warm and strong held her while she sobbed.

Mr. Warneke's chest was big and warm, and he let her wipe her tears and runny nose on his shirt. He smelled like Old Spice. Her dad wore the same cologne, and her heart skipped a beat thinking it might be her father. But it wasn't Walter, it was Mr. Warneke's and he gently took her back into the house and sat her on the flowered couch in front of the perfectly placed coffee table. Mrs. Warneke came over and replaced Mr. Warneke who was firmly clearing out the basement and marching Ilah up the stairs to her room. Nancy couldn't move. She heard cars come and go picking up very silent post-traumatic spin-the-bottle kids. She heard Mr. Warneke's deep voice scolding his daughter. She heard the grandfather clock chime twelve times. She was helped to her room and gently covered with a soft blanket. She cried herself to sleep.

Chapter 17

High School Days

As she looked back over the years trying to put into words the events, feelings, joy, and pain, she could only describe those high school years as amazing! Not much changed at home, but the experiences, people, and friends who entered her life remolded that frightened little girl into a women. Not that she didn't challenge that "new woman" often in the years following graduation but the crevices in her inner person filled with some pretty good putty that allowed her to fill her life with moments she would never have dreamed of. Had she continued to look in the mirror and saw nothing of value, she never would have moved past the pain.

Her freshman year was part of the fifties' era. She was to be a "cake-eater" from DeVilbiss High School. It was the home of the Tigers, known for breeding successful adults, high scholastic achievement, and fashion statements. She definitely felt out of their league! If she felt invisible most of time, this big school with its affluent students, champion football team, and cashmere sweaters would probably make that a permanent state.

The bus left the corner of Berdan and Douglas at seven in the morning on September 7, 1956. Elvis Presley was playing second billings to stars like The Platters, Jean Vincent, and Frankie Avalon. Rock and roll was everywhere, the Korean War was over and Ozzie and Harriet were the symbol of the fifties generation's perfect family. Poodle skirts, bobby sox, dog collars, pony tails and neckerchiefs exemplified the comfort and customs of American life. Communists were the "terrorists" of those days but seemed so far removed from daily life that it was just a black-and-white newscast. There were panels made up of men judging nervous compatriots who for some reason had been investigated and found to be without conviction that the "C" word was unspeakable.

Nancy's biggest worry that day was not whether she would be there in time to catch the bus---- nor whether Cindy Morrison, her best friend would meet her----- but whether she going to fit in, wear good enough clothes, and make new friends. She wondered who her teachers would be. She was so nervous that she almost threw up after she ate Mom's lumpy cream of wheat. Dad had already left for work. She didn't have to go through the inquisition about the new skirt with six kick pleats and new sweater she was wearing. Mom had scraped together a few dollars from teaching piano and Nancy had saved some babysitting money, so they had their arguments ready should they be needed.

Seven o'clock on the dot, the bus pulled up to the crowd of kids standing sleepy-eyed at the bus stop. Cindy had arrived just two minutes before the bus let out its belching exhaust sound. Nancy didn't really know any of the other kids. Marvin and many of the kids from the party at Ilah's had moved or been sent to private schools. Lots of the kids on the bus seemed to know each other, laughing and telling stories about their vacations and summer romances. Ilah was attending private school somewhere in Michigan for Jewish young ladies. She had called Nancy a few times after she had left for home. Over the years they lost track of each other. Nancy wondered if Ilah and Freddie had continued their infatuation with one another from a distance. The distance may have been imposed by her parents to keep that from happening. Ilah was promised to Mark and Mark to her, but from what Nancy knew about them both she didn't think the old traditions of "chosen partners by parents" would fit into their plans.

The high-school halls were a maze of twists and turns that were broken into a sort of "H" formation by a center court. There were four floors and the room numbers jumped from odd to even without warning or for no other reason than to confuse frightened freshman. Cindy's first class was her home room on the first floor. Nancy's was Algebra I on the third floor. Nancy found room 106 and figured that 306 should be right above it on the third floor. So wrong! She climbed the winding staircase nearest to 106 and when she looked at the number of the room across from the staircase on the third floor, it said 330. She was getting a little worried as the crowded halls were thinning out with students entering their classrooms. The big clock in the middle of the hallway read 7:56 a.m. The first warning bell rang, and she began to perspire. She hated to be late to anything. In fact she always arrived to most appointments way ahead of time. That has stayed with her to this day, and she still gets teased about it from her kids and friends. She hurried down the hall to the right, but the numbers were all odd and began to climb 333---335---337. She turned so quickly that she ran right into a big guy who sort of looked at her like a gnat who had irritated him as he walked into one of the classrooms. She was too shy to ask him where room 306 was, or maybe too embarrassed. *It has to be the other direction,* she said to herself as the clock jumped ahead to 7:58 am.

Two minutes – the two minute warning, last chance for a touchdown – fourth down – the rookie is going to be late for the kickoff! The numbers went down, but were all odd 329---327---325. *Rrrrrrrrrring!* Last bell!

The halls were empty except for Nancy in her new blue sweater and beige skirt with six kick pleats.

This is great! What should I do now? Go in the bathroom and cry (if I can find the bathroom)? Go in one of the odd-numbered classrooms and ask the teacher (too, too embarrassing – my luck, I'd pick a senior class and be laughed out of there? Go home and feign an asthma attack of something (but I don't have asthma)? Keep looking for the classroom and try to explain why I am late. She chose the last option. She never was good at multiple-choice.

She surmised that the even-numbered classrooms were probably on the other side of the courtyard, and she would have to go downstairs to the first floor, as the only connection to the other building was on that floor.

They should give you a map! Stupid way to build a high school! This is not how I want to start out! Everything goes wrong.....it never fails!

She stomped down the three flights of stairs to the first floor, getting more red- faced and angry by the minute. Around the corner and up the stairs to the third floor – there it was, Room 306, right across from the stairway.

As she reached out her sweaty hand to enter and face the music, a gentle, somewhat hoarse voice asked "Are you lost, my dear, or are you running an errand for Mr. Grogan?"

She turned and saw a silver-haired tiny lady, shorter than her own five foot, two inches, with kind blue-grey eyes surrounded by white-rimmed glasses.

"This is a very difficult place to navigate when you don't know the layout," the woman continued. "They should give new students maps so they can find their rooms." She smelled like lavender and had a slight German accent.

Before Nancy could tell her she was lost and not on an errand for Mr. Grogan (must be the algebra teacher), the lady opened the door and took Nancy's hand, leading her into the classroom. .

Mr. Grogan looked ten feet tall and almost that wide. He muttered a hello between marking equations on the chalkboard. The students rustled in their seats, and Nancy could hear the whispers and a few giggles as, with her sweaty palms and kick pleats, she made the grand entrance holding tight to the little German lady.

"Mr. Grogan, this young lady, Miss-----sorry, dear, I've forgotten your name," the little lady said..

"Nancy" she responded so softly she could barely hear.

"Naaaaancy, rolling the a's across her tongue, was going to class as I was coming from the office with a load of papers. I should have put them in a box but I was in a hurry and dropped them all near the front door as the kids were coming in. They were scattered everywhere, and this young lady saw my plight and helped me pick them up and carried them to my classroom. That is why she is late. I am so sorry, but she was doing a good deed. Please excuse her tardiness."

Nancy wanted to tell him the real story, but this one seemed so much better, and she really probably would have helped her pick up papers if it had happened that way.

"Very well, Ms. Gehring, thank you", he boomed as he pointed to an empty seat in the first row. Nancy would always be in the first row, having the awful last name of Ball.

Nancy took her seat and laid the pad and pencil she had purchased for her first day on the desk. She fiddled with the pencil and stared at the desk that had the initials JK/MB scratched into the top. She did not want to look at either person on her right or left, as they for sure had seen through the ruse and knew very well that she had been lost.

Ms. Gehring winked at her as she left, and Nancy smiled meekly. She wanted to hug her but that would have been the topper to a pretty rough morning so far!

Eddie Carpenter, one of the few friends from DeVeaux that knew Nancy, had watched the whole thing from his seat one person to the left of another with the last name starting in "B". Eddie had been one of the brave boys who actually asked a girl to dance during dance class on Wednesdays at DeVeaux Junior High School. Nancy confided in him more that any of her girl friends. From the first time he walked confidently over to her and held out his hand to invite her to dance, Nancy walked to school with Eddie, shared her painful home life with him, debated with him on the debate team, and bonded with him like the brother she had always yearned to have. She always put on a happy face and portrayed her life to be similar to the perfect lives she thought her girl friends had. She didn't feel she had to do that with Eddie. After a lecture swimming with equations they barely understood, and firm instructions to read Chapter One if they were to make any sense of it at all Eddie caught Nancy by the arm as she was looking at the floor trying to make a hasty exit to the next class.

"Hey, don't you say hello to an old friend? I almost was late too. This is the craziest building. The only reason I found my way was my aunt works in the office and thought I'd better get directions when I saw how big this place was."

"I'm sorry, Eddie. I didn't see you. That lady was so nice to help me out. I wonder if she is a teacher here? Are you as scared as I am? It is so good to see a familiar face. Cindy had a class on the first floor and I just got so mixed up!"

"Okay, already! Where is your next class?" Eddie asked.

"It is my home room, number 223. Ms. Gehring----oh, my God, that was her, my home room teacher! The kids will think I am a suck up! I can't go in there!"

"Geesh, you are a wreck! The kids probably could care less. Even if they do, this is a big place and you will make lots of friends because you are always nice and people like nice people," he said, placating her.

Eddie Carpenter was going to be a lawyer for sure. His father and grandfather were both very prestigious lawyers in the area. He always had an answer for every question and a "B" grade never found its way to his report card. Everyone knew he would be a great success and probably would live in a big city like New York or Chicago in a penthouse.

Ms. Gehring smiled as the freshman English students shuffled into her classroom. Shelves of books lined all the walls except the front one with the traditional chalkboard. The only thing on the board was her name written in lovely cursive – "Ms. Eloise Gehring" – English Composition I, Advanced Class." That is all the chalkboard was used for during the time Nancy was in her class. Everything came from her lectures and the assignments she handed to the students on sheets of paper each week. Most of the assignments were readings, followed by written compositions related to various styles of writing. Ms. Gehring's image as a sweet little lady changed when she was in class to a strict, no nonsense professor who expected the very best effort from everyone in this advanced class.

The students had been chosen for their grades in elementary English class, contests in which they had participated, certificates for papers chosen for their excellence, and good citizenship. She made sure everyone knew everyone else's accomplishments and talents. She expected commitment, energy and perfection from this group of fourteen-year-old restless, rock n' roll-loving, saddle-shoed kids. Ms. Gehring's love of writing, especially poetry, had been handed down through her mother and her grandfather. Both had read to her from the time she was able to distinguish words from gibberish.

Nancy's grandfather had exchanged poetry and letters with President Truman, who had a little-known love of writing. She always wondered what had happened to the tin box her grandfather had shown her with letters tied with a piece of nylon----was it hidden or lost?

Those letters would have been a treasure she would have enjoyed as she became more aware of the value of the written word.

Ms. Gehring not only rescued Nancy from a very embarrassing moment, but instilled in her a respect and awe for literature and research. Unfortunately, she only had the pleasure of her influence for one month.

Chapter 18

Crossing the River

"We're moving to East Toledo," Walter announced. "It's closer to work and they raised the rent here. We can't afford it."

We can't afford anything, Nancy said to herself. The East Side – that is a foreign country! All the "cake-eaters" referred to "those people across the river" as poor, dirty, living in shacks, and belonging there. *This can't be happening!* She would move back with the Warnekes. With Ilah at private school, there would be a room, and they always liked her cleaning.

"You'd better start packing because I found a house to rent on Mason Street and we haven't paid this month's rent here," her father announced.

Ethelyn looked at her three girls with the resigned, no argument look she always gave to keep the peace, what little there was of it. Nancy started to make the offer to call the Warnekes herself to make arrangements but gulped it down---just to keep the peace. She ran out the door, heading toward Cindy Morrison's house, completely forgetting that Cindy had moved one week after starting school to Lambertville, Michigan. Her parents had found a log cabin on Sterns Road and had always wanted to move out to the country. Cindy had been excited about moving, as she loved horses. She would be just down the road from Douglas Meadows and could ride every day. Nancy had visited their log cabin one time and was impressed by the homey feeling and the old spinning wheel they had found at a flea market that sat near their big stone fireplace.

She couldn't go to Cindy's. She ran over to Eddie Carpenter's house near the elementary school. He was out in the yard raking leaves, and Nancy ran up to him, sniveling and out of breath.

"He's moving us to the *East Side,* for God's sake! He hates me! He says we can't afford to live here! I'm not going there – it's for poor people and gangsters! Nothing ever works out! I love Ms. Gehring's class, and even Algebra is making sense. I don't want to leave my friends." Nancy spouted.

"Hey, those guys across the river play good football, and the black guys know how to rock and roll. Look at the good side," Eddie said with his crooked little smile.

"Who cares about football and black guys singing? I don't want to go over there!" she cried as she wiped her nose on her sleeve.

"Well, I don't see at fourteen, almost fifteen, that you have a lot of choices. You can always learn something, no matter where you go. Just grow up…it's not the end of the world."

Eddie continued to rake the leaves into a big pile and then threw Nancy into it. He jumped into the pile along side her and they began to throw the golden, crimson, and brown leaves all around them like a blanket, laughing and burrowing farther into the pile. It smelled like fall and the air was crisp with the hint of winter's coming. Eddie kissed her forehead and said, "You will always find your way kiddo."

Nancy saw Eddie many years later when she was working in surgery at a urology center. He had contracted a rapid and extremely debilitating form of multiple sclerosis. His muscles had stiffened to the point that they were board like and his extremities were severely contracted into a fetal position. Nancy remembered going into the room where they were performing a cystostomy for a suprapubic catheter placement so that he would not have to endure the changing of the urethral catheter to empty his bladder that he required for almost three years. He didn't recognize her at first nor did she recognize him, until they both smiled and she rushed over to the gurney to give him a hug. His voice was so weak it was barely a whisper. His eyes looked at hers and he smiled that crooked little smile and whispered, "Still lost, kid?" Little did he know how very lost she was at that moment – but that is a story for later.

She bent close to his face and heard him say "Always thought you would wind up as a doctor or nurse someday kiddo-you were always good at taking care of people".

Trying to blink back the tears, she whispered, "I wish I had magic to make people whole. I only can offer TLC, tender, loving, care —it helps, but doesn't do much to change the disease process. I've thought about you many times and wondered what you were doing and where you were."

"I got to do what I loved as an architect and build other people's dreams –until---until this danged MS made me as stiff as a board and cranky most of the time. I married and had two girls seventeen and eighteen now, but my wife couldn't take seeing me turn into this spastic, agitated, person, so she left several years ago." He looked at her with those deep blue eyes and beyond her into another happier time.

"Oh, Eddie, I am so sorry. Sorry we didn't keep in touch after I moved. You were my buddy and a place I could always go to whine about my little troubles. Time went so fast during high school and beyond... I have three kids and am divorced, too. Life goes way to fast!"

"Not fast enough for me, kiddo …..not fast enough for me."

Eddie died the next year.

Chapter 19

Mason Street

The kitchen floor reminded her of scrambled eggs with ketchup. The back yard was small and ended in an alley that ran in back of the houses on Mason Street. She put her few things in the front upstairs bedroom and found out the closet went almost the length of the house. It would be a great hiding place for her and her sisters. Erin and Ali had the room adjacent to Nancy's at the head of the stairs. Erin's Ginny dolls took over one corner of the room, and she adopted an old chest that had glass doors for her future rock collection. Erin had grown almost as tall as Nancy and her feet had grown twice as fast. Nancy delighted in calling her "Big Foot" whenever she could get away with it. Not that she even wanted to acknowledge this ten-year-old was related to her at all, especially around her other teen friends, but they often had to defend each other, and she really loved her sisters.

The third bedroom contained their father's cot and a dresser. He kept the Venetian blinds closed all the time, so it always seemed to be ominous and cold – not a place to enter or trespass. Their mother slept in the dining room on a cot in the corner of the room.

Nancy never saw them sleep together. To a kid that didn't seem to unusual but later in life she recalled him going downstairs and her mother telling him to go away from her, muffled and eerie sounds in the night – not the screaming and profanity she always listened for so she could run to the rescue. It was another sound she couldn't understand. She was too fearful of what she might see, so she just listened awaiting the change of tone that would call her to action. It must be similar to soldiers in combat zones, never quite getting into REM sleep, always waiting for the sound that would pull them into fighting readiness. Experts say if you do not fall into REM sleep on multiple occasions, you will hallucinate. Nancy wondered if some of the things she remembered were real or just hallucinations. It certainly felt real.

This was the period of her life that was such a mixture of amazing joy and tremendous sorrow. The drama of life was so heightened during those pubescent years. It was wrought with hormonal surges, peer pressure, bonding with friends because of vows and experiences that will never again occur in the same way. Entering the doors of Waite High School, Nancy felt frightened and alone. When she graduated four years later, she felt hopeful and confident.

She lived one life at school and a totally different one at home-- when she was home. She spent many days and nights at the home of her best friend, Karen, whose mom was single and worked with Nancy's dad at the arsenal. Karen was short and busty. Nancy had grown four inches in her freshman year and was very skinny and non-busty. They were Mutt and Jeff and had a batch of friends, Sarah, Joyce, Peggy, Sharon, and Jill with whom they did everything Nancy learned to love football and black singers, just like Eddie said she would. They adopted a token male, tall and skinny with pimples and kind of brainy, into their club called the "Crazy Suedes". They shared their homes (all except Nancy's), their secrets, boy troubles, their clothes, and their fears. There were also a group of guys, Al, John, Stevie, and Tom who went to catechism at St. Thomas Church, and Nancy adopted them as her "big brothers". Al had a souped up '57 Chevy turquoise and white with chrome fins on both sides. He let Nancy drive it one-hundred miles an hour into a football field. The field was not the planned destination, but she was frozen to the wheel after flying over the dip in Seamen Street, so frozen she couldn't turn the wheel when she ran out of street.

Nancy excelled in school, enough to make the Honor Society, become a queen attendant, President of the Zetelethean Literary Society, Secretary of the Junior Class, acted in several plays, and JV cheerleader for a very short time until they found out she couldn't do cartwheels.

Nancy was blessed with the ability to be part of and have friends with the "brains", the "nerds", the socials", and the "jocks" without the terrible consequences the which kids nowadays are subjected. Yes, they had those jealous and callous moments when they were cruel to each other, but they always seemed to heal and rarely heard of a kid taking a gun and shooting up their classmates and himself in desperation. If there were any kids who suffered from ADHD or depression, it wasn't publicized or even noticed back in the fifties. They didn't have cell phones or computers, so they spent time face to face at games, meets, social events, sock hops, proms, parks, and each other's homes. Did they have the same problems, fears, hopes, dreams, and insecurities? Perhaps they did, it just was expressed in different ways. Fell so hard that she became pregnant and in the terror of that discovery found a somewhat questionable "doctor" who would help her alleviate the pregnancy for one-hundred fifty dollars and no questions asked, no paperwork or parental permission needed. As if she would have ever told anyone, not even Bob, and especially her dad. She believed that her mother somehow knew but never allowed her to know that she did. She found her shaking in bed one night with a very high fever and a "period" that lasted much longer than usual. Nancy had horribly painful menstrual periods until she actually delivered her first live child at age twenty-one. She would pace the entire house from one end to another moaning in pain, roll onto the couch with a heating pad, then up again to pace at least for one to two days each month. Ethelyn believed that aspirin and an enema fixed most any ailment so the girls had scads of both when they were growing up. Nancy ran from the enema can when she had her periods but agreed to the aspirin.

Girls in the fifties had few career choices. The number-one career was that of a housewife and mother. Some were brave enough to pursue teaching, nursing, and secretarial work, or waiting table in a restaurant. Those were about the choices. Even women that were talented musicians and singers took a back seat or were managed by men.

Despite those limitations, it was a great time in history. Elvis's career was exploding; the movies were extreme "chick flicks," action, war, or cowboy films; the industrial strength of the united States was skyrocketing; and blacks and women were standing up for themselves.

Nancy lived in that world at school, at school events, and at her friends' homes. At home, the situation changed. She became the victim and the caretaker. Sometimes she pushed her luck as she confused her external position with the one behind closed doors.

There were only a few times she or her sisters took the chance of having friends come to their house, as they never knew what mood their father would be in or what he would say. He often made sexual comments that would totally embarrass their friends and them as well. Once, Erin risked having a slumber party at their house. Her father became angry at something she did or said and began beating her in front of her friends. Their mother would always try to smooth things over and repair the damage but it is hard for someone to heal your pride and an aching heart.

Bob the football co-captain came over one day unexpectedly just about a week before the junior prom. He wanted to take his "going steady" ring back and go with someone else to the Prom. He and Nancy sat on her dilapidated couch with the burn holes in the covers while her dad proceeded to show them some movies. If it was to cheer her up it certainly didn't as it was a musical clip that showed a woman seducing the milkman called "When the Milkman Comes to Our House". Not only was Nancy's heart broken that Bob wanted to break up and she had lost her date to the Prom but also she was so embarrassed as they both sat there stiff as a board, trying not to watch the movie, but afraid to holler "turn it off!" or leave the room. Nancy always wondered if Bob had found out about the pregnancy and wanted to dissect himself or if there was any hope that day of salvaging their romance the "milkman" did it in forever.

Years later at one of the High School reunions Nancy saw him again and they danced one dance. He had married and moved to California also had three children. He was a Lineman (for the county). He said that he wondered why we had ever broken up. That was a lifetime ago, and it really didn't matter. Nancy heard he was injured in an accident at work. She remembered he was a great kisser and a terrific football player.

Don't you wonder how your life might have been so different just with the change in a decision, choice of a different path, or someone who enters your life and turns it in another direction? Some tend to believe that we have an imprint, somewhat like an outline of our lives that determines paths that are open to us. There is a list of possible decision trees and an element of surprise. What we do after that paints the portrait of our lives here on earth within that imprint. Energy surrounds the painting and frames it for all time. That energy stays here and can influence others as they come and go while we return to the master designer. How we believe or don't believe in a higher power gives us the brushes and palate with which we will paint the portrait of our lives.

Nancy had taken a job the summer of her fifteenth birthday at a Taystee Freeze owned by the mother of the Crazy Suedes' token male, Ron. Nancy had a pony tail and still was skinny and tall enough to pour the mix into the giant machines to make soft ice cream. She and Ron had become good friends as they grappled through their first two years of high school. From the day Nancy walked into Algebra class as the new kid from the "cake-eater" school who had moved to the East Side – a whole different world- she felt like she belonged more than she ever felt at DeVilbiss. In those years, the more affluent kids came from homes in that school district and even though some of her friends from DeVeaux went there, she felt lost, out of place, and inferior. At her new school, she fit in because she was with people who had the same feelings and often the same situation she had at home. Kids with single parents, dysfunctional families, poverty or near poverty who struggled to make out in life the best they could. Many were kids who might have to make the choice between finishing school and working to provide for the family--- kids who looked out on a refinery or an alley instead of a garden from the window of a bedroom they shared with three other siblings, kids that had to go to a booth at Don's Drive-in to study because of the turmoil at home.

Teachers had to be tougher because they dealt with kids that were fighters and who didn't see where learning about Shakespeare could matter in the life they knew would not change. Some were more fortunate than others, and their life in the middle class was stable and loving. There were blacks, Hispanics, poor, and not-so-poor, and they all seemed to be okay.

Karen was another of the women who made a difference in Nancy's life. Her mom worked with Nancy's dad at the arsenal and she was gone much of the time. Karen had older sisters who were very beautiful and had boyfriends who now would be called "hot". Nancy loved staying at Karen's little house, trying on her sister's gowns, talking to all hours in the morning, and trying to get a glimmer of attention from the sisters' boyfriends.

One time when Nanny was visiting, Nancy asked her grandmother to sew her into a pair of khaki pants so that every little curve would be outlined. Nancy had taken one of her dad's white long-sleeved shirts, rolled up the sleeves ever so neatly and tied an impressive bow just below her midriff with the tails dangling at the bottom. She curled her long hair with plastic rollers (new on the market) so it fell just below her shoulders. Nancy never wore make-up, but today put on a little of Mom's red lipstick. Fortunately, she had avoided the pimples of adolescence; unfortunately, she had freckles and had been unable to erase them with lemon juice and sunlight.

Nancy knew that Karen's sister's boyfriend was going to be at their house waiting for Patty to come home from work, and she was sure she could use her feminine wiles to win his heart away. She had a key since she practically lived there and she knew that she could get out of the house and back before dad saw her in those tight pants. Nancy swore her grandmother to secrecy. Nanny just grinned and reminded Nan that she shouldn't be too disappointed if he didn't fall head over heels in love with her right away. Nancy walked the seven blocks to Karen's house with all types of scripts running through her head. She agonized over how she should pose when he came in, how to talk in a deeper sexier voice, how to tilt her head so the kitchen light would highlight her hair. What a plan!

It took her a little longer to get to her house because she had to take smaller steps so the pants wouldn't rip.

She finally arrived and entered the house, put on some dreamy Elvis tune on the Victrola and waited. She stood in the kitchen which afforded the best ambiance for the rendezvous, and tossed her hair to keep it full until she got a little dizzy. Back then, when she was nervous or anxious she would get a strong urge to eat. She glanced at the clock and figured she had about ten minutes before "Mr. Gorgeous" arrived.

Hmmm – wonder what is in the frig? I could eat really quickly so my stomach doesn't growl when he grabs me to kiss me? she mused.

The refrigerator didn't have a lot to offer. She saw a small dish with what looked like hamburger in it. She loved raw food, especially meat. She even would eat a sliver of raw liver (poem??) when mom would have it out on the counter to thaw. Yes, that sounds pretty barbaric but she couldn't help herself – some prehistoric gene of some kind, she supposed. She grabbed the dish, rationalizing that there wasn't enough left to make a burger, and was shoving it in her mouth just as he came in the door. It tasted awful! I tasted like something between old oatmeal and rancid meat.

She gagged and spit it into the sink just as he came in the kitchen and said, "Hey, what are you doing here? Did you get kicked out? You must be hungry 'cause that is the dog's food you were eating! What a kook!" He plopped on the sofa laughing his guts out while Nancy tried to clean up the mess and wished she could vanish into thin air.

So much for the seduction!

Karen and she laughed so hard later that the embarrassment wore off. Nancy almost split her pants open as they lay on Karen's bed starring at the water spot on the ceiling and talking about boys, clothes, movies, and dreams. Karen married a boy down the street and moved away. Nancy didn't hear from her until a few years ago and the Crazy Suedes got together to remember those years when life stands still, friendship seems infallible, and a boy's kiss can melt your heart. They drank chocolate phosphates at Franklin Soda Shoppe, Nancy got to touch Elvis Presley's foot at a concert, they rode in Karen's Uncle Bully's convertible through Don's Drive in, they danced in their bobby socks at the sock hops, and no matter what life was doing around them, they were lost in the pink cloud of youth.

The Taystee Freeze gave Nancy a reason to stay away from home. She did have mixed feelings about leaving her Mother, Erin and Ali, but the freedom and lack of fear every day outweighed her tendency to take care of others. Ron's mom, Vera, was another of the women that made a difference in her life. Ron was her only child. She and her husband seemed so different from one another. She was classy and beautiful, graceful and proper. He was a farm boy with a rugged and at times grumpy disposition. Their family life seemed so different from Nancy's that she migrated toward them out of curiosity and also attraction. Ron worked at a drugstore on Main Street and was sure he would be a Pharmacist some day and have his own store. Ron and his dad had similar dispositions.

Harold, Ron's Dad, was very kind to Nancy. He saw that she was a very hard worker, as he had been all his life. Nancy worked tirelessly after school until closing time and on week-ends. He would come and take her to chicken dinner while someone else would mind the store. Harold and she used to sit out by the quarry in Williston and he would tell her stories of his boyhood on the farm. Though he was always very kind to her, there were moments when he would be very cross with Vera and others. It would remind her that you never know what secrets hide behind closed doors.

Many stages, many actors – some better than others- and many costumes in life's play.

Vera was Ron's mother and became Nancy's dear friend for life. She was beautiful, intelligent and a very accomplished business woman. Her two sisters were beautiful and accomplished as well. Nancy needed work that would pay more than the twenty-five cents and hour babysitting paid. It just wouldn't bring enough money to help at home and buy a couple of outfits so she would fit in with the other girls that were popular at school.

You have to have costumes for the roles you play in life, especially when you are fifteen, quite unsure of yourself, and needing as much attention as possible. Ron, the token male member of the Crazy Suede's introduced Nancy to his mother, and they just seemed to hit it off from the start. There was an opening at the Taystee Freeze on a busy street not too far from the school. It didn't seem to matter whether kids had permission from their parents and before she knew it she was working after school and on the week-ends. She learned how to fill the "mix" machine for the soft ice cream, turn out perfect crème de menthe and hot fudge sundaes, and fill buns with the best ten cent hot dogs in town – "All Meat Schmidt's Best" it said on the label. Baseball teams, truck drivers and hungry shoppers from the new Mall down the street would buy ten hot dogs at a time. Vera would come and bring Nancy her favorite cup of shrimp cocktail from the Howard Jonnson's Restaurant down the road. Nancy loved the little glass dessert cups the cocktails came in and saved them for many years, long after the Taystee Freeze became Edy's and eventually was torn down to make room for another gas station or Rite Aide.

Myrt was an older lady ---older probably meant about forty to Nancy at the time. They worked together in the evening and would laugh and eat the "mistakes" (the wrong order or one that didn't weigh enough). There was lots of hot fudge and many laughs. They would draw straws to see who would "go to the dump" with the trash and share girl talk and the drama of teen life and middle age. Jill was a pretty young lady that lived in a trailer court behind the store. Vera and all of the ice-cream girls worked very hard, went home smelling like ice cream and mustard, and took off their shoes at the end of their shift to wiggle aching toes and arches.

Nancy had fallen in love with the co-captain of the high school football team. He had muscles and was a terrific kisser, not really into studying, but that was overtaken by the excitement of being "his girl", wearing his junior class ring wrapped in thread and painted over with nail polish until it was a perfect fit on her finger. There were the high moments when she watched him run the field for a touchdown, and the panic when he wouldn't get up quickly from a collision with a Neanderthal from the opposite team. "Necking" consisted of "making out" at the drive-in movie, kissing until you could barely breathe, and doing more than your Catholic priest would approve of.

Bob never knew, nor did she tell him that one awful, rainy night in October, 1957, she walked into a dimly lit room in an old house in Bono, laid on a cold table and allowed a sinister looking poor excuse of a doctor (if he was a doctor) inject saline into her uterus causing violent cramping and pressure to end the life growing inside her. She was terrified – terrified that what she was doing was so awfully wrong, terrified that she would be found out and beaten more horribly than ever before, terrified that she would be struck down by God and an army of angry angels, terrified just picturing this tiny embryo being burned, drowned, eliminated by her own fear and selfishness, terrified that she would ruin her insides and never bear children again.

The doctor had bad breath and the most horrific bedside manner. He smoked a cigarette as he went about the "job," ignorant of her pain, ignorant of her terror, ignorant of her tears.

"Take some aspirin when you get home and these pills for about five days. You will bleed for a while, but it should go away in a few days. If you get sick or a fever do not mention my name. If you are asked how this happened tell them you did it to yourself – because you did, sweetie" He placed his hand on her convulsing belly and she wanted to run as far away from him as she could.

"If you tell anyone," he continued "I will deny I ever saw you, and I will write your parents about this, so you had better keep your lip buttoned up," he snarled and pulled her up from the supine position on the cold table.

The dimly lit room began to disappear into an ever increasing black hole. The room seemed to whirl like a merry go round and his wicked voice sounded like he was walking in a tunnel. He laid her back on the cold table, and she felt the gush of warm liquid ooze between her legs and onto the table. She wanted to vomit but tried hard to breathe through her mouth, taking short tearful breaths.

"Come on, you have to get out of here. I have other clients. Roll over on your side and get up slower this time."

She robotically did what he said and stumbled off the table holding on to a sink nearby to get her bearings. He had placed a large pad between her legs, and it was quickly filled with blood.

"Get dressed – hurry up – here's another pad. You can go out the back door. Remember, button your lip". He turned as he waved her to a door at the other side of the room.

Her legs felt like rubber bands, and she grabbed onto a fence post as she staggered out into the cool evening air. She was eight miles from home at least. Her friend Bill had dropped her off when she had begged him for a ride to her "cousin's" house to supposedly baby sit. She crouched near a large tree and tried to push the second pad into her panties. She felt like she was riding a horse it was so heavy with blood and tissue.

As her head cleared slightly, she felt the cramping begin again and bent down after walking just a few feet from the house. A car turned into the driveway and she crawled behind another tree. That probably is his next victim, she thought.

Don't go in there – don't do it- keep the baby – it is not worth it! she screamed in her mind, almost opening her mouth to yell at the two shadows that ran into the house.

God, what have I done – Oh, God, I am so sorry. Please, please forgive me! I couldn't let anyone know. He would have killed me and the baby – his temper – he would have killed us! Oh, the tiny little thing – please tell me it didn't feel anything, Oh, God – I just want to die! Her heart beat so loudly she couldn't hear the footsteps approaching her cautiously. A hand grabbed her shoulder and arm and another covered her mouth. She could see nothing as the moon had hidden behind a cloud and the "someone" or "something" was behind her. "It" had a deep thick voice and breathed into her ear as "it" whispered, "Don't speak or move – I was driving by and saw you come out of there and crouch behind the tree. Thought ya' might be one of them girls that bastard takes in and does bad stuff to. If I take my hand away, don't scream or talk. I can take you to get help if ya' want me to"

She shook her trembling head "yes" and he slowly moved his hand away from her mouth. He continued to hold her arm and shoulder as she turned to see what "it" was.

The cloud inched away from the moon just enough to show that he wasn't at all a scary monster. He had a short beard and a cowboy hat. He pulled her over to a wagon sitting in the yard and he smiled as she began to sob.

"Oh, now, don't do that – it'll be okay. Where do you live? I can give you a ride closer to home. Don't suppose you want your folks to see you out this late with a guy!" he snickered.

Not in the mood to laugh at all she wiped her nose on her sleeve and whispered courageously, "I'm all right – I can walk home. I just was paying him for helping a girlfriend of mine and bumped my leg on something and it hurt! I can get home all right. I walk a lot around this town." She started to pull away as his grip loosened... and immediately fell as her legs turned from rubber bands to soup.

Maybe she tripped over her Pinocchio nose as it grew with the fabrication of her tale.

He bent over and picked her up. He was strong and determined and she felt a moment of comfort allowing her head to rest against his shoulder. "C'mon, I'm gonna put you in my truck and take you home. If ya want to walk so dam'd bad I'll let you off a couple of blocks from home."

Her dress was damp as he sat her down on the seat of his truck and she could feel the nausea rise up in her throat as the dizziness returned. She bent forward like she had learned in first aide and grabbed hold of her knees as the cramping crept up from her pelvis. They were stronger than the horrible ones she had with each period and she moaned as they spread across her abdomen like a giant evil wave.

"Maybe I should take you to a hospital – you don't look too good and your dress is full of blood – What did that guy do to you? – I'll go in there a punch his lights out!" he snarled as he pulled himself up into the driver's seat.

"*No....no...* you can't take me to a hospital ---j-j-just home. I'll be all right, just a bad time of the month!" she stammered.

"Yeah... right! That creep has people comin' and goin" and they don't look happy when they leave. I drive by here a lot and it sure seems like there is something shady goin on." He growled as he turned the key and the truck ground hesitantly to a start. "I thought about callin' the cops, but I don't know what to tell 'em."

"Please, just take me home..... on Mason Street..... you can let me out at the corner...please." Her voice was weak and childlike. She was a child doing adult things in a scary place alone in a stranger's truck….terrified.

"Okay. But I think you should tell someone, ma'am." The truck eased forward and no one spoke during that eight mile trip to Mason Street. He glanced at her now and then, but she was somewhere else, trying not to feel the remorse, the pain, and the nightmare that she had created.

"Here you are, kiddo", he said as they pulled in front of a house about a block and a half from 1926 Mason. "You're sure you're okay?" In the streetlight shining through the window he could see her pale face and dark circles under her eyes. She looked about fourteen or fifteen, skinny, with a pony tail that looked a little worse for wear.

Her hands were trembling as she reached for the door handle turned toward him and said ever so softly, "Thank you very much I am sorry I am such a bother. What is your name?

"Tim," he whispered.

"Thank you, Tim. I'm Nancy. I have to go. God bless you"

She stepped gingerly out of the truck and turned to walk cautiously down the street, stopping every now and then to lean against a tree. Tim watched her until she walked up the steps to one of the houses in the middle of the block. It was one thirty a.m., and the moon had opened up its shutters to cast shadows on the houses and the trees. He wondered about her. What would happen to her? Would she be okay?

"I guess I'll never know," he said as he drove slowly away, looking back toward the empty street.

The door made a creaking sound as she tiptoed into the house. It was dark, and she prayed that everyone was asleep.

Thank God, we don't have any dogs or cats to announce our coming and goings, she thought as she felt another wave of cramping spreading through her lower body. This one was worse than the last and it caused her to kneel down beside the steps, biting her lip so as not to allow the groan that begged to pour from her gut. The pads had reached their capacity and warm liquid began to run down her legs. She took off her sweater and tried to wipe up the blood from her legs before it reached the carpet.

I've got to get up to the bathroom but dad or my sisters will hear me. Her heart was racing as she slowly eased herself up the stairs. Once in the bathroom, she reached for a towel and dipped it into the cold water in the toilet bowl. Turning on the faucet would surely waken him as his cot was on the other side of the wall where the sink stood. Cautiously wiping as much of the blood from her legs and groin she wrapped her clothes in the towel and made the journey, unclothed and trembling, into her bedroom. There was a school bag in the closet she hadn't used for a while since it wasn't "cool" to carry your books in a bag. She put on a flannel nightshirt, which felt like a comforting hug, some clean underwear and a fresh towel, and quietly placed the blood saturated clothes, towel and pads in the bag. She crept into bed and pulled the covers up over her head. There she chocked her sobs into her pillow and finally fell into a deep troubled sleep. She hadn't dreamt of the scary tuba chasing her for a long time. There he was, laughing at her, and slowly running toward her. He clawed at ther clothes and forced his cold appendage inside her. Violent cramps rose in her pelvis and his cold hand over her mouth almost halted her breathing. Trying vainly to struggle out of his angry grasp, she heard in a low pitched growl, "Jesus Christ! Shut up and lie still!

She awoke just as he was done with her. The morning light was just beginning to peak through the venation blinds in her room. She was lying in a pool of blood and felt like she was going to faint once again. The nausea and the reality of the night before came into her consciousness as she heard her mother calling from the landing.

"Nancy, aren't you going to get ready for school? I have cream of wheat on the stove. Hurry, you'll be late. You shouldn't baby sit on a school night. Your father was wondering where you were so late. You didn't leave a number. Come on, get up." Nancy heard her footsteps disappear into the kitchen.

She tried to get up but was immediately tossed back into the bed.

"I'm going to pass out... Mom, come up here please, I don't feel good!" She tried to shout but a hoarse little squeak was all she could muster.

Erin came bounding up the stairs with Ali crawling behind her.

"What's wrong wwww… oh, my goodness, look at you! You look like a ghost! Mom….Mom… come here, Nancy looks awful!" Erin tripped over Ali, who was trying to peak in the room, and ran down the stairs.

Mom came up to see the "ghost' and gasped when she saw how pale and drawn her daughter looked. She went to the bed and felt her head as she always did when she thought there was some bug attacking them.

"What happened to you? You are cold as ice and white as your sheets! You don't have a fever but your hair is all matted and wet. When did you start feeling….Oh, my goodness, your sheets are full of blood! Are you having your period? This isn't normal…you always have a terrible time with your periods, but this is not normal! We need to take you to a doctor and see what is going on… I'll get some aspirin…maybe and enema… oh, dear… you look terrible!"

"She sure does." Erin chimed in. Ali shook her head in agreement.

"So happy you all agree." *The perfect out,* she thought. *Thank heavens for a history of terrible menses.*

Ethelyn had left to get some aspirin from the bathroom.

"Don't really need an enema, Mom. I have cramps enough!" she shouted weakly.

"You will have to stay home from school. Do you think if you soak in the warm tub of water you will feel better? Erin, you need to start for school, so finish your crème of wheat and off with you. Kiss, kiss."

Erin grudgingly went down the stairs and slammed the door just a little.

Mom drew warm water in the old bathtub then helped Nancy into the bathroom. She kissed Nancy's forehead and said, "It will be all right. Once you have a baby, those cramps and horrible periods should go away".

The sting of tears welled up in Nancy's eyes as her mother closed the door. The thought of drowning in the tub looked like a good option compared to the pain and remorse she felt. She had lied so much that she was sure that if she did drown, hell would be opening up to swallow her for eternity. She had killed a human being. How could she ever be the same? The salty tears ran down her face and into the water and her heart burned in my chest.

Ethelyn knew. Nancy was sure she knew. Her mother never asked but Nancy was sure she knew.

Chapter 20

Sometimes, Very Close to Normal

She really thought it was her football captain's baby. They had never gone far enough with their love making to produce a child. The real truth was buried in a horrifying dream and parts of her life she totally erased. If shadows haunted her and therapists dug deep enough to bring back nightmares in her life she discounted, she would cover them with excuses and obsessive behaviors. He was the co-captain of an amazing football team. For a time he had shared kisses with her that sent hot flashes from her head to her toes, laughed at her silly jokes, danced with her at sock hops without stepping on her toes, and gave her the honored place at football games as the "girl with his class ring". For a short time-- much too short--- Nancy had that scene in *Happy Days* that made everyone want to have been part of the fifties in high school , magical, exciting, and totally feeding that hungry teen-age ego. For a time, the real world seemed to have gone away, and the times happened that are forever remembered as "glowing", "mystical" and "magical". Why would she ruin that memory with telling Bob, seeing his fearful reaction and, perhaps never being with him again?

When they danced that one dance so many years later she looked up at him and said," We were so young, so caught up in the aura of the fifties maybe we didn't know enough to really know what we felt." They hugged and parted.

Those years at Waite High School were mixed with many awesome happenings. It seemed that, if there were bad times at home, they paled compared to the friendship, the dances, the pajama parties, the loves, the tears, the chocolate phosphates, the music, the sports, the classes, the teachers, the hopes, the dreams, the transformation of a girl into a woman – the future.

Nancy had decided, being a hopelessly caught up in caretaking, that the medical field was the profession that could bring her the applause, the satisfaction, the prestige she so longed for. Her grades in school were excellent. During those years there were dreams that were troublesome, sexual dreams that consisted of my being held captive and ravaged by a nameless and faceless ghost. To this day she does not know if anything really happened to her but they affected her relationship with men forever, despite therapy, despite loving persons in her life. Scars always leave a mark. Some fade barely to be noticed yet they are still there.

Nancy received a scholarship to Ohio State University for the first year of pre-med! She couldn't believe it. She was going to be a physician. She was going to be the kind of doctor who came to your house any time you called, got paid with a basket of eggs or a cup of coffee when you had no other way to pay. She was going to be the kind of doctor who got kisses from kids and old people, who delivered babies in the home, who discovered cures for horrible diseases, who maybe, even won a Nobel Prize. She was terrified and excited, unsure and confident, humble and boastful all at the same time. Her mother and sisters would be all right – mom could take more trips now that Erin and Ali were in school. Dad wasn't home very much. He often was coming home late in the evening and disappearing on Saturdays to officiate at games and help with the Boy Scouts.

Their lives were the epitome of a paradox. Anger and rage when the doors were closed fears about not being able to pay the bills, phone and heat turned off at times, father sleeping in a cot upstairs near his daughters, mother sleeping downstairs on a cot in the dining room, no pets, no friends over, no vacations. Holidays were full of shouting and beatings because mom spent a little money to make things pleasant. Outside of those doors, however, Walter was the handsome photographer, the charmer, the usher at church who helped old ladies to their seats, the omnipotent leader of the Boy Scouts, a member of the Sea Scouts, the volunteer fireman, the good dancer.

Their mother was the caretaker guiding sight impaired people on errands and trips, the piano teacher with the amazing touch, the sweet neighbor that would be there if you needed her, the missing person, the chain smoker, the one who set the place for him and quietly put the untouched dishes away when he never showed, the one who found ways to give her girls nice clothes and turn the phone back on so they could call their friends, the one who made sure they were able to have those very special teen-age memories.

Nancy and her sisters were the "good eggs", the achievers, the attentive kids in class, the supporters, the caretakers, the genuflectors, "the give-until-you-drain yourself. No wonder they were all so confused about boundaries, about their self-image, about most everything. Nancy would go to college with the knowledge that she might have to give it all up if a "rescue" was needed.

During those four years in high school there was only one occasion where Nancy drank alcohol. It was never in their home. Their dad had never taken a drink, that they remembered, and Ethelyn rarely had occasion to even order a drink outside of the home. They never entertained or went to parties, other than tagging along to a wedding when dad took pictures. Booze wasn't even a part of their lives.

There was a dance hall in a remote area on Route Two not too far from a deserted point near Lake Erie where the guys used to go shooting guns with Nancy's co-captain boyfriend--- close to the dreaded spot she would abort their child.

Samson's didn't really care if you were old enough to drink. As long as you didn't have a pacifier in your mouth and weren't wearing diapers they, allowed whoever paid the dollar fifty to get in to do whatever they wanted, short of busting up chairs or having an orgy on the tables. The music was country and western with an occasional country rock song. The mix had become popular with the introduction of stars bred in both worlds. The lights were models of kerosene lanterns with the lowest wattage bulb in them. There was a long horseshoe shaped bar and pillars holding up a ceiling with saddles, lariats, and other cowboy memorabilia adorning it. Nancy went with a few of her not-so-usual friends on a dare. She was scared out of her wits that her dad would come barging through the door at any moment and drag her to the car, beating her not-to- bright head all the while. The overwhelming need to fit in to any crowd made the image of her father recede as she wiggled into Al's 1957 Chevy with six other confident looking fifteen year olds. The "gentleman" at the door grinned toothlessly and eyed the three girls in the group up and down resting his bloodshot eyes on their butts or their boobs. The three giggled and huddled close to the boys who all seemed to know what they were doing. The greeter herded them over to a table near the bar.

Nancy thought, *This is stupid, I shouldn't be here. I don't even like bars and never have tasted a beer. I hear it tastes awful. I am in so much trouble if he catches me here.*

One of the guys, Eric Sweet, who was a big teddy bear and used to dress up as Santa during Christmas Holidays to visit kids in their homes (he sometimes was drunk when he arrived) said to the waitress who wiggled over to the table dressed in cowgirl boots, short shorts and a blouse with very few buttons, tied conveniently under her breasts, exposing her midriff, "Give us a pitcher of Stroh's and six glasses, ma'am." His eyes nearly came out of his head as she leaned over near to his face and said with a deep, throaty voice – "Want a tab, Mister?"

Her cleavage was so near his mouth, they thought he was going to jump inside her blouse any minute. He kept some semblance of composure as sweat beads began forming just above his lip, and he answered "Yeah, I mean yes, ma'am".

Johnny Cash was warbling some song about lost women. The beer came, the beer went, and the beer came and went again. One of the girls, Sarah – who was quite a popular majorette, ran to the ladies room pale as a ghost, holding her mouth to keep from hurling on the tables she bumped into on her way. Eric was getting louder and louder, bragging about his many escapades with the ladies, cars, setting fires, racing, and stealing hamburgers. The room as well as the people moved in a fuzzy haze. Nancy had the most unusual feeling of power and lack of fear. The knot in her stomach that consistently lay ready to unravel into painful anxiety went away. She was attractive, could dance any dance, could flirt and converse with strangers, laugh and feel free. Steve, one of the guys who had come along, took her out on the dance floor and they were the stars – like those couples on

American Bandstand that got to dance on a pedestal above everyone else. The music was louder, Steve was handsomer, and it didn't matter that he was shorter than her. It didn't matter that she bumped into people on the dance floor. It didn't matter that her sweater wasn't cashmere or her boobs were small. It didn't matter that her dad might find out where she was and cause a scene. She felt sexy, dangerous, and fuzzy all over. Steve danced her toward a post at the back of the hall near an exit door. He began to kiss her and grab her in several "off limits" places. He smelled like smoke and burped beer a couple of times in between trying to put his tongue down her throat.

Nancy responded for a moment, feeling "in charge", desirable, and a strong urge to drag him out through the exit door and let him go "all the way" Then a little voice said, *Thought you wanted to be a doctor, thought you loved the co-captain, thought you were afraid of your dad, thought you were a good girl.* Maybe the beer haze was wearing off. Maybe she needed more. Maybe she should think about what she was doing and get out of there. It seemed like more than the few moments it actually took for all this to happen, for the voices inside her somewhat foggy head to jump in and out of her brain and see-saw her feelings from fulfilling primitive instincts to self preservation to absolute distaste.

She pushed the heavy-breathing, slobbering Steve against the post and scanned the room for enemy combatants. Everyone was in some level of oblivion, dancing, necking, smoking, drinking, and passing out. Steve had called her some kind of name that she felt was undeserved and staggered toward the bar, looking back with a sneer on his face as though he had just climbed Mount Everest or something. The feelings converged into nausea and a violent urge to hurl her guts. She saw the "restroom" sign and almost knocked down two people before she reached the door. Pizza and beer churned together do not make for a pretty site after they have been partially digested, but there they were, on the floor of the bathroom. Two girls who looked even younger than her called her similar names to those Steve had expressed as they exited, stepping gingerly over the debris. She hadn't quite finished and this time she made it to the toilet where the remainder of the contents of her heaving stomach---- including, most of her intestines---- she surmised, emptied into the bowl. The stinging in the back of her throat and the acidy odor continued to create dry heaves.

I'll never do this again. It wasn't worth it. What was I thinking? Suppose Bob finds out. Suppose Dad finds out – I am such a dork! Those guys don't care about me – they don't even care to see if I'm okay. Steve will tell everybody. I'm dead! Oh, God. Here it comes again! I need to get out of here. Need to clean up the mess out there. She grabbed for paper towels and emptied the rolls cleaning up the vomit.

Another thought slithered in as her digestive system calmed down. *I never felt that way before – in charge, no fear, no qualms, not even caring. There must be a way to get that feeling back without getting sick."*

As quickly as the thought flashed through her mind she discounted it; washed her hands and splashed cold water on her face. There were no more paper towels so she took off her sweater and dried her face and hands as she left the restroom, attempting to look like she was only in there to adjust her hair and makeup. She spied Steve and the rest of the group picking up their coats and arguing about who was with it enough to drive.

Nancy walked over to them avoiding looking in Steve's direction and said, "I'll drive – you guys are too boozed up."

Of course, she didn't have a license and had never driven without a sober person telling her what to do. But she was the caretaker and needed so to be the rescuer, even though none of them appreciated it. Al dangled the keys to his souped up '57 Chevy and dropped them in her clammy hand.

"Go for it, kiddo – it's a pretty hot car so be easy on the pedal," he slurred. His eyes were glazed over and he weaved enough that Mindy had to lean on him so he didn't fall. They both weaved enough to keep each other semi-erect as they all moved out the door to the parking lot.

The moon lit up the parking lot enough that the group could locate

Al's prize '57 Chevy. Car enthusiasts would die for one in such fabulous condition. Because Al's father was a successful commercial lawyer he chose to shower his only son with "the best of everything that money could buy". They had what you would call a mansion in Oregon, a growing upper middle class suburb on the East Side of Toledo. Al's mother had left his father two years ago. Talk was that Mr. Jones had "wandering eyes" for the ladies and the Mrs. had her fill of his escapades. Al never talked about her and accepted his father's penitent gifts readily. Nancy watched while the group piled into the car and arranged themselves.

Al sat in the passenger seat next to her and mumbled just before passing out "Don't hit it too h-h-haaard, on th' highway, cause ther' are copsssssssssssss".

Nancy loved the smell of a new car and the feeling of control she got when she was behind the wheel. She blinked her eyes and took a deep breath as she turned the keys and heard the glass packs on the mufflers rumble as she gingerly pushed down on the gas pedal. As she looked in the rear view mirror, she could see the bobbing heads of her passengers as they wandered in and of there beer comas. It took very little pressure on the pedal as the car lunged backwards. On her left was an old Ford that had seen better days, and she barely missed adding to its already dented body as she backed out.

"Whew, I didn't even notice that car next to me. I'd better be careful" she muttered under her breath. Steve moaned a little as she stepped on the brake and his head swerved like a rag doll's head.

"They're all like the scarecrow in the *Wizard of Oz* in this car, except me – I'm the one with the brains," she whispered, chuckling to herself.

The brain is an amazing instrument. Cells wired for every sort of thought, emotion, action, smell, taste, reaction work with efficiency and precision to allow us to perform our daily activities and make decisions. When alcohol or other substances attack the cells in the brain, it muddles up the wiring and causes chemical reactions in some people which can wreak havoc with decision making, reaction time, and our ability to perform safely.

Route Two was dark and desolate in those days, with only an occasional light from houses quite a distance from the road and a few businesses. It had only two lanes without any markings for no-pass zones as there are today. When she finally was able to back out to the parking lot without taking lives, she jerked the car from first gear into the other gears convulsively. The passengers who barely could hold their heads up on their own went through enough gyrations to cause serious spinal damage as she tried to coordinate clutch with gear shift and gas pedal. Not only does this take practice it is performed much more efficiently without alcohol or other illicit substances clouding the brain.

It had rained slightly, and the road was just wet enough to make the tires lose some of their traction. Headlights stirred up a slight mist that eerily outlined the beams in front of the Chevy. A few on coming cars caused her eyes to burn as she clutched the steering wheel even tighter than the death grip she already had on it just to keep the car on the road. The car seemed so much larger from the driver's seat without the buffer of Al's lap that she had all she could do not to just pull over and wait until someone else in the car woke up enough to drive. There were several crossroads along that stretch of the road. She glanced down at the speedometer to make sure she was going the speed limit, but the arrow was stuck on "0".

I have no idea how fast I am going, I don't have a license, and I barely know how to drive, she mused. *I can do this. I'm not stupid.*

The window was steaming up from the drizzle and change in temperature. She glanced at the dashboard with its different buttons and knobs. She had no clue which one to push or turn to clear the fog. Just as the car was approaching Coy Road, she tried to wipe the steam off the inside of the window with her hand. A car approaching the intersection crossed in front of theirs just as she caught a glimpse of the stop sign. She swerved to avoid hitting the car, and instead of hitting the brake, she stepped on the gas. The car slid across the damp pavement and bounced over the small ditch on the left side of the intersection. The sound of metal crashing against the dirt and the jolt of the car convulsing through the ditch rattled the contents of that '57 Chevy, including the semi-conscious passengers.

198 Nancy Jasin Ensley

"Holly Cow!! W-w-what in the hell are you doing?" Al bellowed as his head hit the convertible top. "*Jesupete! Give me the wheel!*" he cried as he grabbed the steering wheel and lurched toward her.

Nancy was crushed against the door by his two-hundred twenty pounds as she tried to find the brake with her foot. Al slammed his foot on the top of hers, and she let out a screech like a cow being branded. The gas pedal was stuck under their two feet at this point and the car was almost airborne as it plowed through a field on the other side of the ditch. Somehow amongst the screeches of the other kids in the car and the accumulated produce from the field around the wheels and the undercarriage of the car, Al managed to locate the brake and the car stopped about twenty yards from the road. The passengers sat dumbfounded for several moments as the rain played tinkling music on the damaged metal. When they finally realized they were all still alive, they all began to laugh uncontrollably. Tears were streaming down their cheeks as they piled out of that poor Chevy. It was buried up to the lower part of the doors in muddy, disheveled soybeans. The engine was smoking and it smelled like a wet dog.

"Some driver you are! Look at my car, will ya....heck of a mess!" Al muttered.

"Some car with no speedometer and no way to turn on the defroster! You're lucky we weren't all killed! I never want to drive again!" Nancy hollered, crying and laughing at the same time.

"My dad's gonna kill me when he has to come tow this outa' here!" Al lamented in a not-too-worried tone.

Everyone was talking at once. Sarah threw up again and Steve kept repeating "dumb shit!" over and over. Nancy was not sure if he was referring to her or someone else but she did take it personally.

They walked home, all six of them huddled together. They hardly spoke. The cool early morning air was mixed with a misty rain which was quite sobering, literally.

Had she remembered how terrifying it was not having any control..... had she remembered how in one moment a quick decision can change your life.....had she remembered, things might have been so very different.

Chapter 21

Dr. Who?

Her grandmother taught her that work was your penance and your privilege. It was part of the design that God had for you, so not to work would definitely not put you in the favor of the Holy One. Starting at a very early age Nancy earned a percentage of the two cent refund for any soda bottles she could carry to the grocery store. Her earliest recollection of entrepreneurial endeavors was when she was five years old. The family was living over their father's store on Main street in Atlantic Highlands and Nancy was toting bottles in her little red wagon with the wobbly wheel down main street, excitedly anticipating the jingle of coins in her pocket. Occasionally, she would stop at Aunt Lizzie's cruller and custard shop just to breathe in the sumptuous smell of baking crullers and creamy lemon custard mixing in the vats. So as not to spoil this child, Aunt Lizzie would allow her to sweep the floor in the shop in exchange for a bite of cruller balls (left over bits trimmed away from the crullers to be placed in the showcases to sell to real customers) or a tiny cone with a small squirt of lemon custard. She would remember that wonderful odor mixing with the breeze and teasing the senses of passers-by when she reminisced about good places to go in your mind. One day in her travels she had collected more bottles than her little red wagon could hold. The shopping bag she had "borrowed" from the five and ten cent store down the street from their shop wasn't what you would call a quality product. It was straining to hold the ten or more excess coca-cola bottles when it broke apart enough to allow one of the bottles to crash on to the sidewalk. This portion of the sidewalk had irregular sections that left gaps which could easily cause a tripping hazard. Subsequently she went down right on top of the broken glass hands outstretched toward the sharp pieces jutting up from the pavement. What she recalls was someone lifting her up and both arms held over her head. Bright red blood was oozing and gushing from her hands and elbow. Large pieces of green glass protruded from the wounds (green and red – how festive!) She must have been howling pretty loud because the drunks came weaving out of the bar across the street, probably concerned that it was a "raid" or something.

Babysitting was not nearly as lucrative a profession as it is nowadays when she was eleven (legal babysitting age in the forties and fifties.) One of her grandkids made thirty five dollars per hour at a job last week – that's more than she had made in most of her career! The young couple in the upstairs part of the duplex on Kershaw had a little eight month old boy who Nancy only saw sleeping in his crib, sucking his two middle fingers, when she babysat for them. They had some magazines in a rack near a big overstuffed chair where she would sit, except for the several trips to the baby's room to check on him. To her amazement (and primitive pleasure) the magazines had pictures of nudist camps, their participants, and articles on how much freedom there was in belonging to one of their clubs. People are very interesting without clothes, especially when they are airborne hitting a volley ball or lounging on the beach. It was a very good desensitizing experience for the future exposure to scantily clad patients and encounters with all parts of the anatomy the medical field would provide. Her mother always wondered why she was so eager to baby sit for the couple upstairs as they always left dishes for her to wash, dry, and put away, dusting, and other chores without further compensation.

Opportunities present themselves so that we can look at the parts of who we are that might lead to difficulties. Nancy's tendency toward compulsiveness and overdoing contributed to her successes and also to her failures.

The Ohio State University campus sprawled along the river and up through East Columbus with masterful grace. The lawns were manicured and forest green, with white and red mums in full blossom surrounding old and new buildings mingled among majestic oak and maple trees. If the trees could talk, they would tell stories of intense students with horned rimmed glasses plowing through calculus and physics books; the giggling young ladies in their skirts, nylons, high heels, and silk blouses walking by attempting to get everyone's attention; the lovers holding hands and stealing kisses under the shade of their branches, whispering promises they probably would break in time; the guys from the football team punching each other as they each tried to tell the funniest joke or talk about that cute redhead that just joined the cheerleading squad. Ah, if those trees could talk! Then there was the freshman student, in shock over the size of the campus, fearful of not knowing anyone, and insecure as to whether he or she could make it through four to six years with minimal scarring.

Wow, that was Nancy! Her gut was knotted and tender. She had no idea where she was supposed to go, who she was supposed to meet, and whether she should just find a bus and go back to the east side of Toledo. or try to head in one direction or the other and ask someone for directions.

Entering students for premed were to report to Chatham Hall, wherever that was. A map was enclosed with the acceptance letter that Nancy had received one month after graduation from Waite. That day was so memorable – a partial scholarship and ability to take out a loan at a low interest to go to medical school at Ohio State University brought tears to her eyes and a lump in her throat. It was both exciting and scary. Her mother had not been feeling well and nothing had really changed at home. Ethelyn had lost weight, and the doctor was encouraging her to go to the hospital to have a hysterectomy. She wanted to wait until graduation was over and Nancy was settled with friends in Columbus. They could not afford both the partial tuition and the dorm charge. Friends who lived near the campus rented Nancy a room in exchange for cleaning the house and other chores. Of course she accepted and was very grateful for the offer. No drinking allowed, no wild parties, and keep your room neat and clean, were the major rules of order. The Blossoms were a lovely middle-aged couple with no children and two poodles they considered as valid replacements.

People from other countries---- Japan, China, Indonesia, France, and England-- attended the University for its educational diversity and for its excellent medical, agricultural studies, and engineering colleges. Having been quite sheltered as far as ethnicity Nancy stared at everyone she passed on her way to registration.

Chatham Hall was one of the oldest buildings on campus. Its clock tower glistened in the sunlight, and the double doors opened into an elegant foyer with study rooms and classrooms extending from the four long hallways. Even the smell of the oak paneling reminded her of a one time visit to the Toledo Club for a meeting (the doorman gave a look of disdain to the four students from English class who were to meet to discuss Shakespeare with an expert member of the club.) As she looked up toward the ceiling of the foyer, paintings of famous men in medicine lined the walls. All the portraits were somber and austere. They seemed to be saying, "You had better have your wits about you if you think you can make it here".

It didn't last very long. Not because she didn't "have her wits about her," but because her mother was rushed to the hospital for emergency surgery about two months after Nancy had started classes. She took what was meant to be a sabbatical to be with her mother and never returned. Something kept her nearer to home. Though she regretted not reaching that goal of becoming a country doctor, she had the most amazing medical career. She shared birth, death, pain, joy, recovery, agony with so many – every emotion living, dying, and healing can display---- that she felt blessed.

Chapter 22

Trading in Her Blue Suede Shoes

Nancy walked hesitantly up the ten steps to Croxton House with several other young girls who appeared much more confident of themselves than she. It reminded her of that first day in first grade, when she almost turned around and willed herself invisible, and Eddie, the school's janitor, was sent by an angel to rescue her. No Eddie on this warm August day.

I shouldn't need an angel at eighteen years old to carry me forward, anyway, she flogged herself subconsciously. Her boyfriend, Ron, and his mother were close behind, escorting her to begin her nurse's training at the Toledo Hospital School of Nursing, so it would have been difficult to run or disappear without embarrassment.

Ron was the same young man who was the token male member of the Crazy Suedes club all during high school, and the son of her boss, and friend, Vera, who managed the Taystee Freeze, where Nancy had worked. Ron and Nancy became a "couple" after her break-up with Bob, the football player.

Ron was tall and thin, had pimples, was extremely smart, and the other five girls in the "club" agreed that he would be the least threatening male member of their very exclusive entourage. The mission of the club was to support one another in those agonizing boy/girl first loves, keep up on the latest fashion statements and gossip, and wear, at least once a week, blue suede shoes with the little zipper on the side.

Ron was an only child and his family appeared to be so "normal". What a contrast to the turmoil at Nancy's house! On the surface, all seemed so *Ozzie and Harriet* perfect, but appearances can be deceiving. There were no battles or screaming matches, no burn holes in the couches and chairs, no belts being unbuckled and used as weapons. Meals were peaceful and orderly. Ron's grandmother lived with them, made multicolored rugs from her three girls' dresses and made the flakiest pie crust she had ever devoured in her life. The secret ingredient was bacon grease, believe it or not. She was a delight, full of kisses and compliments – a gem of a lady. She reminded Nancy of her own grandmother back in Jersey, whom she missed terribly. Their Boston terrier, named King, had the habit of passing the most ungodly farts! If they could have bottled it tear gas would have paled in its wake. King always seemed to let one loose when he was sitting next to Nancy, as she demurely attempted to hide her fear the family would not like her. Nancy was sure they thought she was the culprit and needed some medical attention for her problem.

She had grown to love Ron's family, even the odiferous pooch. . Nancy had never heard Vera, Ron's mother, utter an unkind word about anyone. When Harold, Ron's father, used to take Nancy to chicken dinner when she would be working the late shift at the "Freeze", he would tell her told stories of his life on the farm in Elmore – about driving the hearse wagon with bodies when he was fourteen, working in the fields before and after school, hard, physical, back breaking labor. Nancy winced at times when he would be gruff and unpleasant to Ron's mother but she never said a word and just listened obediently. She and Ethelyn were so similar in their resilience, temperament, and patience. Beyond all else, they deserved much more tenderness then they ever received.

Ron showed qualities from both parents. He was a friend throughout high school and picked up the pieces of Nancy's broken heart after her "secret tragedy" and loss of the football captain. He accompanied her to the junior prom when she asked him to go. Her intentions were partly to be able to show off her pink gown with layers of islet lace and to make Bob so sorry that he had traded her for that busty babe that was his date that he would beg her to forgive him. That never happened, so Ron became her beaux and later her husband.

Training to be a nurse at a three-year institution in the late fifties and early sixties consisted of classes at Toledo University in the mornings, working on the "floors", as the hospital departments were called, and classes in the afternoons. Then, it was a quick meal in the cafeteria ("porcupine balls," leftover hamburger stuck together with gooey rice, were to be avoided unless near starvation was present) and back to work on the floors until seven or eight in the evening. Some of the students stayed on until eleven o'clock for a gargantuan one dollar and twenty-five cents per hour. There were clinical labs during most afternoons where the students learned basic procedures such as making a bed with perfectly mitered corners, giving an injection of saline to your favorite orange and taking blood pressures with the eventually banned mercury blood-pressure cuffs.

Most of their learning about real nursing occurred on the floors with real patients. They learned that mitered corners on sheets rarely took away the pain of a fractured arm or leg. It was a soft voice helping the patient relax, being able to give medication when it was needed, and the touch of a hand that made it a little easier to bear. Hardly any patient the students cared for had a bottom that looked like an orange, so giving an injection involved much more than what they learned in the lab. Feigning confidence few of them had in the first year of training, the "probies" learned that presentation was half of the skill set of a good nurse. The practical experiences built their ability to tackle any challenge even if it had not been covered in the textbooks or the labs. There were no excuses for tardiness, absenteeism, or even having your seams in your white nylons askew. There was no such thing as "the end of your shift" or "not my job" entering anyone's conscious thought. They were given three midnight passes and two one o'clock passes a month. No trading was allowed. They were not cumulative, nor were extensions of the time negotiable. If a student was called out for some infraction of the rules, she lost her passes.

If rules were broken, students were campused for a month. That meant they had to stay on the grounds of the hospital, the University for classes, or at Croxton House (the student nurses' dorm) for that month. Excuses and explanations brought not a single tear to the eye of the instructor.

Midway through her first year of training, Ron asked Nancy to marry him. Nancy had dated no one except Ron since her breakup with the football captain. Her parents and sisters had moved to

Davenport, Iowa, because the Rossford Ordinance Depot where their father worked had closed. The government had decided to consolidate several military depots throughout the country. Nancy wondered, even with her naiveté about politics, why they would combine weapons' ordinances which would make them a bigger target for a bomb, but figured Uncle Sam was wiser and knew what he was doing. She had made Ron's family her new family and spent her time off from school and work, at their red-white-and-blue cottage in the summer, and weekend Sunday dinners at their home on the East Side in the winter. She didn't have a driver's license. She could in no way afford a car and really didn't need one. A couple of the older girls at Croxton House had cars, so others could usually hitch a ride if the occasion arose.

Her instructors did not realize she was engaged, as that would have been an unforgivable crime. Students were to concentrate on their education, on becoming a caregiver, not on boys or other forms of entertainment. Nancy's engagement ring remained on a chain around her neck covered by the extremely well starched white collar, attached by buttons held together with brads to her extremely well starched blue checkered uniform, with extremely well starched white cuffs attached with buttons and brads. All this was covered by an extremely well starched white pinafore held together with ten sets of brads and buttons.

It took an extra thirty minutes and calloused fingers to put the uniform together every day. The students had contests to see who could do a uniform in the shortest period of time. Sally Reese won every time setting a class record of twelve minutes and fourteen seconds.

There was one close call with the hidden ring when Mrs. Ludwig, Nancy's med-surg Instructor noticed the chain peeking out from under her collar during a question-and- answer session on one of the floors.

"What is that around your neck, Miss Ball?" she asked as she leaned forward to get a better look. She smelled like cigarettes and camphor and, for a moment Nancy thought about her mom and wondered how she was surviving way out there in Iowa without her protector.

"Miss Ball, what is that chain around your neck?" she repeated a little more curtly than before.

Sweat ran down Nancy's armpit as she wrestled with telling the truth or making up some story. Neither sounded like a good solution, so she mumbled, "I have a cross that belonged to my grandma. It is very special to me because I lived with her much of the time I was growing up in New Jersey." She knew Mrs. Ludwig was from the east coast, as she had held on to her "ya" and "twalk" pretty well.

"New Jersey----you're from Jersey?! What part? I'm from Trenton. I really miss the shore and the deep-fried crab and oysters, don't you?" she leaned back in her chair as she relaxed her overpowering demeanor.

"I miss so much about Jersey, the shore, the hills, New York, the food!" Nancy answered with faked over-enthusiasm. She did miss those things but not as exuberantly as she stated. "We're from Atlantic Highlands" she added.

"Oh, the highlands......just beautiful! We'll have to talk more about home, Ms Ball. Make sure you have all the beds made in hallway C with perfectly mitered corners." She concluded by standing and waiving a much relieved Nancy toward hallway C.

Nancy believed Mrs. Ludwig suspected it really wasn't her grandmother's cross dangling from the chain. She figured her instructor let it slide because of their common roots. Who knows? Nancy felt she really didn't lie, actually. She did have a cross on a chain her Nanny had given her years before. It was in Nancy's jewelry box back at Croxton. She missed her grandmother. She missed the tire swing and the chicken coop and the moments during those years that relieved some of the pain.

Three years of nurses' training and so many stories! The young women certainly grew in many dimensions when life was laid in front of them without any window dressing. It was bare, and often unforgiving. They saw it all. A human being brought to life with a slap on the bottom after its agonizing passage through a virgin birth canal, the young man burned over seventy percent of his body when chemicals exploded in the high school chemistry lab, the ravages of cancer devouring cells with glutinous abandon, the creeping paralysis of Gullian Barre, the tears of relief when the surgeon states, "He will be back to new in a few days," the tears of disbelief when the surgeon states, "We did all we could, but..." So much to accept, decipher, ingest, absorb, and forget. In three years some of them aged twenty years, some of them left to find a less trying way to make a living, and some of them appeared to change very little.

It was a Friday night in October and a dense fog had covered the Toledo area. In order to make a little change, Nancy was babysitting for one of the doctor's ten kids. After the final reluctant three-year-old accepted the tenth and final summons to bed, Nancy snuggled with some pillows on the overstuffed couch with a magazine and a few sighs of accomplishment.

The doctor suddenly burst through the door, followed by his petite wife, and announced, "There's been a terrible plane crash. Football players from a college in California....lots of injuries........some died. Nancy, you come with me to the hospital. They need all the help they can get," he stammered as he threw her sweater over her shoulders and guided her to his car, the engine running.

The headlights tried to cut their way through the soupy grayness. They were passing buildings they knew were there but could not see, giving an eerie loneliness to the journey. Nancy's heart was racing as she tried to visualize what might lie ahead. The student nurses had read about disasters during their training but had never really been part of one. Hospitals had very little preparation in those days for actual disasters. Nurses, doctors, pharmacists, dietary staff – everyone available was called into the local hospitals. Every gurney, extra intravenous supplies, dressings, surgical trays, were brought to the emergency rooms and the orthopedic and med-surg units of the hospitals. There were very few intensive-care units in the hospitals, even the larger ones. The few units that had been established were the bare bones of the high-tech units of the future. A burn unit was just in its infancy at one of the local hospitals.

The plane, a small Cessna used for short distances, held thirty two passengers. The pilot had been cautioned that fog was thickening at the airport and takeoff might be a problem, even with instruments intact. An investigation later found the pilot's license was not current and he misjudged the length of the runway, causing the plane to skid onto the rough and spin out of control. The fuselage crashed against some trees, slicing the back of the plane into a burning inferno.

The young men from Cal Poly football team had been joyously replaying their win over the top team from Bowling Green University. The coach was patting Al Montoya on the back for his amazing tackles. Al, a handsome dark haired two hundred sixty pound defensive back, was of Italian descent. He was a senior and had been offered a position as one of the line coaches on a pro football team in California. He had given his class ring to Casey Robertson back home, and he was looking forward to her praise in the form of hugs and kisses when he arrived. His best buddy since grade school, Ted Anderson, was cutting up with four other players in the back of the plane, showing off his dexterity by spinning a football on his index finger. They had one of those friendships that withstood the test of time and the interference of trials and tribulations. Ted had dropped out of school after his freshman year to deliver papers and work at a local butcher shop to help his mother. His father was more interested in Jim Beam than with providing for his wife and five kids, so Ted chose to drop out of school to provide his total earnings of forty dollars a week for his mother to buy food. Al would bring his lessons to Ted late at night and tutor him so he could keep up with his classmates. Al and his family held potlucks and bingo games to help out the family. Ted's mother went to secretarial school at night after working all day in a restaurant. When she landed a good job at a large law firm, Ted was able to return to school. Because of Al's assistance, Ted excelled in his classes and was allowed to play on the football team.

The coach was still a little worried about the plane leaving with the thick fog engulfing most of the area like an evil ghost enveloping prey. Coach Rolson was a big man who loved cigars almost as much as he loved football. His coaching style was tough and vigorous, but extremely fair. After playing several years as a quarterback at Ball State, he opted to go into teaching and coaching after several knee surgeries. His dream of playing for the pros was vicariously fulfilled as he watched many of his players be drafted for teams or sought after as coaches.

"Are you sure you want to take off in this soup?" he asked the pilot, who seemed uninterested.

"No problem, I can get above it – ain't no problem" the pilot answered aimlessly, without looking at the coach.

"Well, you need to know that this is precious cargo – just beat BG in a big game, so these boys can't wait to get back to California to celebrate"

"Humpf, " the pilot grunted. "We take off in ten minutes – better heist yourself into the plane"

"Okay ……….. but, are you s…..never mind. Guess you're the pilot." Coach muttered as he disappeared into the fog, heading toward the plane.

Al had just closed his eyes to get a little sleep as the plane's engines churned and propellers cut their way through the dense grey fog. The runway lights were barely visible and the take off lights laughed back at the plane as it slowly taxied into position. Joe, the pilot, had made sure he got a good swig of whiskey and a couple of uppers before he slipped into the pilot's seat. The tower continued to send messages to "stand-by" and "not clear for take-off" when they noticed the plane had left the parking area against orders. .

The pilot pulled back on the throttle and began to taxi down what he perceived to be the runway.

Twelve thousand pounds of metal, fuel, and football players headed at an angle toward the woods on one side and grassy field on the other. The right wheel caught the edge of the runway as it veered onto the field.

The pilot attempted to control the plane as he overcorrected, trying blindly to find the runway again and headed straight for the woods. At eighty five miles an hour, the plane's left wing sheared across a big oak tree and splintered. Pieces of metal, propeller and gasoline flew across part of the runway and the woods. Sparks from the contact ignited the back of the plane as it spun back across the runway and into the field on the opposite side. The right wing dug into the soft dirt in the field and broke in two pieces, one of which sheared off the burning back portion of the plane. Both portions of the severed plane screeched to a halt after sliding almost two hundred feet apart from one another.

They heard it in the tower---- that awful squeal of metal breaking apart and the impact of an immovable object with one that is moving too fast echoed with eerie reverberations onto the ears of the air traffic controllers in the tower. They heard it but could not see anything except for an instant when they thought they might have seen fire.

They heard it inside the plane as bodies fell on one another; bones were smashed by flying metal, suitcases and the weight of big muscular men. Screams, unearthly and helpless, combined with the breaking apart of the plane merged together in the thick, soupy, night air.

Emergency calls to all police and fire departments in the area came in at 11:04 p.m. Because of the dense fog, the first rescue team arrived at 12:07 a.m. All emergency crews were hampered by the poor visibility. It wasn't until early that morning when the fog lifted that the vastness of the wreckage could be appreciated and all the injured and dead victims could be accounted for.

At 12:42 that morning, the first ambulance arrived at the hospital emergency entrance. Nancy's heart was pounding so loudly she was sure she wouldn't hear instructions as to what this meager student nurse could do. It was the first time she or the classmates that had been contacted to help had seen anyone burned so badly. The entire right side of the person on that first stretcher was blackened with patches of red angry flesh bulging through. What looked like a bone was protruding from the right upper arm. The bone was jagged and charred. There was no active bleeding (she surmised due to shock), and the person was moaning pitifully. The odor was sickening, and she tried to breathe through her mouth to keep from vomiting.

Someone shouted "Start an IV of D5W in Ringers on this guy. Cut off his clothes and give him some Demerol!"

More ambulances and some cars were arriving, and the ER began to look like a war zone. People were scurrying everywhere, shouting orders, dropping equipment, attempting to calm those with less critical injuries who were sobbing uncontrollably.

Nancy felt like she was in a dream for a moment – a nightmare. Then something happened. She couldn't explain what snapped inside her, but she methodically grabbed tubing, IV solution, alcohol, and needles from the cart. She wasn't frightened; her heart continued to pound, but now it was with excitement.

As she approached one of the burned and disfigured young men on the stretcher, his eyes held a look of panic she would never forget. She laid her hand on his chest and said, "I'm Nancy, a nurse and I am going to take care of you. I have to start an IV in your arm or ankle so I can give you some medicine to make you more comfortable. I won't leave you alone."

He blinked his one eye that was not burned and tried to say something. She bent down near his face. The smell of burned skin and flesh was overpowering, but it didn't bother her now. She focused on his face.

"Don't let me die……" he whispered, his throat so badly burned from the fire the words were barely distinguishable.

"I promise" she said with all the confidence she could muster. "I promise. What is your name?"

"T…te…" he tried to push out of his swollen trachea.

With only one observation and no practice, hitting a healthy vein with a sixteen- gauge steel needle, that was standard at that time, would have been quite a feat. After cutting the clothing away from the swollen and charred body of Terry, or Ted's –she couldn't be certain of the name—she had a few areas left to choose from were veins could be seen or palpated. Alcohol was poured on gauze and she found one vein on the inner side of the left ankle. While mouthing the "Our Father," she pictured the angle at which to attack the vein Ms. Patton had demonstrated on the dummy arm. The needle looked as big as a sword as she gritted her teeth and charged like Sir Lancelot. Dark red blood slowly dripped from the hub of the needle and she quickly connected the tubing and opened the valve wide to allow the fluid to pour into T-bone's (That's the nick-name she finally gave him) dehydrated body. She ran to the cupboard that contained the narcotics. It usually was locked but no one seemed to care on this awful night.

Demerol. What is the other name? Meperidine. That's it, she quizzed herself as she grabbed the precious vial while looking around for someone that looked like a doctor to give her the dosage.

T-bone tried to cry out ---- only the tiniest squeak would come through--- as someone covered the burned areas with impregnated gauze to try to keep the fluids from oozing from his tissues.

The hallways and rooms were filled with people, stretchers, portable X-ray equipment, supply carts, and IV poles. The wastebaskets were overflowing and blood soaked bandages, covers from trays, and supplies littered the floor.

"This guy has to go to surgery or he'll loose his arm" a man in blue scrubs callously commented as he continued to cover burned areas with gauze.

"Are you a doctor? Can you tell me how much Demerol to give him? Maybe you should be careful what you say in front of him......... he can hear you," Nancy spouted.

"Well, Little Miss Nightingale is going to tell the mean doctor what to say, are you?" he sneered.

"I j-j-just need a dosage so I can help him," Nancy stammered while trying to look him right in the eye.

"Give him 150 mg IV. What's your name?"

She tried to think of a reasonable alias, but nothing came to her.

"Nancy Ball" she answered confidently

"Ha – I'll bet you get a lot of teasing about that last name!"

She didn't comment. She went to the IV and slowly pushed the Demerol into the port. T-bone closed his left eye. The panic softened in the right eye where the eyelid had been burned so badly the eye remained opened.

The doctor winked at her and pushed the stretcher toward the elevator.

She watched for a moment and wondered if she would see T-bone again.

Turning back to the crowded middle hallway, she robotically

cleaned fragments of metal from gaping wounds, started or attempted to start five or six IVs with those dreadful needles, held trembling hands as doctors sutured, debrided, set bones, started blood transfusions, intubated and tried to answer the hundreds of calls coming in from the media, frantic family members in California, and other hospitals. It was not the usual Nancy that night, not the girl who worried about being liked by everyone, unsure of herself and tending to be overcritical of everything she did. That night, she *was* a nurse. She felt confident and willing to attempt anything in order to help the injured. Not only did they all have to face the disaster with every fiber of strength they could muster, they also had to face pain, suffering, sorrow, and death.

Later, much later, when the halls were cleared and all they could hear was the broom pushed by the maintenance crew swish-swishing" the debris – when they felt their arms and legs turn to rubber and their eyes fill with tears they had gulped down for hours, their hands began to tremble ever so slightly, they came down from that crises place and the weariness overtook them. They would succumb to oblivion.

Five patients died at Toledo Hospital that night, six student nurses left the profession, and Dr. O forgot to pay Nancy for babysitting. One of the survivors was Ted , who she fondly nicknamed T-bone. Nancy took care of him and his best friend, Al, for four months. Ted was transferred to University of Michigan Hospital for skin grafting and therapy. He gave Nancy a tiny silver football on a chain that she kept for many years. Al was at the hospital for thirteen months. Practically all the bones in his left leg were shattered during the crash. Multiple surgeries could not alleviate the infections from contamination, and his leg finally became gangrenous. The night before his leg was to be amputated Nancy sat with him and they prayed the Rosary together. Al was one of the kindest, most polite men she had ever met. Though he was as big and muscular as a bear, he was a teddy bear to all who met him. Some portion of his spirit was amputated along with his leg. He gradually turned inward and became sullen, angry and withdrawn. His chance to coach with the pros had passed, and with it a part of him died. Nancy heard that after he was transferred back to his home in

California, he sued the hospital, the airlines, even the Red Cross who came to the crash site that fateful night.

Nancy prayed for him and all the young men who were lost and injured.

It was late in January, 1960. The snow lay like whipped cream on the cars parked on the road outside Croxton House. Slow Poke, Nancy's pet turtle had ambled up on the plastic hill inside his tiny pot, probably looking for sun in which to bask and snooze. Several of the other girls were in various stages of preparation to make their way through the tunnel to their assigned units. Someone had been assigned to wake up Sally Reese and was cautiously preparing to throw a stuffed animal from a safe distance away from her doorway toward her snoring body. You see, Sally slept so soundly that when awakened, even with the most gentle of alarms, she would thrash about wildly and leap from the bed with the look of a tiger ready for the "kill" in her eyes.

Nancy had two buttons missing from the starched cuffs of her uniform and was praying that no one in the emergency room to which she had been assigned would notice, especially the unit supervisor. There were three or four people in the waiting area. A black man with a towel wrapped around his hand; a thin, frazzled looking young lady with matted brown hair and wrinkled sweatshirt and pants holding a tiny baby wrapped in a soiled blue blanket; and a large woman who was obviously very pregnant pacing back and forth across the room. There were no ambulances in the bay. All seemed pretty quiet.

"Mrs. Thompson," the ER nurse called from the door that connected the waiting room with the patient-care area. The pregnant lady grunted some obscenity under her breath and plopped into the wheelchair the nurse provided.

"How close are your contractions, ma'am," she asked politely.

"So damn close, I can't count them anymore. I told that blonde at the desk this kid was ready to hatch, but she just told me to take a seat. *You* try to take a seat when someone is pushing against your butt like a bulldozer!" Mrs. Thompson replied demurely.

"We'll get you right in a room to see the doctor, ma'am"

"Here comes another one! Whewwee! That was a whopper!" Mrs. Thompson hollered as she attempted to crawl up on the exam table.

The receptionist had paged a doctor from OB to come ASAP. The drowsy-eyed resident, Dr. Thorndike, who had never seen a birth let alone performed a delivery, arrived in his crumpled scrubs. He looked as though he'd seen a ghost as Nancy lifted Mrs. Thompson's portly legs into the stirrups.

Nancy had dutifully taken a history and found that this was number eleven for Mrs. T and number zero for Dr. T.

"Where is the OB Doc?" he whispered as Nancy opened the package with exam gloves for him.

"He can't come down. He's in the middle of a C-section," Nancy whispered.

"*What!* Ah……..what time did your contractions start, Mrs. Thompson?" he asked, recovering nicely.

"About two hours *ahhhhhhh*……Aye…..Aye…*aye!*" she yelped.

"Doctor Thornton………………is that a foot?" Nancy looked at him as he stared at the gaping opening and the small appendage pushing itself out among the secretions.

Doctor Thron……. Doctor, are you okay, should I get some help?" Nancy asked as she eased herself toward the exam-room door.

"Nnnnnn oooo! Give me a towel, nurse!" he yelped almost as loud as Mrs. T, who was by this time repeating a sonata of *aye, aye, aye's*.

A small bottom and another foot had appeared.

"Push Mrs. Thompson……….*push* hard!"

"Gimme a sucker!" Dr. T yelled at Nancy's wide eyed, frozen body.

Why would he want a loli….Oh…………suction… that's what he means. She grinned as she pulled a small bulb suction from the cabinet and some towels.

Dr. T was crouched in front of the birth canal like Yogi Berra at the plate.

Nancy placed the towels in his shaking hands, grabbed hold of Mrs. T's hand, and poised the suction bulb ready for the tiny head to appear. Sweat was dripping from below Dr. T's surgical cap as he gently rotated the limp little baby until the head appeared. The infant boy was as blue as the doctor's scrubs and wasn't crying. The lifeless body looked like something from another planet, with the bloody placenta oozing out behind him.

Dr. T looked suddenly much older than his twenty ears. He grabbed the suction bulb and turned the baby to one side while he suctioned fluid from the baby's mouth.

"C'mon, little guy......c'mon.....breathe," he begged.

Nancy had seen the doctors on Ben Casey hold the infants upside down and slap their bottoms but wasn't sure if that was just part of the show or a proven clinical method. She noticed that the baby's ribs were retracting showing he was trying desperately to take his first breath. Dr. T must have watched the same show, because he cautiously turned the baby head-down and patted his tiny bottom.

She would never forget that sound---- the almost imperceptible squeak and then hoarse little cry. Within seconds the blueness began to change to a dusky white and then a hint of pink as oxygen filled the baby's lungs and bloodstream. Nancy quickly handed Dr. T two clamps and a sterile scissors for separating the cord, wrapped the beautiful boy in towels and handed it to Mrs. T, who smiled and kissed the cheesy wet head of her son. She had been so involved in the last violent cramps of labor and delivery of a huge placenta, that she had not noticed the frantic looks in her attendees' eyes when there was no sound.

Dr. T went on to pursue a career in Anesthesia.

One of Nancy's very best friends during nurses' training and beyond was a wonderful girl she met on her first day at Croxton. Everyone was so excited and frightened. Entering a new world and living together with hundreds of girls, away from home, some of them for the first time, made for mixed emotions and a propensity to talk excessively as they explored their rooms and kissed their families good-bye. Kitty was going steady (secretly of course) and had occasional spats with her beaux, similar to those that Ron and Nancy were experiencing. They were so young and naïve. Whatever were they thinking becoming involved in a relationship before embarking on a three year journey to the unknown?

Kitty, Nancy, and several of the girls on the third floor became buddies. They talked until the wee hours of the morning, shared their pain when they lost a patient or saw things that made them shudder, hugged each other really hard when one of their significant others disappointed or hurt them, helped each other get in and out of trouble when the need arose, studied and ate together, covered for and played tricks on each other, shared clothes, borrowed make up, and critiqued boys ----that is, men!

One of the girls, Jackie, who was engaged, spent many days of those three years announcing her departure from the school only to be convinced (with much urging) to remain and finish the course. One of the most adamant of those beseeching her to stay was Kitty. No one would let Kitty forget the day Jackie and Nancy returned from work only to find that Kitty had left to marry, with only a few months left in her senior year. She wasn't marrying the man to whom she had been dating when they started as probies. That relationship had ended by the middle of their first year. She had fallen in love with the son of one of her patients. Jackie was shocked and was planning some sort of revenge if she only could find Kitty. This amazing nurse, one of the best Nancy had ever known, settled down with her true love, had four wonderful children and took her entire training over again after the children were in school, graduated with top grades and pursued her nursing career. Even through illness and death in her own family, personal surgeries and pain, her strength and kindness held their friendship so dear.

They graduated, all seventy one, minus Kitty, in 1962.

Chapter 23

Stephanotis

Nancy worked for a short time on the orthopedic ward at The Toledo Hospital. There was still an iron-lung machine in front of the nurses' station. Polio had been arrested by a vaccine just one year before she graduated. President Kennedy had rescued the Cubans, and the Beatles were crooning their way to stardom. She was to marry on August fourth and was spending the night before her wedding at Ron's Aunt Mabel's. It wouldn't have been fitting for her to stay at Ron's house as she had been doing since starting to work as a real nurse.

She felt as though the train was about to enter the kitchen as it roared along the tracks behind Mabel's house. Though it seemed as though her eyes had barely closed, it was already 5:10 a.m. on Saturday, August 4, 1962. Graduation was over, and she had taken an evening shift position on the orthopedic unit of Toledo Hospital. She was placed "in charge" immediately after her first evening, and she believed that was the last time she would ever be "in charge". She always perceived herself as a follower, never wanting to lead nor having the confidence it took to be a leader. There she was, green as can be, in her starched white uniform and cap----in charge. Little had changed from her clinical rotation to that unit during the student years and the present. There was one chair in the nurses' station for the physician, and a locked cupboard where the head nurse, a former member of the army nurse corps, horded priceless supplies. Two L-shaped hallway housed forty eight patients in various states of traction, casting, turning beds, cranial tongs, and consciousness. Many trauma cases continued to be placed on the unit, as the intensive care units and trauma centers were just beginning to be formed. All the ladies who worked on the unit had tight biceps and could beat most anyone at arm wrestling because of their having to lift patients and heavy metal traction bars and weights.

The train whistle could be heard in the distance as she tried to ignore the sound of her heart beating in her ears. She needed to capture just a few more moments of sleep. The wedding dress hanging on the door frame reminded her of the huge step she was about to take in a few hours.

God, I am not really sure this is what I should do. What if the flowers are ugly? Who ever heard of stephanotis? I'm not sure he loves me....I mean loves me enough t... Stop it! Stop it! You said yes, now you have to follow through. Everyone is scared when they are about to get married, I think," she mused as she sat on the edge of the bed crunching the carpet between her toes.

The weather forecast was for heat and humidity, but no rain, thank heavens.

Ron and Nancy traveled to Gatlinburg, Tennessee for their honeymoon. Nancy continued to work the evening shift on the orthopedic unit at the hospital. Ron worked part-time at a local drug store while completing his education in the College of Pharmacy at the University of Toledo. They rented a small house on Willard Street not far from the Nancy and Al airborne fide in his '57 Chevy. They brought with them baggage from both of their young lives. Nancy's bag was full of needs----to be recognized, to be in control, to feel loved. Lake an amoeba with its pseudopods hungrily absorbing and speck of nourishment, she over-achieved at work by taking charge, missing meals, making sure that she was the best, the super nurse, the super women. When she came home she would scrub the walls, dust and vacuum, make sure everything was in place. She doubted Ron's love for her because her expectations were insatiable. Ron was short tempered and weary from his burden of studying, attending classes, and working. Both began to feel inadequate and misunderstood. They shared joyful moments and intellectually were compatible, but the forces of their dispositions pulled them back and forth in a tenuous relationship.

Nancy knew Ron had a volatile temper well before she accepted the beautiful heart-shaped engagement ring. She'd had plenty of time to get to know him. During high school, the Crazy Suedes shared chocolate phosphates at the Franklin Ice Cream Parlor, pizzas at Cipriani's, slumber parties where no one was allowed to sleep, the excitement of necking at the drive-in with the boy of your dreams, the heartbreaking moments when he wanted his class ring back. They all vowed to be friends forever and a day and to never steal one another's boyfriend. Ron was not a "jock," more of a "brain." On of the smart ones who play in the band, sing in the choir, get straight A's, join debate teams and Spanish clubs. He was tall and skinny and was an only child. The members fo the club were all a little "brainy." Though Nancy had been allowed to join the freshman cheerleading team, her cart wheeling skills and flipping in the air lacked a certain finesse, so she moved on to the less athletic choir. She was no songbird, but could blend in with the altos. She had a propensity for "blending in". Ron was in many of her classes, and they both had their eyes on the health field and college. His house was on the way the group usually took from and to Waite High, so he began walking home with them and was adopted by the Suedes. He also shared a love of phosphates. When her sophomore year was fraught with the pain of the boyfriend breakup and, unbeknownst to Ron, the nightmarish abortion, he was there to recue her. He took her to the junior prom, where Nancy wore layers of pink eyelet lace with a strapless bodice. The skirt fell just above her thin ankles, and her feet had plastic high heals that looked like Cinderella's glass slippers. Her hair was chestnut brown with the tiniest red highlights, and she had cut it to just shoulder length, curled under in the current pageboy style. Ethelyn offered her pink cameo earrings to top off the perfect outfit. Nancy went primarily to show Bob that show had survived the breakup and also to make him regret the loss of such a prize. He was there with busty Lois, who she was sure couldn't hold a candle to Nancy in dancing prowess and beauty. She was sure Ron saw the "come hither" looks toward Bob when she was slithering up to the punch bowl with her most sultry walk, the glances his way while they were dancing, and the silence on the ride home as the reality that she had lost Bob forever dawned on her. Ron never said a word. She felt safe with him. She really needed someone "safe," someone who had his head on straight.

When Nancy met Ron's family that cinched it. They seemed to be all that a family should be----caring, financially secure, no battles, Mom, Dad, a son, and a dog. She had grown to love Ron's mom working at her Taystee Freeze, and she felt Vera cared and respected her. Nancy worked very hard, gave more than one-hundred percent----she had to show the world that she was worthy, that she was an okay human being, that she was strong and resilient, that she was so much more than the person she felt she was inside.

When you choose to look through rose-colored glasses, as some put it, you lose your peripheral vision. When you take them off, ther real world come into focus, and it is so very difficult to see things realistically. Add to that anything that plays with your brain, such as alcohol, sleeping pills, marijuana, cigarettes, sex, drugs, gambling, and nothing is as it really is. Decisions are base on distorted perceptions and somnolent synapses. Ron showed some warning signs of uncontrolled temper early on in their courtship, throughout their high school years, and into her years of nurses' training. Nancy certainly brought dysfunction to the relationship, too. She needed praise, applause, and confirmation. She wrestled with never feeling good enough, always waiting for the next "shoe to drop," and restlessness. He became critical of her actions, her thoughts, her need to be right. They had fights, arguments, and silences (those were the worst), always making up and vowing not to let it happen again.

He was jealous. She was insecure. She was jealous. He was insecure. It was certainly the set-up for a perfect storm. They were great actors. To the rest of the world, they were the couple to succeed. Their delusions of grandeur based on what everyone else observed led them to believe they should marry and that it would last forever. Nancy had seen her mother and father weather their stormy, violent relationship for all those years, and they were still together. Why would she think that relationships would be any other way? It was part of her. She came to admit that she had a certain secure feeling, deep down inside, when chaos was whirling around her. Subconsciously, she thought----she knew---that if it wasn't there, she might even create it. They were intelligent beings, Ron and Nancy. They could talk about everything, but expressing their inner feelings accurately was beyond them. Anger, frustration, and fear colored their ability to be rational and reasonable. She was not sure where his came from, but she most assuredly knew from where her instability arose. The catalyst for the end result began with drinking grasshoppers at the cottage on the lake. That beer at Charlie's during the summer of her sophomore year couldn't hold a candle to the freedom she felt when that creamy green mixture of gin, crème de menthe, and half-and-half slithered down her throat, engaged with the blood vessels in her stomach, and rocketed to her brain. It was as if all the anxiety melted away. She felt attractive, confident, "in place" instead of "out of place", mellow, and happy. A second one wouldn't hurt her. She would keep it to that, just two. She didn't want to look like a "lush," especially in front of his parents. Well, that was a stupid thing to think. Ther had never been any booze around her house. Her parents didn't drink. Her uncle got drunk now and then, but no one ever accused him of being a drunk…. just tipsy.

Chapter 24

One, Two, Three

"I think it's time---my back feels like it's splitting apart, and I think my water just broke!" It was minus three degrees. Nancy had just been out with Ron to choose their Christmas tree, pendulous abdomen and all. She couldn't sleep, so had decided to scrub the walls going down the stairs to the basement of their bungalow on Willard Street. The small suitcase with soft blue pajamas (a side gift from the baby shower from her good friend, Karen), toothpaste, toothbrush, and the white knitted outfit to bring home their first born was thrown hastily into the back seat of the car. Nancy was stuffed into the front seat, grabbing hold of Ron's hand, the dashboard, the door handle, anything she could squeeze when the waves of viselike cramps spread from the tip of her pelvic bone to each vertebra and across her flanks, grabbing hold of her swollen belly and pulling the fibers of each muscle into a rock-hard ball. It was amazing to her, even after witnessing all types of childbirth that women endured this struggle repeatedly despite swearing to kill the men with sperm that wiggled its way into an egg that caused this being to stretch a uterus to monster like proportions, push organs out of its way, obstruct bladders in such a manner that makes peeing become a top priority, and leave behind stretch marks that nothing but a shroud bathing suit could hide. They said you forget the pain, but she thought there is a type of amnesia that sets in with the sleepless nights, pacing, burping, changing, and rocking that follow childbearing that gets pushed to a portion of your brain, deluding you into thinking "The next one will be easier, tootsie."

When she held that tiny six-pound-five-ounce boy in her arms she cried, and his father cried. He was handsome—every toenail and fingernail, every chin, the precious way his little lips would pucker, the way he would yawn and open his eyes and look at them. She knew he could only see a hazy outline of the humans, but he looked as awe struck as they were. She was sure he was wondering what had happened to that dark liquid, warm, world, where only muffled sounds could be heard and you were fed by osmosis through that cord thing. He now had hungry feelings and his arms and bottom were wrapped up with some fuzzy stuff, so all he could do was push air through his lungs and throat to let the world know that this "coming out" was not the very best of both worlds.

Each birth had its own special wonders. Each child entered a special place in their hearts. Even the loss of what the doctors surmised were twins stayed nestled someplace inside, kept alive with the might have been parts of their lives.

Number two decided to wait until she was bigger than her brother before beginning her journey. It was January 30, 1965 and a freezing rain had left ice paintings on the trees and wires. Like crystals, the frozen water sparkled in the moonlight as the electricity shut down and Ron and she lit candles and the fireplace of their new home in Michigan. They were so excited about the ranch house on a whole quarter acre of land in a new subdivision, not only because it was a palace compared to their little rented East Side bungalow, but also because they had gotten a terrific deal from Ron's uncle and it belonged to them. A big picture window looked out across the street to a lot filled with cottonwood trees. Behind them there were just two houses and a few others on that street. They had spent the night at Ron's mom and dad's apartment in town because of the lack of heat and electricity. Nancy lumbered around the kitchen attempting to help make cookies without burning her huge belly or burning the cookies. Her back ached, but what back wouldn't, having to carry around about forty extra pounds? The lights came back on as the crystals began to melt away and so did her back ache. This was not like the last one--- She definitely remembered the last one, and this was different.

As soon as they arrived home from Ron's parents, Nancy grabbed the suitcase and turned them back around to the car. "You had better hurry!" she snarled between clenched teeth, grunts and pants. As they sped down Secor Avenue, Nancy had a contraction that rocketed through her like, well, like a rocket, and she actually tore the handle off the car door. By the time Ron had dropped her off in admissions, parked the car and was getting her registered, she was crouched in the hallway near the elevators, like Cleopatra on her birthing stool, pushing her guts out. She remembered seeing a janitor mopping the floor nearby with his eyes bugging out. Someone poured her, her now crowning baby and her suitcase into a wheelchair and they were whisked to the third floor. Nancy was placed in front of the white erase board that listed the names of the women in various stages of labor (no HIPAA privacy police in the sixties) She stood up to sputter out her name, age and Para info (how many pregnancies/births) and the nutcracker pushing the wheelchair took that opportunity to turn and run with the equipment. Just as she was managing to force out the last of her demographics to the sleepy-eyed nurse transposing it to the board, it came like a Tsunami----that irresistible urge to push the dickens out of her already stretched vagina.

"Oh----oh---rrrrrrgh!! I'm going to have this kid right here!! *Rrrrrrrrgh!!"* she snarled.

"Pant----Pant, don't push!" the sleepiness suddenly left the nurse's eyes as she yelled for help and pushed a cart under the grunting patient, clothes and all- literally sweeping Nancy off her feet and rolling her toward the labor room. In those days, the husband was left in a waiting area to smoke, drink coffee, pace, take a nap, read the news, or whatever. Before the dejected anesthetist could give Nancy the spinal she was scooted on to the table and she delivered an eight-pound-thirteen-ounce little redhead. Moms weren't allowed to hold the baby in those days either. As if they would catch something from the person they had rented from for nine months! Nancy recalled a brief glimpse of reddish brown hair and perfectly formed lips already parted and searching for the nipple.

In the recovery room something happened. The LPN smiled as she collected equipment to take Nancy's temperature and blood pressure. She had red hair and was tiny, at least from the patient's vantage point on the stretcher. The room seemed hazy and Nancy recalled looking into the overhead light as a warm moist sensation oozed down her legs and than up her back. The light became very bright and suddenly she was across the room, no sensation at all, a slide show drama flashing across her eyes. Dr. Wilson, her OB---the kindest, sweetest man---- was swearing, which he never did. "Dammit, we're loosing her----run the IV wide open—order some blood!" A nurse Nancy knew her from her stint as a student in the delivery room jumped on top of the figure on the stretcher and pushing her fists into its abdomen and pelvis.

Nancy heard her mother's voice with her New Jersey twang echoing down the hallway. She wanted to tell her it was okay, it was wonderful where she was --- no pain, no sensation, nothing, no awareness or thoughts, just like watching a slide show of vacation pictures where you know no one in them. It was indescribable.

Nancy tried to get up as sensation returned painfully to her limbs, body, and brain. She couldn't get to her mother to tell her to take care of the kids. Something was tied to her wrists. As hard as she strained to move, they grudgingly held their grip. Her mother's voice faded as a nurse with a Mercy cap entered the room.

"Well, you finally woke up. Do you know where you are?" she quizzed.

"My mom is down the hall somewhere----I heard her. Tell her I'm okay, I think." she stammered. She really hated the feeling of feeling. The other was so much better.

"Honey, your mother called, but she said she was in Iowa with your son and wanted to tell you she loves you." Mercy nurse reported.

"No----she's here. She is short and talks with an Eastern accent....I heard her!" Nancy insisted.

"You had a really bad time after delivery. They couldn't get your uterus to clamp down----big baby and rapid delivery. You are getting some blood to replace what you lost, but they brought you around. You probably are a little woozy from going through all that." Mercy nurse reported.

She wanted to tell her where she had been, but she didn't know where that was or what it was. It was where she would have liked to have stayed. She was sure the nurse and most everyone else would think she was bonkers. Plus, there was no good way to describe it. She now knew where people go when the agony and fear drains from their faces just before they lost their heartbeat. They were lifted to a place where you can still hear and see but without any cognition or emotion. All the times she had witnessed death there was that brief moment between life here on earth and the afterlife, the spiritual life, the darkness or the light, the transformation –whatever you believe--- when a choice is made for them to return or to move on.

Now there were two. How can one describe the love you feel for your children? No matter what they do, become, obey, disobey, transform into, keep from you, share with you---no matter---they have a place in your heart and mind that cannot be used for anything else. Nancy had seen and heard of parents that never speak to or see their children for some reason or no reason. Still deep, deep within those who choose that path their children remain in that space forever.

Nancy had planted pink, purple, and white petunias along the walks and around the three trees in the back yard. Little green infant leaf buds were straining toward every drop of the occasional warm spring sunshine. March was always fickle in the Midwest. Freezing winds carrying snow blankets could transform into a soft warm breeze teasing you into thinking you could shed winter garb and begin to dig into frozen ground to prepare your garden. April was more like the fairy princess who sprinkled gold dust and then disappears suddenly allowing a little bit of March back into the picture. In her hormonal upsurge of creativity Nancy had planted feverishly and perhaps a tad before the recommended planting date on the insert that came with the ten flats of those gorgeous flowers. Deb started to make her entrance into Cottonwood Lane exactly on her due date, which led Nancy to believe she would be quite different from Sue, who was weeks past her due date, had a mystery about her, and would not let anything stand in her way, from birth. Deb would always be on time, mindful of the needs of the other guy, the perpetual caretaker, persistent in fighting for her rights – a sixties child in every way. Tommy hated to sleep. It was a waste of time. He wanted to learn everything, take it all in. He walked when he was eight-and-one-half months so he could investigate places as high as his little legs and arms could reach. Sue rarely required much attention. She would sit in her infant seat placed in the playpen for hours and just coo at the plastic shapes dangling above her on the play toys stretched in front of her. Tom was sick a lot. From the time they brought him home from the hospital he reacted to the few gulps of breast milk, regular formula, and condensed milk. His poor little nose was always running and he had awful cramps until the doctor suggested a trial of soy milk.

The labor pains were rhythmic and tolerable enough that Nancy chose to eliminate the anesthetic voluntarily this time and have the baby naturally. Ron and she hadn't settled on a girl's name so when the nurse came in with her clipboard to gather that information there was a movie with Debra Paget on the TV in the hospital room. They named her Debra. They looked at her tiny fingers and toes, made sure all twenty were there, kissed her precious cheeks and brought her home to join the others. It had snowed on the petunias and they seemed to be saying to Nancy as she passed their drooping petals "This is *not* one bit of fun!"

Nancy stayed home with the children for nine years. Outside of an occasional private-duty day or night, volunteer work at the local schools, and bowling on a women's league, she spent her time with her children as they played, napped, ate, made homemade bread, made Christmas cookies, experienced adventures and discoveries together, hung hundreds of pictures and schedules on the refrigerator, visited the neighbors and their kids, played games, colored, read books, took vacations, wrapped presents, unwrapped presents, rode bikes, rocked in the rocking chair, left cookies for Santa on the hearth in front of the fireplace, worked on homework, avoided homework, dabbed Calamine lotion on chicken pox welts, went shopping, went to the Lake, kissed boo-boos, put up Christmas decorations, took down Christmas decorations, always together. Ron worked until about nine or ten p.m. at the drugstore, so the "together as a family time" was minimized.

Being the adventurous one---very much like Ethelyn, her mother----- Nancy loved to arrange "field trips" with Erin and her two kids. "Crew Director" was a handle that pretty much described that wonder lust that propelled her to organize and facilitate outings, surprise detours, piling kids, diapers, spare undees, snacks, wet washcloths in plastic bags, baby bottles, coats, mittens and other necessities into a car and take off to wherever and whatever. Nancy's sister, Erin, was and is much more realistic about attention spans of five children under the age of six and a mother's patience. Nancy would call her and say something like, "Hey, the kids are up from their nap. How about taking them to McDonald's and then maybe for a little ride?" Nancy's enthusiasm for five kids dripping ketchup all over the back seat and fighting over the last French fry should have tipped Erin off that Nancy's intentions went way beyond lunch!

One very special memory she had of a particularly challenging jaunt was visiting the Cascades in Jackson, Michigan near the cottage at Round Lake. The Cascades are fountains built into a natural cascade of rocks over which a waterfall continuously plummets. On either side of the rocks are platforms made of rock at various levels and fountains that shoot into the air colored by red, yellow, green, and blue lights. These fountains spewed at different levels according to the music that was played through a speaker system. Naturally, Nancy picked the hottest and most humid evening to haul the kids and very wary sister to a joyful field trip to the Cascades. Not only was it sweltering, but the mosquitoes were out in battalions at dusk as they arrived. They had stopped at the local dairy in Jackson to pump the kids full of sugar to make the drive more exciting with five hyped-up-on-ice-cream munchkins jumping up and down in the back seat of the car. This was before seat belts and acceptable use of tranquilizers (for the adults, of course). So they were off, sticky fingers and all, in a car without air conditioning ----off to the Cascades!

"We are going to have so much fun! Just wait 'til you see these, Erin! These are one of the seven wonders!" Nancy shouted over the screeches in the back seat.

Erin was such a good sport. Despite her many harrowing experiences being dragged all over creation accommodating her somewhat hebephrenic sister's impulses she smiled and said. "I can't wait to finally see-----*stop* wrestling with the girls, you boys back there!---the Cascades."

Nancy thought she detected a little fear in her sister's voice, but brushed it aside because she knew Erin was a captive.

When they arrived, it wasn't quite dark enough for the fountains to begin their dance, so they released the kids to a playground area near a hill adjacent to the waterfalls.

"Let's see who can roll down the hill and reach the bottom the fastest!" Nancy hollered to the kids. The hill was covered in lush, manicured grass and certainly looked like it was inviting them to take the plunge.

Erin looked at her sister as though she was out of her mind and said "Sis, their clothes are already matted with ice cream drippings. If they roll down the hill, the grass will stain their already challenged outfits and someone might get hurt."

"Not if we're there beside them," Nancy whispered, as she stood an arm's length distance from Erin, hoping she would not deck her.

"*Ohhhhhh...........nnnnnnnoooooo*! I am *not* rolling down that hill! *Nnnnnoooooway, nooooohow*! You can roll down the hill if you want, and I'll stay here to pick you up when you break all your bones!" she cackled.

"I wasn't suggesting we roll down the hill, dummy! We can just walk down beside them and make sure they don't run into anything" Nancy explained in her most responsible voice.

"I have thong shoes on and so do you, dear. We could twist an ankle trying to keep our footing on that mountain!" she reasoned

"It's not a mountain....it's a hill. We used to go down mountains in Jersey, don't you remember?" she thought a little reminiscing would do well here.

"I remember, but we were kids then. *One* of us is an adult now," Erin pointed out.

"Cute. Okay, I'll go; you stay here and catch me when I fly off the *mountain!*"

With that Nancy yelled to the herd, with a loud "*Here we go! Last one to the top is a rotten apple!*" (Tom was allergic to eggs, so she didn't want to worry him.)

Now, had she considered the time of day, the dampness effecting the slipperiness of the ground, the sticky condition of the children's clothes and skin, and the most predictable invasion of flesh-eating mosquitoes ---had she considered all the possibilities, she might have chosen a different activity. But impulsivity overrode sanity, as it often did with Nancy, and there they were, huffing and puffing, five sticky, sweaty, nap- deprived, hot kids and one sticky, sweaty aunt/mom conquering the Cascades' hill as if it were Mt. Everest.

"You have got to see this view! The sunset! The hills! The lights from the cascades! Erin, get up here! " The kids joined in, and Erin caved. She only slipped a few times on the wet grass as she grudgingly dragged her nearly six foot frame up the incline.

They were all out of breath. For a moment, that was all you could here, their breathing. Even the children seemed to be struck by the fluorescent pinks, lavenders, and blues cradling the huge orange ball like a mother's arms laying her baby to rest. The tiniest breeze brushed across their faces that were wet with perspiration. A few drops evaporated to cool their skin slightly. In the distance, the fountain's mist teased the hot air like the silken scarf of a dancer. They stood there in that precious moment holding each other, Deb sitting on Nancy's foot with her arms wrapped around her legs, Annette nuzzling close to Erin's soft brown hair, Tom inspecting a vigilant ant as it tried to be inconspicuous to the giants in its path, Sue sucking her thumb and looking up at her mother as if to say "this is nice". Michael evaluating the hills angles determined to find the one that would facilitate the best "roll".

Wouldn't it be wonderful if we could freeze moments in time like these and thaw them out when chaos is all around us? Like the sigh you take after you've finally passed that terrifically difficult test, like the warm glow you feel after making love and his arms fold gently around your waist. *that would be wonderful!* Nancy and Erin mused.

Down they went, one by one. Their giggles filled the air with sweetness as the world spun around and around and the grass cushioned their little bones.

Erin and Nancy ran down the hill gaining speed with every step. Soon their bodies got ahead of their legs and they became part of the Olympic tumbling team. A clump of sticky, grass stained, sweaty bodies piled into the car. Champions they were----they conquered the hill---Oh, pardon – the *mountain*!

On to the *Cascades!* The kids jumped from the car and proceeded without pause to jump to the first plateau, directly into the mist of the fountain, as the music played "The Most Beautiful Girl in the World". After several drenchings they collapsed on nearby benches to view the entire scene once more before departure.

Then *they* came. They saw wet, sweaty, sticky, sugary, immobile flesh and they came in swarms.

"Mosquitoes! Oh, great, mosquitoes! Run for the car, kids, and get in fast. Keep moving your arms." Erin and Nancy whisked up the littlest ones and ran to their tank. The mosquitoes had their weapons loaded, ready to inject their venom and suck blood from those poor peasants.

Every now and then, after many years, Erin retells the story of that amazing field trip---one of Nancy's best efforts, if she does say so herself! Erin always closes with her best rendition of "The Most Beautiful Girl in the World"

Chapter 25

The Fox in the Chicken Coop

Thirteen years ....Had it really been thirteen years?? This can't be true.........The look in his eyes when I closed the door...... *How did this happen? What have I done?* She tried hard to focus as the door clicked shut.

She walked to the bedroom past their couch, the dining room table where they had so many meals together, through the small kitchen and into the bedroom----their bedroom---the one they added together. The children were asleep. She prayed they could sleep, as she couldn't. They were so upset, angry, hurt, frightened, shocked ---all the superlatives. They had every right to be all those and more.

She passed the cupboard, opened it hesitantly and lifted to bottle of whiskey from the shelf. Her throat was dry and her hands trembled as some of the liquid missed the glass and dripped onto the Formica.

Ron and Nancy had lined them up in the family room next to the fireplace.

"Your father and I have something to tell you. This is very difficult, but we want you to know that we love you with all our hearts and that will never change." Nancy was sure Tom, their oldest, suspected the roof was going to fall into their hearts and cut their world into pieces. She could see his shoulders preparing for the crash as they stiffened under his shirt. Susie, nearly eleven, pulled the invisible curtain of protective armor down around her.....something Nancy had done so often when she prepared for battle. Debbie, nine years old, always looking for the ray of sunshine peeking through the most ominous of storms, smiled cautiously. She might have hoped they were going to announce a fabulous vacation or at least a trip to the Taystee Freeze.

"Divorce! Divorce!----No!, No!---No!" Tom screamed as he ran from the room, almost running into a dining room chair. "Mommy... Daddy...you.... Are one of you leaving us?" Sue asked, with no tears, just staring beyond their troubled faces to wherever the answer would appear. "Why? Are you mad at Mommy again? You always make up.. It is okay, okay?"

Deb crawled over to her mother and laid her head on her lap. Nancy lost it then…tears, hot salty penitent tears poured, all over her face.

Ron looked at her in that way he so often appeared to look at her. She was the one who asked for this. She was the bad guy. She was the rotten apple in the pie, the coal in the sock at Christmas, the burn hole in the couch.

Every marriage, every relationship, has its hills and valleys. They certainly had a few. To all viewers-- and even deluding themselves---they seemed as close to Ozzie and Harriet as you could get; two attractive, intelligent, college educated people; High-School sweethearts; three beautiful children, occasional cats, dogs, gerbils, hamsters, birds, and a short term with a snake; a lovely ranch house with three bedrooms and a family room complete with fireplace and real wooden peg floors, a two car garage, a beer tap, friends, financial security, petunias in the summer around the trees in our big yard, good schools, amazing parties with the neighbors, dancing, dreaming, making love. belonging to church, running the catechism class, canoeing, camping, vacations, holidays with oodles of presents, stay at home mom, cottonwood trees that would whisper as the warm summer breeze tickled their branches, family, learning to play Bridge, learning to tie shoes, potty training, kissing boo-boos, pictures of a house with the sun shining above it on the refrigerator, progressive dinners. It was all there, the prescription for a good life. What on earth could drive a wedge between all that?

It might seem to you that, despite deep emotional barriers, the "good life" was beginning to take shape. They had a lovely house in a budding community, financial security, three great children, two cars that ran, friends, family, church ----every ingredient for the happy American family. To everyone and to Nancy and Ron as well there should have been every reason to believe they had it all. They were not rich, but they weren't in debt, their kids were healthy and happy, they were intellectually, sexually, and morally the perfect couple. Nancy baked bread, canned vegetables, entertained friends, organized and taught a pre-school catechism class at the Catholic Church, bowled on a ladies league, though she wasn't any champ on the lanes, volunteered as a teacher's assistant for a challenged group of high school students, taught a Nurses' Aide evening class in the Adult Education department, organized parades and assisted with Park programs, worked occasional night shifts at Monroe Community Hospital, had a great meal ready for Ron when he came home at ten pm from the drugstore he co-owned with another Pharmacist, cleaned apartments they co-owned with a group of friends in a rental business called "Scepter", enjoyed progressive dinners with a group of couples they loved, went to dances for the Pharmacy Academy------on and on and on.

Jealousy, self-inflicted loathing, restlessness, anger, temper tantrums, too much to drink, expectations unfulfilled, old tapes, wandering eyes, selfishness, too much to drink, fear, hurt, repressed anger, too much to drink----too much---too much. No tire swing in the back yard.

Nancy's uncle Sid had the affliction. He was the one that used to flick her on the top of her head when she was little as she tried to dodge past his big hand. The family used to bet on how long he could sit upright in his favorite spot at Nanny's house. He would perch on the seat in the dining room in front of the bay window. That window looked right out toward the huge tree that held her tire swing. There he would proceed to down thick red Hungarian wine and beer until his eyes would close and he would snore like a bull, still sitting up.

"I think he'll be down in eight minutes, I'll bet you five bucks!" some one would yell. Maybe that's why people called him "tipsy". He never would fall over, and the kids would dare each other to come real close to him, very cautiously. No matter what level of haze he assumed, he could sense someone in his space and out would come that dreaded hand with it's painful flicker. He died of alcoholism. Nanny loved her "cough medicine"; Nancy's father never drank, but they wished he would have. The seed was there. That seed can grow into a monster that squeezes the life out of a person's accomplishments, family, friends, jobs, and beliefs. It is a weed that chokes the flowers and the fruits of dreams. It can desecrate the earth beneath you until you fall into a black hole of nothingness.

What happened? You know how you see a group of pictures advertising a movie, and they only give you hints of what the whole story is about? That is what happens when Nancy tries to put together the next eight years of her life. Somewhere in the folds of her brain, there are parts of the story that reveal a new picture. The trouble is that she doesn't know if they are real, a conglomerate of memories, or fabrications imagined to try to fill the gaps in the puzzle.

They fought. All couples fight now and then, but these skirmishes became battles, personal attacked, and insults that left them exhausted and resentful. Alcohol was always involved. It acted like gasoline on embers deep in their growing up, prodding them to burst into flames. They never knew what would ignite them. Nancy began to love parties and the attention she could get from other men. She had her shape back, and she could be lots of fun, especially with a few Manhattans as a primer. He was jealous. She was jealous. Jealousy is just a symptom of insecurity and a poor self-image, and they had those elements well-established in their personas. Deb told Nancy she would hide under the sewing machine, terrified by the screaming and anger she saw on her parents' faces. Nancy knew how that felt. She knew exactly hoe her daughter felt. Alcohol wraps itself around the part of your brain that takes all you have learned----restraint, patience, rational adult thinking----and constricts its ability to do its job. Enough of it and it actually atrophies, as well as deteriorates the intellectual part of your brain, the cerebrum. Your world shrinks to a narcissistic, egocentric pile of rubble. Feelings are anesthetized, and any that survive must be doused with more and more sedation as they become too painful to bear. Alcoholism is a disease. Alcohol is the substance that allows, in some people, the disease to progress. It is a disease of the mind, body and soul.

Being Catholic all her life, Nancy never questioned that there was a God, that His son was Jesus, that there were saints, angels, heaven, purgatory, or hell. She never questioned any of that. She always felt that Jesus was her friend, that He was beside her and sent angels to wrap their wings around her and protect her. One day she looked around, and her soul was gone. Jesus was gone. The angels were gone, and she----she was all alone, empty and terribly scared. She proceeded to fill that empty space with more alcohol, with men, with egocentric insanity. It didn't work. It destroyed everything she loved and morally believed. It took her soul, her ability to make good decisions. It too the little self respect she had gained. It almost took her life.

Ashes-
Blow in the wind
The breath of a dying storm
Dried flowers
Leave there pungent scent
Remnants of vibrant petals wilting
Candles
Wax sculptures melting
Around roving apparitions
On the walls of time
Whispers
Tears on the lips of lovers
Lamenting lost dreams
In the shadows

Somehow, her medical background gave her a deep respect and fear of using drugs, though she was tempted when that agonizing pain in the pit of her stomach would not depart, no matter how many Manhattans, Scotch on the rocks, grasshoppers, and beers she drank. In fact, they all probably made the pain worse as she ate less and dumped alcohol into a raw and irritated stomach. She couldn't tell for sure that she never took drugs---she hoped she didn't. There are a lot of "hope she didn'ts". One horrible example of how deluded she became is something she found out when her children were adults. In fact, the first person to tell her about this occurrence was her ex- son-in-law.

Didn't she know about Ricky, their neighbor who used to baby sit for them when they would go out? Didn't she remember him coming out from the kid's bedroom? Didn't the kids tell her about the things he had done to them? Didn't she see the looks on their faces when they knew he was coming to watch them? What kind of a mother wouldn't know, wouldn't suspect, wouldn't question? He was the son of friends and neighbors across the street. He was your typical "nerd". Horned-rimmed glasses, skinny as a rail, polite and kind of goofy, like lots of teen-agers. He had a sister who was in her prepubescent plump stage and acted as though she had no use for him whatsoever, like most little sisters of teen-agers. He probably only baby sat for them a handful of times, but those times left scars on the kids that affected them the rest of their lives. Evidently, when Sue told Pat (Nancy's ex-son-in-law) about Ricky and his escapades, Pat found Ricky, now a grown man, and threatened him in such a way, Ricky left town.

After Ron and Nancy left the house, usually for one party or another, Ricky would molest them and tell them he would kill them if they told. The children were stuffed in the back of a car and taken on rides to places where Ricky would get drugs and marijuana which made him even more aggressive toward the children. Nancy's heart turned inside out thinking that she and Ron were so self-absorbed that neither of them---- the mom and dad---- the ones that were supposed to protect them and keep them safe, could have ignored or never suspected any of this. Ignorance is not bliss. Ignorance perpetuated by selfishness is despicable.

There were "affairs", sought after quick fixes for an amoebic ego, tailspins into a dark pit of hopelessness and immorality. They were risky, dangerous, and thoughtless encounters that caused self-loathing and depression. Rationalization becomes reality. Reality that is based on rationalization is a gerbil on a wheel, going nowhere. Running, but going nowhere.

The angels were still there. Jesus was still beside her but she couldn't see them nor feel them. They had to be. She was the head nurse on a neurology unit at a large hospital. She was in charge of others and responsible for people's lives. That part of her that she had put aside to raise their family had broken loose and gotten the courage up to tell Ron she needed to work. She needed to "find herself". She believed that going back to work plus the drinking played a part in the bitter end of their marriage. She would pray to God that the angels protected those she cared for when she came to work after an all–nighter, drank perfume in the car and sucked on Halls cough drops all day to cover up the tell tale alcohol breath. It never ceased to amaze her that many Alcoholics can function, be successful, hide, and convince those around them for years that there isn't a problem. Great cons they are---great cons, especially coning themselves.

The fox in the chicken coop was eating all the chickens. No-one heard their cries, nor felt their pain. Their feathers filled the musty air and blood dripped from his vicious mouth. His eyes scanned the room for more victims. His incessant hunger clouded his vision and his brain. He didn't see the farmer aim his rifle at the artery in his neck pulsating in his madness. The bullet found its mark and exploded against his skin, tendons, blood vessels, and spine. It threw him against the wooden coffins of his prey---with a gurgling moan; he sank into the dirt floor. No one cried when they threw his carcass in the hole---no cross or flowers marked his grave.

So they told those sweet children. The ones they loved with all their hearts. They told them mommy and daddy were splitting up, divorcing, calling it a day, ka-put, over! So they told them, the little chickens, that the fox had taken over the chicken coop. They were no longer able to make good decisions—their animal instincts needed to be fed. Nancy needed men's attention and lots of it. Not their love---men didn't give love---Her father never loved her, so no man really would.

One of the jobs was at the hospital, working the night shift on the neurology unit. She was grooming herself for head nurse without her knowledge and without intent. There had to be angels. No one approached her or reprimanded her for unusual behavior at work. Instead, she was praised by her superiors and given more and more responsibility. The other job had fallen into her lap when she was teaching a nurses' aide class two evenings a week at Bedford High

School for the adult education division. The instructor of the senior high Health Occupations program had to leave her job suddenly. A Registered Nurse with a teaching certificate was needed to teach and organize the program, which included off-site vocational experiences in the health field. Nancy was an RN, but was in the process of obtaining her Bachelor's degree in nursing at the University of Toledo. Because she was finding it difficult to afford the house payments, utilities, and other expenses on her small salaries and the seventy-five dollars a week child support, the opportunity to have a full-time job with benefits was enticing. An arrangement was made so that Nancy could change her major to Education and her student teaching could be combined with the traditional classes. Of course, Nancy had to keep her night job at the hospital, go to school, and work full time as an instructor, besides her extra-curricular activities. Trying to be a mother, a good mother, in the midst of the whirlwind of no sleep, tension, and alcoholism, was like spinning on the tire swing. Eventually, it has to stop and when you get off, the world keeps spinning and you are so sick. During the days when she was teaching, nursing, and studying, she seemed to be functioning normally. She loved all of her jobs. The students responded to her style of teaching realism; her patients responded to her tender loving care, she graduated cum laude; her children were doing well in school and seemed to have adjusted to her crazy schedule and the periods of absenteeism. That is how she saw her world – through rose-colored Manhattan glasses.

Give her a few drinks, and she was off to the races. She was the center of attention. She danced, she flirted, she teased, she put morality, her children, her friends, her job, her life aside for that "glow", that anesthetic that took the anxiety and abdominal pain away. Trouble was it took more and more to get that sensation. She called it a sensation because it was not a "feeling". She had gotten rid of those because you have to act on them. You have to deal with them and she didn't want to, not at all.

There were two of her. The mom that made meals, kissed boo-boos, went to basketball games and track meets. That mom worked two jobs, went to school, kept the house clean; the mom. Then there was the other person was a drunk, a cheat, a loud, show-off egomaniac. One of them was going to win the race---- the race toward sanity or the race toward insanity or death. Though she had never needed much sleep this pace was taking its toll. She began to loose weight, have blood in her urine and pass out just sitting. Her roof needed repair, bills were piling up, and she was angry and suspicious. One night, in a bar of course, she met a man who said he could fix her roof and had a swimming pool at his house. She thought at the time they were really good reasons to marry him so when he asked, she said "yes" without blinking. He seemed to like the kids but she really didn't remember. By that time she could barely remember decisions she made from one day to the next. During the next three years she had exchanged her job as an instructor for a more vigorous job as head nurse on the neurology unit. In the early 1980's she move on to a job with some Vascular Surgeons as their clinical affiliate. She created a monster with that job – which is a trait she needed in order to survive---creating monsters. She worked ten to fourteen hours a day – new every lab result, every history and medication of all their patients, created educational materials, wrote orders, collaborated with consulting physicians, made thousands of decisions each day, drank gallons of coffee and ate pickle and ketchup sandwiches on the run. At work she had to think quickly, make decisions rationally, and respond to emergencies and tedious situations readily. In her personal life she couldn't seem to make one good decision or realize the disaster it had become.

Nancy and Tom, her roofer friend, were married just over a year. He made sure there was a tall Manhattan waiting for her when she came home from work ---how very thoughtful! But he was a con just like her. He found a way to have her sell her house to him when he sold his to move in. He became a source of dismay and fear for her children. He made them chop wood every week-end to heat the house when he turned off the furnace and made them use the fireplace for heat. He harassed the children, never allowing them to sit on their beds to study, to have friends over. He scheduled what they could see on the TV and removed a part from it so they couldn't watch it when he was at work. He put a tape on the pop bottles where the remainder of the pop line was to see if they drank any. It was a nightmare! Nancy was sick, physically and otherwise. What had she done? What was she going to do? She was so ill that her kidneys were washing out all her potassium. She had to go to the University Hospital in Ann Arbor for treatments of some kind. She honestly doesn't remember. She did remember side swiping a truck on one of those trips. Her life at that point in time was a slide show of events that only gave the barest details of the whole story.

Her poor kids. Her son,Tom ,had packed his little suitcase one night during a particularly awful altercation with Nancy's new husband. Nancy sobbed as she watched her son walk to Tom's truck to move in with his father. She felt helpless, exhausted, sick and painfully lost. She could barley drink one glass of liquor without vomiting. She needed to quiet the demons and she couldn't. She was so confused and frightened. Paranoia began to be an unwelcome companion. Things people said to her, or didn't say were misinterpreted. She had to find a way to drink that would allow her to function and settle her nerves. Everything and everyone that meant anything to her was being pushed aside to make way for her addiction. She was not in any way the person she had tried so hard to be. Not in a million years would the sane Nancy have allowed someone to dictate unreasonable rules to her children. The reasonable Nancy would never have allowed her kids to be injured in any way, emotionally, or physically. The rational, intelligent person she thought she was had been paralyzed by the "fox", shivering in a corner, desperate, alone, and powerless. Tom, her dear son, sent away with a little suitcase of his treasures and a few clothes during what should have been the best years of his life. He played his flute in the band, was in plays, excelled in his studies, could cook better than most master chefs. He was compassionate and kind. How terribly painful for him! Her daughters watched and were given orders by a man whom they feared. Watching their mother retreat into a bottle and not stand up for them as she should have was devastating. The disease is chronic, insidious, and selfish.

One of the more stable members of the family at this time was their cat, Tigger. Tigger was striped, with hues of gray and black knitting their way into the fabric of her soft coat. She had an air of aloofness and calm composure. Two of her favorite places were on the back of the couch in the family room and the hood of the car, especially when it had just been driven and the engine heat warmed the metal and her belly. God often sends messages in the strangest way and through unsuspecting messengers.

For several months Nancy had moved into her son's old room with a small space heater, hidden belongings and papers she felt were important under the mat in the trunk of her car. She was planning an escape. She had no claim to her home. Every day was an effort, every night was agony. She had lost thirty pounds and could barely eat. Sleep was a luxury that rarely came her way. She was terrified of every sound, every thought, and every imagined ghost. It took metered ounces of energy and stage presence to get through the day at work.

Whether real or imagined, she suspected a friend of her husband's, a portly beast of a man, to have been hired to kill the girls and her. His name was "Bear" and he really resembled one in many grizzly ways, or at least that is what she perceived. All she knew was that they had to escape with whatever they could load in their car. Her neighbor and dear friend offered to help along with a mentally ill brother of an acquaintance, as members of the transition team ---one good choice, one very bad choice. The mentally ill brother of a friend haunted Nancy and her girls for several months after they moved with his unpredictable, crazy actions. Nothing she did made any sense but at the time it made absolute, delusional, insane sense.

It was Wednesday. The girls were in school. The clouds allowed tiny streaks of sun to move across the dining room floor. She didn't go to work that day. Methodically, she dusted and vacuumed, put away the groceries, made the beds and walked toward the family room. The last thing she remembered was looking for Tigger. She needed to hold her and feel her warm fur against her aching chest. The curtain came down at that moment. There was no recall of the next few moment's events. The next thing she knew there was a loud "thud" and she saw

Tigger on the hood of her car. Vomit was hanging from her mouth and sprayed over the dash and seat. She could barely focus as the world spun around her. Her hands were shaking and ghostly white.

"Tigger-----I forgot about Tigger" a voice seemed to echo through the turbulence.

"Door is closed----got to open the door." the voice said urgently

"Garage door opener---push it" the voice commanded and something lifted her trembling arm to the opener on the visor.

"Open the door Tigger needs to get air" it said, more gently than before.

The shaky pale hand moved toward the handle and opened the door.

"Turn off the car" the voice seemed to be far away now.

Tigger's soft tongue licked the face of her master lovingly. Nancy's head pounded as she tried to focus on something. A cool breeze moved across the garage floor and picked up the pungent smell of vomit, threw it into her dripping nostrils and brought back some level of consciousness. She wiped her nose on her sleeve and saw the blood, her blood. She looked at the clock and panic pulled her heart into her stomach as dry heaves tore into their muscles. It was 2:05 pm.

My, God –I have to clean this up………must have forgotten to open the door and passed out----he'll kill me----can't let the kids see me like this.

She dragged her limp body to the door and staggered to the bathroom, filled the tub with hot water and bubble bath and crawled in, clothes and all. Part of her wanted to allow the water to fold around her and just go to sleep. She had to fight doing that with all her might.

2:31 PM.....have to get the car cleaned up………bleach or Pine-Sol.....so dizzy ...c...c...can't let them know...can't...the flu…….I have the flu and just threw up in the car before I could make it in the house……………forgot to turn off the car when I closed…………… but I hadn't been anywhere!.....store in the morning………what happened?.. I never start the car before I open the…………door……. my head is pounding………carbon monoxide----should call the poison center, but have to clean up the car…….Tigger……where is Tigger?

She jumped the hood of the car.....saved my life..........what's left of it. I couldn't have done it on pur.......No! I would never do that to my kids! I'm a good mother! I...I.....we have to get out of here. I am so frightened, She stumbled to the cabinet under the sink throwing the wet clothes in the washer on her way. Grabbing some towels and pine-sol she ran to the garage. There was Tigger, lounging on the car hood as if nothing had happened.

"Bless you. buddy" she whispered as she breathed through her mouth so as not to heave again from the smell. She stuffed the cleaning rags with particles of half digested food and the remains of her episode into three plastic bags and pushed them deep beneath the other garbage in the cans outside the garage. Realizing she had nothing on as she glanced up and saw the school bus turning the corner onto Cottonwood, she almost tripped over Tigger as she ran back into the house to throw on some sweats. She glanced in the mirror as she pulled the Bedford T-shirt over her mangled hair.

God!....I look like a ghost.... I'll scare the kids to death. She pinched her cheeks to coax a little color into them and dabbed a little make up on the dark areas under her eyes. Her eyes starred blankly back at her and for a second she thought she was dead and she was looking at the world from another place again.

A Hall's always was a good cover up for alcohol breath, so she searched feverishly in her purse. She found an old one were the wrapper had become part of the lozenge. No time to fuss getting the wrapper off, so she popped it into her mouth, wrapper and all.

Friday, 7:15 PM.........another silent dinner...another long and stressful day at work----clutching fear -----trembling hands and moments when she thought she would pass out. Not able to drink without vomiting and suffering agonizing back pain. Trying to get through the day without anyone noticing how sick she was, emotionally, physically, and spiritually. Paranoia eating at her brain, frightening nightmares and confusion, knowing she had to get the children away from this man. The agonizing reality that she had lost their home, lost her son, was losing her girls, and worst of all...she had lost her friend, Jesus. She didn't feel Him next to her as she had for so much of her life. Her thoughts were scattered and decisions took every ounce of energy she had. She blamed herself. She hated herself for getting them in such an awful mess. What she didn't realize was that the one thing she craved, alcohol, had clouded her mind and led her down a path to a cliff's edge.....a path from which she had plunged and was still falling.

Days were like a slide show. Blank frames pushed between pictures of daily life, scattering the congruity of the story across the screen in a collage of disarray. Her five foot seven inch medium frame was falling prey to anorexia and syncopal episodes. How she continued to function in any manner now confirms the belief that God carries you when you can no longer walk on your own because He has a destination for you and is determined that you reach it. She weighed less than one-hundred ten pounds and didn't realize how that looked until one of the doctors she was working with asked her to pose in a black leotard with white outlines of the arterial system painted on it for an educational videotape. She surely wasn't chosen for her beauty but for her resemblance to a skeleton. Many memories of that year were missing.

It was as though someone else was winding up a robot that obeyed the commands "get dressed" "go to work" "go home" "get undressed" over and over. She bedded down in her son's old bedroom with a space heater, sobbed into a pillow every night, and barely slept as clutching fear, real or imagined heard footsteps in the hallway, real or imagined---heading toward her girls' rooms to kill them and then turning to do her in next. She continued to hide papers she thought were important under the spare tire well of her car. She couldn't let the demons have them. Her husband let her know over and over again that nothing was hers – the house, the furniture, the flowers----nothing. If she tried to leave, an enormous friend of his named "Bear" would find her and make her disappear along with her girls. He called one of the doctor's for whom she worked and accused him of having an affair with her. Desperate, totally frightened and ashamed she got herself in a worse mess attempting to escape by asking help from a man who needed help himself. She shared with a friend the mess she was in and the friend said she had a brother who would help Nancy move as much as she could to an apartment she had found several miles away. What made her think she was capable of making a decision was ludicrous. She was physically, mentally, emotionally, and spiritually bankrupt. She thought she must be an amazing actress or people were just to busy with there own stuff to notice that no one mentioned any change in her work, her efficiency as a nurse, or her ability to care for others. If they did, it was lost in one of those blanks that were occurring more often. Looking back it was the way she grew up ---changing roles as quickly as a flick of a finger. Another person would take over at work, directed by God's loving hands, keeping those for whom she was responsible safe.

Her friend's brother, Dell, seemed quite nice and eager to assist the damsel in distress. What she did not see was how frightfully ill he was. After helping her move some of the furniture, he made her pay with sex, stalked her in public and urinated on the porch of her apartment when she slammed the door on his hand. They chose a day that they knew Tom would have late loads from the trucking company for which he worked. Nancy pretended to go to work and waited at the end of the block in her car, hidden by a large elm tree, until his truck turned the corner and headed down Knepper Street. Nancy's neighbor and friend came rushing over to help her throw their things into the car and onto Dell's truck. As they backed out of the driveway of the only home Nancy could call her own, she stared at the three trees Ron and she had planted in the front yard, one tree for each of the children. Through burning tears and the hollow nauseated feeling in her chest, she backed out of the driveway for the last time.

There always are moments of sunlight in a bleak and dismal day. They are there------ you just have to push the clouds aside and catch those fleeting moments, treasure them and allow yourself to laugh at the idiosyncrasies of life. Lock, stock and barrel they moved what they could pile into the two cars and a truck to an apartment not far from the high school. The entrance to the complex wound back to a secluded area between two streets bordered by a huge field that no one mowed. Hopefully, Tom and his muscle men wouldn't find them, not that he would even care to, as he had their house free and clear, most of their furnishings and a full refrigerator. She couldn't tell what she felt or if she felt anything. She was emaciated and ill. Dragging her body to work, trusting very few, every part of her mind and body begging for a drink to anesthetize the scattered fireworks in her head, only to vomit violently after the first gulp. Gut wrenching abdominal cramps, and distressing hand tremors woke her from the few treasured moments of sleep each night. She fainted sitting at her desk at work without warning as her potassium dropped to a dangerous 2.3 (the normal is usually 3.5 or above). Her heart would race and it felt as though it was turning somersaults in her chest. It felt as though her head was floating off her shoulders. She surely looked disjointed much of the time but no one said anything except "You really are getting too skinny!"

She wanted to die--- no, she wanted to live, just not this way. The most frightening part of this was that she couldn't feel Jesus next to her anymore. The one comfort she had all her life during those awful moments of despair and fear was that Jesus would hold on to her, protect her, carry her when she couldn't walk through the quicksand. She couldn't feel His presence. She had lost Him---she had lost herself. Her son had escaped to his father's to finish his last year in high school at Bowsher. She could only imagine how angry he must have been with her. He had been with his friends from shortly after he was born. He had watched her dissect their seemingly perfect family and introduce scary strangers into their lives. She had allowed booze to wash away good judgment, her role as a mother and wife, their home, and their security. To this day, though they have patched up some of the wounds, she lost a piece of him that she might never be able to retrieve. She loved her kids with all her heart. The penance was greater than any priest could bestow--- the loss of precious moments in their growing up, lost jewels in the crown of motherhood she strove to wear so proudly.

Parting those clouds so the sun could peak through wasn't easy in her sad state. Nancy brought home a kitten one day after work which Deb appropriately named Asti Spumanti. Asti loved the field behind their apartment where sweet fuzzy treasures could be pounced upon and brought home to be hidden behind the couch, only to be found with rare vacuuming of that area. She was so proud of her "spoils" they couldn't be cross with her. Nancy derived some pleasure watching the girls sitting out on lawn chairs in the sun in their bathing suits, enjoying the "girl talk". Deb and Sue had racks of clothes lining three walls in the room the girls shared since the one small closet was bursting at the seams. It looked like a Jewish clothing factory. Once Sue and Deb found some red and yellow striped socks and bright red shoes with sparkles, stuffed the socks so they looked like real legs were inhabiting them, attached the shoes and slid them under the bed so they looked like the scene from *The Wizard of Oz* where the house falls on the bad witch and all you could see are her shoes and stockings peaking out from the wreckage – there is a picture somewhere. They laughed hysterically when they called Nancy into there room. They barely could sputter out between giggles "The witch is dead! The witch is dead! The wicked witch is dead!" It felt good till the paranoia made Nancy wonder if she was the witch and they really wished she was out of their lives. Those moments of sunshine seemed to bathe away some of the darkness if only for the briefest of moments.

January of 1983 was bitterly cold. The girls and their poor excuse for a mother had plodded through the holidays with a skimpy tree adorned with one string of lights and a few ornaments Nancy was able to buy. Fortunately, her Ex's mother and father–in-law continued a tradition of gift giving and cheer at their now remarried son's lovely home, so some semblance of normalcy surrounded the kids.

The woman who had battled all her life to be a whole, respected, good person had laid down her arms and was handcuffed by a nightmarish disease. There were many blackouts and times when Nancy would find herself in situations so terrifying, confusing and dangerous that she reviled herself with shame and disbelief. The bottom of the pit happened one Saturday when the kids were spending the week-end with their father. It was the week before Christmas. That had always been her favorite time of year. Even as a child, despite her father's ranting over having to put up a tree on Christmas Eve, despite his anger always ruining every holiday; despite his violent reprisal for any purchase or gift her mother dared to sneak under the tree, despite all that, she loved the story of the baby in the manger, the glimmering decorations in the stores and the music drifting through the streets and in the churches. She would stare out the bathroom window at the star that was told to mark the cave where her friend Jesus was born, and some of the sadness would melt away.

Now, she no longer looked up to the sky for the star. She had to fill the emptiness and despair, the loneliness and self reprisal with something. The bottle was half full of whiskey. She had drunk a half bottle of Pepto-Bismol, put on a sweater and some pants, rubbed some pink rouge on her hollow cheeks a few moments after she kissed the girls and watched them walk to their father's car. The brown liquid called to that hollow place.

"Drink me. I will make the pain go away. Drink me." It seemed to say as she poured it into her glass.

"No ice. I will just sip it with no ice. Maybe I should take one of those sleeping pills the doc ordered with it. Maybe I should call Erin….maybe I should….." she whispered as she saw nothing but that glass of brew calling to her. She could taste it….feel it going down her esophagus and into her gut…feel that warm sensation as it grabbed hold of her body and brain and cried "More! More!"

She didn't remember going to the bathroom and grabbing the bottle of sleeping pills. It was almost full ----- she had refused to take them for fear of becoming addicted. She didn't remember downing two or three glasses of the booze or the three pills she swallowed with them. She didn't remember driving haphazardly down snow covered roads. She didn't remember going to a bar with mud wrestling for entertainment. He offered her a drink. He saw she was alone. He saw the dazed look in her eyes and the purse she had clutched in her trembling hands. He helped her to his partially wrecked van and grinned, showing his mangled teeth surrounded by a poorly kept beard. She recalled watching the road pass below her through the hole in the van floor. He was throwing newspapers in bundles out of the window of the van as it weaved along the dark slippery roads. It was cold and she shook violently. She didn't remember why she woke up in a filthy one room apartment in downtown Toledo. The faucet made a dripping noise on the dishes piled in the sink. It sounded like a drum in her head swollen with hangover. She didn't know why her clothes were half pulled away from her aching body and the smell of vomit and putrid tobacco filled her nostrils. She was lying alone on a mattress on the kitchen floor that was horribly dirty. Her purse was gone. Her soul was gone. Her mind was mush and her eyes were swollen and clouded with fear. Her coat was lying on the sticky floor next to the bed and she wrapped it around her face and sobbed uncontrollably. She had to get home. The kids would be coming home. She didn't have any idea where she was or if some monster was waiting outside to end her life…what was left of it. She threw the coat around her aching shoulders and moved cautiously toward the door. Icy cold bit at her face and legs as she moved into the street. The sign read Cherry Street and the buildings told her she was somewhere downtown. She had no money…no change in her pocket other than one lone penny. She walked from downtown to the apartment in Lambertville. She walked and prayed with every step she took that God would forgive her, help her, save her. The tears crystallized on her swollen ashen face as the wind whipped her about. A church bell tolled in the distance. People passed her as though she was a ghost, barely glancing her way or bothering to move when she passed.

They aren't home yet, thank God, she told herself as she struggled to unlock the door to their apartment. Her hands were numb as was her heart. She threw her clothes in the washer and stood in the shower with the hot water turned up as hot as she could stand it. She couldn't wash the filth away. She couldn't scrub hard enough to uncover the person she tried so hard to be. Her tears and agonizing cries for help echoed against the shower walls and slowly swirled down the drain. Wrapping herself in a thick wool robe she had received several Christmases ago, she attempted to make strong black coffee spilling much of it as her fingers seemed to be opposing the directions from her weary brain.

The girls came home and gave her a conciliatory half hug. They went to their room to finish homework or something. She sat huddled in the chair next to the tiny tree with one string of lights and none of their treasured ornaments. Just like the people she passed on her journey home, the girls barely noticed her. Why would they? They barely knew her anymore.

Nancy's dear sister's divorce was final. The kids were at their father's, it was ten degrees below zero, and the roads were icy, especially in the suburbs, on January 8, 1983. She and Erin were sitting in the dark, staring at the forlorn tree. Nancy had vowed to never attempt to drink again or to take any sleeping pills. She deluded herself into believing that night was all a dream and that she had fallen asleep after the combination of booze, sleeping pills and Pepto-Bismol. Blackouts are not dreams. Nightmares are often real.

"Let's go to a single's dance" Erin broke the silence amidst the chilling wind pushing its way through the seams of the door.

"What? I hate those things – men in gabardine pants smelling like Old Spice and talking about there x-wives with there bad breath! Noooo way!" Nancy retorted.

"There is one in Rossford at this motel. It would have to be better than sitting here feeling sorry for ourselves" her sister attempted to sound enthusiastic.

"I look like hell, feel like hell. Who would want to dance with me?"

"You do not----come on----we can always leave if it is too geeky." She pushed Nancy toward the bedroom. "Now change----wear something warm to cover those skinny bones".

"Okay, but if it is a disaster, we will leave----right?"

"Sure----no pickups, no take homes, no promises" Erin slithered into the bathroom to fix her hair which, by the way, was always perfect. She always looked stunning, even when camping the few times she attempted it ---she always looked together. Nancy didn't know how that curly headed kid with the bunny rabbit face turned into this beautiful woman. It must have been those vitamins Nancy had pretended to take, but spit into the garbage and covered up in Kleenex.

They sat at a table in the dimly lit bar of the motel after sliding down the expressway, wondering what on earth they were doing out on a night like this. The car barely got heated up at all by the time they pulled into the parking lot. Nancy had ordered a seven-seven and pretended to sip a little of it, fearing the nausea and retching would begin and make a scene. She drank in the aroma of the booze as the 7UP bubbles tickled her nose. She wanted to pour it into her stomach so badly. She wanted to feel the warm sensation of oblivion. She didn't remember her vows to never drink again. She put it down on the table gently as though she needed to caress it like that last touch of a lost lover.

The dance was in the basement of the motel, and they could hear an occasional note from the records being played by the DJ slip its way up the stairs into the bar.

"Let's go home---I'm not into this" Nancy pouted indignantly.

"We're here. There's a cute guy at the bar, let's see if he is going downstairs." Erin was always looking at the bright side!

The "cute guy" had gotten up accompanied by another guy, who wasn't as cute at all. The two headed down the stairs toward the music. The "cute guy" half-heartedly glanced their way as he exited, which they took as an invitation.

They paid for their drinks and Nancy clutched her full glass as though it was a life preserver, taking it down the stairs as gingerly as she would have carried the wine chalice for the priest at Communion. The room was large and dimly lit by signs advertising different types of beer in arrays of fireworks, waterfalls and clouds moving across the neon sky. Metal folding chairs lined each side of the room like a sixth-grade dance class. Several men and women sat starring hopefully onto the practically empty dance floor. Some of the women wore blouses to expose their cleavage, some turtlenecks to give the "hands off" message. The men were an array of short bald guys in gabardine trousers, pot bellies, and an occasional guy-just-let-off-the farm. There were a couple of "posers" leaning against the pillars near the bar. These were the Sears catalogue models that donned every bar and gathering place in town. They displayed their masculine prowess by posing, flexing there muscles and wearing the tightest jeans so as to best display there tight butts and other wares. They never danced, just posed. They never spoke to anyone, just by their cocky smile and raised eyebrow so as to make the girls swoon who dared to come within their space.

The metal chairs were cold and made them shiver a little (or maybe it was the aura of the room). It was as if they had gone back in time. Back to those awful pre-teen dances where you were terrified you would be the only one left sitting on the cold metal chairs, the only one not chosen to dance. Another one of those times you wanted to become invisible, and instead seemed to stand out, with everyone seeming to be laughing at your poor untouchable self. It didn't take long for a fairly presentable looking gentleman in a non-gabardine suit to ask Erin to dance. She always drew looks from others. She was tall and regal. When she entered a room, heads would turn. When she smiled, it lit up even the most dismal surroundings. There Nancy sat, staring onto the dance floor like the other poor lonely souls that had not been asked to dance.

"Laaaadies' Choice" the DJ shouted over the mike. "Laaaadies' choice---c'mon girls, give that man a whirl"

My God, let me out of here! Nancy said to herself. Just as she was about to run to the ladies room and hide, she heard a voice a few chairs away, "I wonder if ladies *do* really ask guys to dance?" he said as he leaned forward from *his* cold metal chair.

Never afraid of a challenge, Nancy stood up, straightened her skirt, attempted to puff out her chest at least to a thirty-six B, and walked over to the challenger, stood in front of him and quickly evaluated the prospect. At a closer look, he was younger than her, quite a bit younger. She almost stepped back, ready to change the attack to a retreat.

"Well, are you asking me to dance, ladies' choice?" he asked.

Nice eyes---wonder if he's shorter than me----too young---it's just a dance---say yes---what the heck! she conversed with herself.

He stood up and gently put his arm around her waist, took her hand, and started to move onto the dance floor. A tingle went up her spine when he touched her waist and took her hand, which she attributed to the fan in the ceiling rotating above them.

A little taller than me-----really cute-----way too young-----stop talking to yourself----he'll think you are a nut case-----which I am----just enjoy the moment, you dork!

He stood a respectable distance away from her body as they danced gingerly around the floor. Nancy saw Erin dancing with the cute guy from the bar, and she winked at her as she glided past them. Nancy wasn't sure if they talked. She thought they did---of course, she thought she probably babbled, as she tended to do when she was nervous. Why was she nervous? She needed a drink. Where was her drink? But she would get sick. She would never see him again. He was even younger up close. He had a beard like those Mennonites have, sort of extended side burns. His eyes were piercing and deep set. He looked like Richard Geer. She supposed this would be the only dance as he surely saw she was older than he and probably sure she escaped from some asylum the way she was babbling. But for some reason they kept dancing, and talking, and he moved a little closer with each dance. His cheek touched hers and somehow her gold earring came loose and they wound up crawling on the floor looking for it and laughing as she accused him of biting her ear and dislodging the earring. They never found it. She never attempted to take any more sips of her drink and, thank God, he never offered to buy her one. He sipped on a coke most of the evening between dances. She learned he was coming out of a messy divorce, as was she, that he lived on his boat in the summer and was renting a room at a guy's house not to far from her apartment in Michigan.

Nancy's sister and the cute guy from the bar were having a good time so they all decided to go to Frisch's for breakfast. It was now about two am as they met in the parking lot and ran into the warm, almost empty restaurant. Nancy's dancing partner's ride (his present roommate) had ditched him, so Nancy offered to take him home since it was not to far from where she lived. The cute guy was kind enough to pay for all the breakfasts and Erin hitched a ride with him as she was happy to see her dejected, emaciated sister laughing again. Nancy wasn't too worried about Erin riding home with a guy, as long as he didn't have gabardine pants and talk about his ex-wives.

God sends angels in all forms. Some are invisible but you feel their breath upon you in moments when all seems lost---a sensation of peace, and resolution that pushes beyond the pain and confusion. Others come in human form, no wings or trumpets, no long-flowing iridescent gowns. They don't know they are angels. God weaves people into your story to pull you along, to inspire you, to rescue you, or to just be a quite presence in your life. Some of them even look like movie stars.

Chapter 26

Gary, Indiana

The call came about four o'clock. Nancy was seeing a new consult for the surgeons she had worked for the past several years. She had resigned from her position as head nurse of the neurology unit and had taken a job as patient educator for two very busy vascular surgeons. Of course, she had to create another monster – her usual M.O.--- and the job had blossomed from patient educator to clinical nurse specialist. She had become a clinical affiliate, allowed at that time in hospitals, giving her privileges similar to those of the physician assistants of the present day. The surgeons spent most of their time performing surgery and Nancy took care of the patient's orders, education, reviewed all their charts before and after rounds, took out lines, started IVs, prepared educational materials, helped with research, collaborated with the referring physicians, answered thousands of pages, scheduled surgeries, drank tons of coffee, ate pickle and ketchup sandwiches, ran up and down flights of stairs all day, rarely emptied her ever expanding floppy bladder, ran to codes and emergencies, read x-rays and learned to read the new CAT Scans, prepared Amnion dressings from "borrowed" placentas, knew every lab result, x-ray and special procedure result, memorized the history and demographics of every patient, took out stitches and staples, assisted with minor procedures on the units ----you name it, she would do it, as long as her nursing license allowed it. She loved the versatility, the responsibility, the excitement and the rewards of comforting patients and families. The adrenaline rush kept her going at work

Outside the world within the hospital, she was powerless. Her world had crashed around her and her soul was empty. Inside the hospital, she had praise and control; outside the hospital, she searched for it in all the wrong places. Men came in and out of her life. They became her addiction, now that "the bottle" was no longer her friend.

It didn't matter if they cared for her, as long as they paid attention to her. She had control in the bedroom—she was good at that they told her. They told her things she needed to hear, even though they just said what they thought she *wanted* to hear. . Not that she received anything from it except the fact that she was "good" ; she never felt good. There were many roles to play. She never knew which one was really "her" Was she the confident "girl Friday" for famous surgeons, the flirtatious "party girl", the "good mom" who wanted the best for her kids, the little girl who was always ready for a battle, beaten by her the enemy – herself, or the hopeless drunk who could no longer drink to drown the pain?

Four o'clock – a 911 page. She pushed the button to view the page and quickly found a phone in a nearby nurses' station.

"They've taken Mom to the hospital. She had emergency surgery for bleeding around a tumor in her colon. She's in surgery now. Can you and Erin come?" Nancy's sister, Ali, in Iowa said haltingly.

"We'll be there as soon as we can! Meet you at the hospital. Tell her we love her!"

Nancy called Erin, and by six-thirty pm they were on the road. That trip was an adventure in itself. Nancy's 1982 Pontiac was a good friend. It seemed to know that she was hurting for money and did it's best to keep running despite lack of attention. After filling the tank at a Marathon station they headed toward the turnpike. It was cold for April and darkness rolled over the sun like pie dough being mashed by a rolling pin. Women are very tuned to the sounds their cars make and "Penelope" the car, was making surging sounds whenever Nancy had to decelerate or accelerate. There were no "trouble lights" yelling from the dashboard, so they clipped along at about seventy miles an hour while Erin watched for police cars. They would definitely play on any officer's sympathy that dared to stop them, tearfully letting him know that they needed to get to their mother as soon as possible and would definitely be more vigilant in watching the speedometer if he would excuse their transgression so they could be on their way. They were worried. Alice had told them that Ethelyn's hemoglobin was less than six when she arrived at the hospital. Her abdomen was bloated and she looked pale as a ghost. Though neither of them had ever actually seen a ghost, they imagined ghosts were extremely pale. Not knowing the surgeons at this hospital, by reputation or otherwise, added to their worry.

It was about 11:50 p.m. when they approached Gary, Indiana. Nancy always sang the tune from *The Music Man* about Gary whenever she started to see signs that they were nearing the town. Just as Nancy was about to burst into the chorus, that sound came from the engine – a *whwhwhwiiiiirrrrrr* like someone sliding across ice. *Whwhwhwiiiiirrrr* – there it was again. Penelope began to decelerate 70----60----50----40---30, despite Nancy pushing the gas pedal to the floor. It kept slowing down as they eased the Pontiac off the turnpike toward one of the exit ramps.

"Sounds like a belt is loose or something" Erin offered.

"Maybe if it cools off, we can get it going again – even if it is a belt, we are in the middle of nowhere in Gary, which is a spooky place in the daytime let alone the middle of the night!" Nancy was sure these words were consolingly.

"Put on your hazards. Maybe someone will come along and see we need help." Erin offered.

"Don't think I want to risk the two of us being found helpless by some crazy person!" Nancy offered consolingly.

"Well, we have to do something. Do you have a flasher or flashlight?" Erin sounded a little aggravated.

"No, you are not walking to try and find help. We are supposed to stay near the vehicle – that is straight from "Road Sense" Nancy offered, again, consolingly.

"Try starting it again----it may have settled down. We have to get there. Mom rarely calls us to come. This is serious." Erin looked tearful.

Nancy climbed into the driver's seat and turned the key. A very loud nothing happened. Not even a grind or groan. She turned the key again, and there was a brief sputter, then nothing.

The night sky had settled into the palm of the eerie brown, grey haze of pollution from the factories so typical of that area in those days. Crickets chirped contentedly in the tall grass of a nearby field and the chilly air mixed with musty smells of human and industrial waste in a nearby dump reminded Nancy of the pathologists' lab where cadavers are dissected for autopsy. That certainly caused them both to shiver a little as Erin stared at the dash as if "hypnotism" would work on Penelope.

"Let me give it one more try ---it's not out of gas, and I just had the oil checked, They told me they put in a new carburetor." Nancy mused

"Sounds good to me" Erin said encouragingly "It's creepy here!"

Nancy turned the key in the ignition at the same time she said her favorite prayer, "The Guardian Angel" prayer. She turned the key cautiously without stepping on the gas, thinking that she may have flooded it by pushing on the gas b pedal multiple times when it was decelerating. The engine started right up, and they turned toward some lights they could see in the distance. The girls let out a sizable "Yippee!" when the speedometer began to respond to a gingerly applied foot on the gas pedal.

They had no idea where they were going or what they were going to do. As they passed abandoned stores with broken or missing windows, a grocery store that advertised *"Cigarettes-----Cheap"* on the front door with bars peaking out from behind the sign, they realized they had absolutely no plan at all. Both were praying silently that they didn't have to stop for a traffic light, though the littered streets seemed to have swallowed up their humans. Well, not *all* their humans! There it was----a red light at a corner near a hazily lit bar from which emerged two very tough looking ladies of the night. One had big frizzy blond hair and lips smeared with gold lipstick that shone in the light from the street lamp. The other was very well endowed and covered with all kinds of beads, earrings, and bracelets. Nancy and Erin barely breathed as the ladies walked toward the car.

Nancy tried to remember some karate moves she had seen on TV. Erin was staring at the dashboard again – probably wondering if Penelope would magically sprout wings and propel them out of there.

" Wat chyal doin' girlies? Out lookin' for some fun??" The blond peered into Nancy's window and shouted.

"Ya'll tryin' ta move in on our territory? Huh!" she shouted even louder.

Nancy took a chance and opened the window a crack and squeaked "No, absolutely---no—we---ah we ---our car n-n-n-needs some gas ---c-c-c could you tell us where a g-g-gas station is, pleeeeeze?"

"Ha, Ha, Misty ---these squirts want us to help them!! Whadya think of that ---us helpin' somebody –ain't that a puddle of snot ---ain't we just full of luv an' charity!??", she slurred, swatting her cohort across the back.

Misty drew her fist up as though she was going to let Blondie have it, and Nancy stepped on the gas as hard as she could. Penelope whirred as loud as a jet warming up for take-off. Suddenly, the old Pontiac lurched forward and headed down the dingy street. 30-40-50 mph. Then it happened again----*wwwwhhhhiiiiirrrrr*-----50-----40-------30----

"Oh, my God, she's dying again!!"

"Put it in neutral! Stop stepping on the gas pedal! For heaven's sake –do something!" screamed Nancy's adorable little sis.

"I am doing something! *It is not doing anything!*" Nancy retorted, lovingly.

"Look----There's a Gas Station on that corner," Erin screeched.

There it was, like an oasis in the desert. In fact the half lit sign said "Gas Oasis."

Penelope slithered toward one of the gas pumps, gave one miserably weak *wwwhhhiirr* , and stopped. The station was desolate and run-down. One gas pump was missing its gas nozzle and the display portion where prices and different octane levels of gas were ripped off and unlighted. In the corner of the lot, there was a small booth with bars on the windows and a slumped over figure at the desk.

"Do you think he….. she….. is dead?" Erin asked. From their vantage point the body didn't seem to be moving.

"I'm going to go over there. You cover me" Erin stated bravely.

"Cover you…………with what? A damn bottle opener? Sure I'll cover you……………with a scream for help!"

Erin stepped carefully out from the safety of our injured auto.

"Wait, I'll go with you." Nancy offered.

"Someone has to stay with the car. We are in the worst of the worst neighborhoods."

The walk to the small, dimly lit booth seemed like a mile as Erin tiptoed across the twenty feet separating it from the car. The figure in the booth stirred and began to attempt some semblance of sitting up. It was a man or boy. A dew rag held down frizzy brown dreadlocks which covered his brow and parted over glassy eyes that seemed to be having an awfully hard time focusing. A burned-out cigarette dangled from his mouth like an appendage of one of his teeth. Erin hesitated when he came alive, not sure whether to run back to the car, wet her pants, or keep moving forward towards her quest for information.

"Yeah", he offered in a gravelly, slurred tone.

"We are having some difficulties with our car and wonder if you can help us. Do you perform any type of service here? Can you give us directions to the turnpike from here? That is….if you can get us started. Our mother is in the hospital, and we need to get there." Erin said in her most appealing voice.

Way too much information for this dude! He rolled his eyes, flicked the cigarette from his mouth to somewhere in the booth, and spoke over the mike that was perched in front of him.

"Lady, lady. Ya gotta slow down so I can get what yer sayin'."

"The *turnpike*! A big road…cars and trucks going fast….. the *turnpike*!" Erin yelled.

"Ya mean the *toll road?*" he retorted, lurching forward on the "toll road" words as if the microphone couldn't get the message across loud enough.

Nancy was riveted to the window of the car which was open just enough to hear raised voices. When she saw the booth person lurch forward in the booth, she came out of the car like a cop in a chase scene.

"Hey! Hey, you! Don't be yelling at my sister like that!"

They both looked at Nancy as she stomped across the lot shaking her fist at the booth person.

Eth must have said to herself, There she goes again, taking charge….

always has to be in control....can't let anyone do anything! At least that's what she would have said to Nancy if she wasn't exhausted, frightened, and lacking coffee.

"I'm fine! This gentleman is letting me know it isn't the *turnpike...* it's called the *toll road!"* She made sure the words were yelled very close to Nancy's ear.

"Okay, Okay, just wasn't sure you were safe. Uh....is there any service here...uh, which I doubt very much."

The body had slumped back on the desk, so they assumed that was the answer to that question. They walked back to the car, both of them sure they would be spending the night there not sleeping, one of them holding tight to their only weapon, the church key. They sat in the car with the doors locked not saying much. They stared out toward the dingy alley and broken-down storefronts.

Tap.....tap.

The girls jumped and grabbed each other, not daring to look toward the sound on the window near the driver's seat.

"Don't be scared," a deep, kind voice whispered through the tiny opening in the window they had left for some air. "I saws you as I was passin' by and you looked like you was lost."

Erin and her sister cautiously turned toward the voice. He was a black man, about sixty or so. His hair was white and it capped off a smiling face with glowing white teeth. He had a jacket over a shirt that looked like it had seen many launderings. In the dim light, his eyes under white eyebrows seemed so kind and unthreatening that they felt each other's grip relax.

"We can't seem to get our car started, sir. Are you the gas station owner? We need someone that can get us going again. We have a half-tank of gas, so that's not it..... it just seems to fizzle after a few miles, decelerates, no matter what I do with the gas pedal." Nancy reported

"Well, now.......let me see what I ken do, ladies. Would you all open your lid and ah'l take a look see" he drawled.

Nancy pulled the latch to the hood and the man bent over the engine with a tiny flashlight. Nancy whispered to Erin, "I hope he can fix it enough so we can get out of here"

"Me too" she yawned as she leaned her head on the seat back.

"It looks like your carburetor is sticking. I'm gonna spray it with some engine cleaner an' see if that gets it goin' for ya all" he spoke from behind the opened lid.

He didn't go to get anything. They didn't think he coincidentally had engine cleaner in the pocket of his jacket...just in case. But, when he said "start 'er up", Penelope obeyed, and the engine purred like it had many years before.

"You got to keep 'er around fifty miles an hour till you can git to a shop, okay?" he said as he leaned toward the driver's side of the car after closing the hood.

"Oh, thank you, thank you so much........How can we thank you, you see Mom is ill and we are trying to get......." As Nancy talked she turned and reached for her purse to offer some payment for his help. Erin was also trying to help find the purse in the array of suitcases hastily packed and a bag of chips that had spilled in the back seat.

When they looked up he was gone. No one was in the street or on the sidewalk. They looked toward the booth with the body still and lifeless ----no one anywhere. Where had he gone? He was just there! He couldn't have disappeared that quickly. They didn't even get to thank him.

"I think he was an angel" Erin said "I mean a real angel....there are angels, you know."

"Do you think so? I believe there are things we never can explain. Somehow, God took care of us." Nancy wanted so much to feel close to Him again.

They obeyed and stayed at fifty miles per hour all the way, finally limping into a gas station just east of Davenport, Iowa where their folks and sister lived. Penelope decelerated and decided to "nap" just as they came down the hill and pulled in front of the service center.

Ethelyn survived the colon resection for cancer and a blood clot in her leg. She was a survivor. Nancy and Erin stayed until she came home from the hospital, cleaned the house as best they could, left instructions with Alice on the care and feeding of a post-operative patient, and prayed that their father would be kind to her. It seemed he spent very little time at home while they were there.

The evening before their mother's release from the hospital, Nancy was extricating papers crammed under Ethelyn's bed when she had this urge to call the young gentleman from the singles' dance. He had given her his number after they had talked until the wee hours of the morning in front of the house were he was staying, never thinking she would call – neither of them in a place to think of having a relationship. Nancy pushed the thought aside and began the task of cleaning her mother's bedroom. Ethelyn had saved every *Reader's Digest* invitation to join a contest and win millions and stuffed them under her bed until the bed tilted to one side. Nancy thought it had lost one of its rollers, but when she looked under the bed the sea of contests poured out from broken boxes. Unrealized dreams, broken promises, bruised hearts and bodies often are assuaged by hoarding. Forts are built of seemingly insignificant items-- books, figurines-- to replace the loss or barricade the pain of life's disappointments. Ethelyn pushed them under the bed, the bed where she had always retreated to quite the ache in her heart and in her body from the undeserved beatings and accusations. The ashes of her dreams fell into her tiny ashtray as she sat on a crooked bed with a cigarette, breathing in the smoke like the aftermath of a blazing fire she could never quench.

Tears fell onto the papers as Nancy stuffed them tenderly into plastic garbage bags. She and Erin set them lovingly in the corner near a chest of drawers. They could not throw them away. They could not stop the pain they felt for their mother. Nancy pulled up the shades on the window and the sunlight reached through the dusty window caressing the now level bed.

"H—hi, may I speak to John?" Nancy asked haltingly when she finally mustered up the courage to call the man from the single's dance. She had searched for the crumpled napkin that held his phone number and found it buried under mascara, checkbook, some pens and old lifesavers at the bottom of her purse. She had stared at it after dusting off the purse fuzzies and finally got the courage to dial.

"This is John?"

Oh, my God! He answered. I feel like a dope calling him. He's way too young...and I'm in such a bad place right now. I don't kn......

"Hello, is someone there? Is this one of those stupid survey things?! If it...."

"Hi....It's Nancy.........from the single's dance.......the one with the gold earring.....I just called to say that I am in Iowa right now. Our mom had emergency surgery, and we had a terrible time getting out here----the car kept loosing power, and there was this angel....... well, it really was a man...but he disappeared after he magically got our car to run......we were in Gary at midnight-----god-awful place, especially at night. Erin had a church key she was holding as tightly as she could to use as a weapon....some weapon, huh? Are you still there?"

"Wow, that's some story.........I can't believe you called! I didn't think you would even remember me! Is your mother OK? I hope so. Your car......an angel? Where's Gary?"

"I'm sorry, I always talk too fast. Yes, she is coming home today from the hospital after having a colon resection. She had cancer, and her hemoglobin was very low. I'm sorry to bother you....I just was thinking about the night we met and how much we, I guess, I talked. I just wanted to thank you for a great evening."

"I had a great time too. I hope your mother will be alright. Give me a call when you come home. That is, if you want to call".

Do I want to call?!! You bet I do, she said to herself.

"I'll let you know when I get back, and maybe we can go for a coffee at Frisch's" she sain, boldly attempting to make a date.

"Sounds good to me!" he seemed enthusiastic. At least she took it that way.

"Bye"

"Bye. Um... thanks again for calling." the sound of the dial tone.

Her palms were sweating and her heart racing. "I hardly know him. I shouldn't have called. He's too young and we're both just exiting from failed relationships. There's something about him, though. I have to stop thinking about this and take care of this place before Mom comes home."

For the briefest of moments, Nancy thought of a drink to calm her nerves. Nausea instantly pushed the thought from her mind. She had to clasp her hands together to stop them from shaking. She hoped that Erin was too preoccupied with having to manage her family by herself, since her husband had callously left all of them, lost in another life. Nancy loved her sisters with all her heart. She tried to hide her addiction and insanity as best she could. Believing that a "dry spell" would cure her and she soon would be able to drink in moderation was a lost delusion.

Ethelyn was pale and weak. Erin and Nancy stayed for a few days to make sure she ate and rested. Dad hovered some and was unusually kind to her while they were there, making her chicken noodle soup and turning her pillows. There was this side of him that they loved. This was the charming and tender Walter that ushered at church, headed the Boy Scouts, took pictures at weddings, and worked from dawn to dusk, barely missing a day in twenty-five years. The fox in the chicken coop always lay waiting in some dark corner of his soul.

Chapter 27

Could I Have This Dance?

Could I have this dance, for the rest of my life?
Would you be my partner every night?

God was there all the time. He knew the sad sack of a woman needed a nudge in the right direction. He puts people in our paths. We just have to slow down and notice them. He really never leaves. We all have a spiritual part of us no matter what religion or persuasion. Even those who profess disbelief have a part of them that defies explanation.

They had coffee at Frisch's restaurant; cups and cups of "bottom of the pot" chewable coffee. Something about him prompted Nancy to pour her heart out. All the stuff she couldn't handle, the stuff she could, the kids, the ex's, the parents, the work, the finances (or lack thereof). They talked about everything but the booze. She never mentioned the booze. Never even came to mind that all those things she discussed were affected by her drinking and insecurities. She never mentioned the unbearable craving for a drink. She never mentioned the unbearable need to stop the pain and the embattled feelings inside her. She didn't tell him about the desperate need to feel that warm paralyzing sensation as the alcohol deadened the synapses connected to reality.

There was a young man living in the apartment above them who would bounce his basketball in the living room above ours every night about seven thirty in the evening. Deb, Nancy's daughter, who normally would not jump at a request from her mother, would literally leap up from her spot on the couch, or bolt from her room offering in the sweetest of voices to run upstairs and tell that "jerk" to stop his dribbling. Every time...........

Nancy found out many years later that his thudding was a signal that his parents had left the building and Deb should come up to share a "joint" of Cannabis with him. Pretty slick!

After several dates and oodles of talks, John had moved in with them. Nancy thought she asked the girls if it would be alright, playing on their sympathy for the poor guy who would have to chisel himself out of his boat frozen in the lake during the winter months. He never interfered with her decisions or discipline with the kids. He would give an opinion if asked, but quietly went off to a neutral corner during a discussion or argument. He had the patience of Job with one menopausal, dysfunctional, alcohol deprived middle aged blond and two hormonal teenagers, with pent-up anger from recent and remote injuries.

They were all injured. Perhaps the camaraderie that brings people together in a disaster was healing them all in some way during those years.

The girls would leave for school. Deb boarded the school bus on the mornings when her sister absconded with the Camero. Chills would raise goose bumps when Nancy would hear that 350 engine's roaring start. Whatever possessed her to purchase a car that actually levitated when it started, before its tires would screech like the start of the Indy five hundred, is beyond comprehension, especially for a couple of action seeking teenagers. A patient rep from work, who was also a single mom with two boys, said her boys were working now and had both purchased new cars. She wanted to get rid of this "cool" Camero – it had been a good starter car for them and she wasn't asking an arm and leg for it. Nancy's finances, along with her decision making skills, were in the pits, so she bought it without a question as to its mechanical health or history. It could do zero to seventy miles per hour within twenty feet, and it used about one gallon of gas to do it! The girls were taking care of Nancy during those years. They are amazing young women. Each of them found a way to cope with the ghosts that haunted them.

Deb took on the caretaker role – the one who people are drawn to when they are in need because they know she will find a way to help them. It is a draining role to play, with a script that seems endless and overwhelming at times. She invested in years of counseling and self awareness programs that helped to dissipate some of the anger and fear that came with the bedlam in her life.

Sue excelled in school and in her profession as a pharmacist. Analytic and independent, she masked her insecurity and resentments with an air of confidence and detachment. Volcanoes erupt without warning when crevices in mountains are exposed. That part of Sue, that angry part is nothing like the sweet, intelligent, women she grew to be. That other part of her, the part that begs to heal, produces eruptions that boil to the surface causing loved ones to retreat from the lava as it spills over into their lives.

Tom was living with his father, playing in the band at Bowsher High, and excelling as a student. He, too, chose to channel his pain and anger into work, advancing to great heights in his career. He moved several times after college; a collage of experiences; becoming part of several loving families and developing extraordinary cooking skills.

Children heal quickly, but scars left by unrest and division in their families either fade till they are barely recognizable; cover superficially, so that the wound leaves a cavity beneath the surface, or erupt into abscesses that drain the life-blood from their souls. Nancy could neither erase the past nor paint a picture of security and perfection she vowed she would provide for them. Her prayer was for the forgiveness, peace, and happiness for them that she searched for all her life.

John and Nancy would lie in bed holding tightly to each other, not wanting to leave those few moments before consciousness takes hold and your mind begins to write a list of "must do", "didn't do", "shouldn't have done", "can't afford to do", "don't have the courage to do", and "what to wear". Making love seemed to be the best way of pushing those lists back into the sub-conscious. One of the few times Nancy felt confident and beautiful was when making love. Calling off work would never occur to her. Work defined her in a way that love making did. She transformed into a fearless nurse dynamo with boundless stamina, the ability to dodge bullets and to make critical decisions within seconds. Such a paradox! The blow up doll inside her with it's many crevices who wanted nothing more than to be unnoticed and invisible was so different from the façade that everyone saw--- the leader, the healer, the caretaker, the all-doing, all-seeing monster she created and felt she had to live up to.

This man somehow opened up a part of her she never knew existed. They could call off work, feigning sickness (not really a fib, as they agreed they were both a little sick in the head) and spend the day making love and feeling amazingly alright with it.

John didn't drink, hadn't for five years. Nancy learned shortly after he moved in with them that he needed to go to meetings. These were meetings for people who had a problem with alcohol. Not for Nancy. She didn't have a problem with alcohol-----she had a problem without alcohol. She needed it, but it didn't need her anymore. If she sipped, gulped, or chugged it to stop the shaking and the overwhelming feeling of dread that would overcome her like a Tsunami, her insides would reject and eject it unceremoniously. Drinking Pepto-Bismol, eating oatmeal, deep breathing, praying did nothing but add to the frustration and the pain. Her moods were all over the place ranging from fearful to hebephrenic, from apathetic to pathetic, from aggressive to regressive. How John, the girls, her friends, and her family tolerated her was amazing. She blamed the ex-husbands, her mom and dad, the priest, her friends, her family, even God for this mess. The few decision-making brain cells she hadn't destroyed were clamoring for an audience with her, but she was too weak and stubborn to listen.

Her paranoia convinced her that John went to those meetings to seek out females. Surely all the hugs were more than friendship. Who would want to go several nights a week or multiple times a day and listen to sob stories from addicts that often repeated the same mistakes over and over? Why would these people who professed to be sick in mind, body, and soul confide their deepest fears and inequities to each other without the oversight of professional counsel? Nancy started to accompany John to observe and critique as well as to monitor the extent and number of "hugs". She was the professional. Hadn't she taken many classes at the University and in nurse's training to be able to evaluate and coach the injured and suffering? Wasn't she the center of the universe around which the world spun in demented delirium? Whispers and stares were about her, weren't they? Her clothes, her figure, her speech, her thoughts were critiqued and insulted, in her mind. Nothing seemed right, and it was everyone's fault, not hers. After each meeting she would leave angry and tense. She couldn't explain why she felt that way. John would ask her what she thought and she would retort haughtily, "Those people definitely need a professional facilitator! It is dangerous to bare your conscience like that without professional guidance!"

"Amazing how it has worked just fine for almost seventy-five years for millions of "sick alcoholics" without a facilitator," he would quietly reply.

"W-w-w-well, you just go there for the hugs and to cruise chicks! You should be cured by now! Five years, for heavens sake-----five years of the same thing----don't tell me it isn't to see other women---all men are the same!!"

"Maybe you should start listening instead of criticizing. I'm going to bed," he would say.

And he did. She just stood there pouting and feeling like a schmuck. Some tiny rational voice somewhere buried under resentments and fear kept telling her she was wrong. *She* needed help, not them. They were getting help. They were trying. She was stuck in quicksand slowly sinking. *Someone please throw me rope and save me! Please, God, help me!* she would cry. There were no tears. Tears wouldn't come. There was a pain in her gut and stinging in her eyes.

The rope that could save her was lying so close to her hands that she could have grabbed it at any moment. God must have had some more for her to do here. She almost missed it. She almost drowned in the ooze of a disease that is devastating, insidious and little understood. Since she was too weak and stubborn to grab it herself, God and a whole swarm of wonderful, caring people lassoed that rope around her and gradually pulled her onto some solid ground. From there, it was up to her to follow them on a path to a life full of promises and challenges, or to turn back toward the swamp and drown in the unforgiving mire of self-destruction.

They were married. John almost was late for the wedding because he had gone fishing in Lake Erie with a good friend, sort of a two man bachelor party. The boat motor decided to die and they waited for many hours for a tow. Nancy thought that John might have had second thoughts and tried to defect to Canada. Tom had gotten involved in a church in a small town west of Toledo after graduation from Bowsher. He assisted the pastor of the church with the service and Erin, Sue, Deb and some friends completed the wedding party. Trying to keep expenses down, Nancy had ordered a sheet cake from a nearby grocery store decorated with bride and groom faces. That day in July was very hot and humid so when Sue picked up the cake, the ruby red lips of the bride décor melted. The groom decoration survived the heat, but the bride looked like a victim of the Amityville horror. Nancy kept covering up the poor soul's face with napkins but one of their friends thought it was a hoot and kept removing the cover.

For the next twenty-five years, John and Nancy were able to travel through majestic mountains on a Honda Interstate, smell the fragrance of pine needles fresh with morning dew in the forest, feel the warm glow of a campfire and stare up at a pristine night sky filled with glistening stars, accept the challenge of a class five rapids in a four man raft, catch walleye, perch, salmon and a few zebra mussels as the evening sunset painted fabulous rainbows across a lake sparkling as the last rays drew ripples in it's depths, laugh with their children and grandchildren and soothe their tears with kisses and promises of a better day, strain their backs and shoulders digging a footer and laying bricks for a workshop; argue, repent, kiss and make up, make mistakes, right wrongs, teeter on the edge, hold on, live ---live---live!

There were times that they almost lost what they had. For five years Nancy's parents were ill and John and she, Erin and her new husband, Ed, took care of them. Because of the things she learned from the books and people in the meetings and from the return of her friend, Jesus, Nancy was able to forgive her father and care for him. She could be with him, as he was no longer the way he was when she was growing up. As his shoulders and spine bent like a tree whose limbs thirstily reaches for the ground water, kindness returned to his eyes and he became docile and compliant. Parkinson's took those hands that struck in anger and rendered the skin paper thin and trembling with any purposeful movement. Ethelyn became more vocal as he withered and began to pay him back with a tongue lashing now and then. Though it was not in her nature to be vengeful, at times she wore this look of satisfaction as he capitulated to her reprimands. They stayed together until the last puff of smoke swirled around her room and she reached up her hand as though she was grasping another's. A sigh was the last spoken word she uttered. Perhaps a sigh of relief mixed with sadness. Perhaps a sigh of joy as the hand of God whisks you into His arms and carries you to His kingdom.

Their father wept. Tears fell onto her casket. Were they tears of repentance, tears of loss, just tears?

One of the nieces put a greeting card with tiny writing that went all around the edges just the way Ethelyn used to write every card, every letter. Her love used every bit of space. Her heart was filled with kindness, generosity and unselfishness. She used to touch Nancy's hand to remind her to slow down. She touched the lives of those who she offered help to so unselfishly. She caressed the keys of the piano in the way she caressed life. She rarely drove over thirty-five miles an hour anywhere. The palms of her hands were always warm from the camphor oil and the garden gloves she wore in order to ease the pain of arthritis. Those hands brought music to so many. They taught tiny fingers to find the notes and to bravely play Chop Sticks with both hands. Their touch was like milk poured gently down the side of an ice-cold glass. It was almost as though she barely touched the keys. Perhaps her hands hovered over them and the keys leaped up to touch them. Her life was concert played by sorrowful violins, romantic oboes, trumpets blasting in stormy staccato, laced with the lighthearted dance of flutes and piccolos. Long after she played her last concert, when Nancy was off somewhere in her thoughts and the speedometer was inching beyond the legal speed this warmth would melt over her hand. It would startle her enough to pay attention to her speed. Whether real or imagined it matters very little.

John managed to hang on when mom passed away and dad was

too feeble to stay in their apartment alone. For over a year they dealt with special meals, catheters, "accidents" with bowels, wanderings at night, numerous adult babysitters, bathing, comforting, trips to the hospital and doctor's offices. They were both working full-time and then some. The days when they would take off on their Honda or make love passionately dwindled. Nancy also spent many week-ends going to Cincinnati to help Sue with her two adorable twins. Sue ad become a Pharmacist, moved to Cincinnati, and worked at a large children's hospital while her husband worked week-ends, so Nancy happily left work on Friday and traveled to Cincinnati to do grandma duty for those adorable kids. Sometimes she would load her father in the car to give him a change of scenery. He would sleep most of the way, waking occasionally to make sure Nancy was still coherent. He fancied himself the co-pilot on their travels. He loved to stop at the Waffle House along the way to partake of a large stack of waffles covered with sweet gooey syrup. Though he was diabetic it seemed that a little hyperglycemia made him more alert with less violent tremors.

That day came when Nancy and Erin had to make a decision to place Walter in an extended care facility. Worried that his wanderings might lead him into danger, exhausted from trying to work with very little sleep, they tried to explain that this was best for him. The look of sadness and fear in his eyes when he said "I'll be good. I'll be better. Please don't make me go" was heartbreaking..

"It's only for your safety, dad. There are activities there and other people your age. It is a very clean and reputable place and Erin and I will come to visit you. I'm so sorry." Nancy tried to comfort him.

The nurses and aides cared for him for eight months. The facility was one of the best. He seemed to do well there, or pretended he was happy. Erin and Nancy would visit him several times during the week. Nancy always made sure she was the one to change his supra-pubic catheter. He liked the attention and trusted her. One week John and she went camping, which they loved. Something seemed to have changed. She felt John pulling away ever so insidiously. Never confident in a relationship, though deep inside she knew he loved her, a terrible fear would engulf her, causing her to question his love. The more she questioned, the more he would retreat. Oh, there were moments when that warm, comfortable feeling of being loved and in love would shine through, but they were occurring less and less. They were both sober. She had finally been blessed with the realization that she was a hopeless alcoholic. They worked their programs individually and respectfully. The wedge of obligations had started to drive them apart emotionally.

Times away from the responsibility of work and life in general would rekindle some of that fire they felt when they first courted. The camping trip was all of that. They cuddled by the fire as the evening chill surrounded them. Hiked through the woods and watched the little white tails of deer darting away from the humans invading their forest.

When they returned, Walter had become very ill with a urinary tract infection. Despite antibiotics and fluids he became septic and semi-conscious. The nurses' aides bathed him tenderly and moistened his parched lips with oil. He remained in and out of consciousness, not eating or drinking for over a week. Erin and Nancy would be there every day to assist with his care. Erin had a difficult time forgiving him. This compassionate and caring woman put her feelings aside to be at his side until the end. . A priest came to visit one evening as Nancy was dozing in a chair across the room from Walter's bed. He sat on the bed and said to Walter, whose eyes were closed and respirations rapid and labored. "Walt I know how much you like women. Those angels up in heaven are the most beautiful women, so why don't you just let them wrap their arms around you –It's time to travel."

Walter suddenly opened his eyes, which he had not done for days. He had a little mischievous grin on his face as his eyes closed, his breathing was less labored and he seemed to relax his body, which had been tense and twitching these past several days. Nancy went home to catch a few hours of sleep. At midnight she received the call that he had died. She and Erin kissed his cool forehead when they arrived. So many feelings raced around inside of both sisters. Both of their parents were gone. Though their lives had been stormy and insecure in many ways, they had done their best---they really had. It didn't seem to matter what they endured, or missed, or feared. At that moment they were two orphans, tiny and vulnerable. They called their little sis, Alice, and hugged over the miles on the phone. No matter what life threw at them, good or bad, they all stuck together and were there for each other.

Shortly after he died they took Dad's ashes back to New Jersey and sprinkled them over Nanny's grave. Nanny's grave was just a short distance from where they had sprinkled their mother's ashes on her mother, Irene's grave. Together, but apart even in death, their remains melted into the earth.

Nancy and John's respite from caretaking lasted only a year when Sue and her three girls moved in with them. Sue and her husband had separated and were contemplating divorce. Pat and she had many battles. There were multiple attempts over the years to patch things up, but there were ghosts in both their lives that kept flying around them and causing havoc.

The grandchildren were an amazing gift they never would have enjoyed had they not stopped drinking and held tight to the AA program. Nancy's compulsive nature hungered for time with them, hugs from them, spoiling them, being there for them. The twins and Erica, (Sue had three girls now) were in pre-school a few blocks from John and Nancy's house. Sue took a Pharmacist's position in Monroe, Michigan. John had never been allowed to partake in the raising of his two children, so having three giggling, screeching girls around was a test indeed. He had tried to become a part of his children's lives, but his ex-wife bore resentments that drove her to keep them from him. Later in life, he was given the gift of bonding with them. He had three sisters, so was somewhat used to being around girls. Five women and one man was an amazing challenge for him. Even the dog was a female! Nancy was going through her female change of life, the girls and Sue were dealing with a painful change. Why wouldn't he be driven to change something in his life?

Things changed. Do you know what insensible loss is? It is the loss of fluid from just breathing in and out, from perspiration on your skin, from metabolism itself. It is difficult to measure but can change the way your organs and bodily functions behave. It is not directly noticeable, but it occurs insidiously. John's family suffered from depression. His sisters, their children, and his children all had some form or another of the painful disease. Many alcoholics suffer from depression and other psychological diseases along with the same chemical imbalance that causes a huge tolerance and incessant craving for booze. The signs and symptoms of depression are like the insensible loss of fluid. They go undetected. There is no conscious control over the cloud that begins to envelope the mind and the soul. What triggers it-- chemical, emotional, situational--- no one is really sure.

John went diving and snorkeling one day out by the islands. He loved the water and his time alone. He and Nancy both enjoyed the boats they had over the years. Fishing, pulling kids on rafts, navigating the Great Lakes, and making love in the cabin or on the deck under the stars were highlights in their lives. If he wanted to be alone, he should be. You should be who you are, even in a marriage. If you fell in love with that person, why would you want him or her to be someone else? Humans are restless and selfish, live for satisfying needs in the moment with little thought of the repercussions of our actions. We eat too much, work too much, drink to much, have to be entertained too much.

When he came out of the water, it was like life had left him. He "snapped". He wanted to escape, run, or hide. He told Nancy that he became someone else; barely remembering what motivated him, what he did each day. He was like a robot that some outside force was controlling. She lost him. She was so busy with life that a brief kiss at night and in the morning deluded her into believing that he was still with her, her partner, her buddy, her lover. He came home from meetings and a class he was taking at the marina later and later. She didn't see him disappearing. Part of her that wasn't running like a banshee taking care of the world felt him pulling away, but she buried the uncomfortable feeling under work, caring for everyone else except him.

Sue got the call from some women's husband. "That man needs to leave my wife alone. They've been seeing each other for a year and it better damn well stop! You tell him that! No more meetings in parking lots and at the Marina! No more!" He slammed the phone in Sue's ear. She held the receiver in her hand and stared at it.

Mom is at work. How can I tell her? I knew there was something going on. He seemed so distant and withdrawn. Poor mom. Should I call her?

John disappeared on a Thursday night. Never came home from his AA meeting. Nancy had frantically called his cell phone dozens of times with no answer. She called his sister who was living in a trailer in a suburb outside of Toledo. Her gut was burning and her heart pounding through her chest. Panic is a terrible feeling. Your adrenalin kicks you in high speed and you are acutely aware of the feeling of impending doom. Three nights. Three awful days. Having to drag to work and be presentable. Don't show the anguish and fear that you feel. You've got to keep cool and efficient for eight to ten hours. Make some desperate calls when you can steal a moment. No luck! Where did he go? How could he leave her? They loved each other. She was so frightened. Can't show the kids. They were going through so much themselves.

The nights were horrible. Nancy couldn't sleep because a vice had its jaws on her chest and was squeezing it unmercifully. Not only was his side of the bed gapingly empty, but also her brain was chastising her for all the mistakes she had made. Spent too much money giving gifts, didn't pay attention to their marriage, too preoccupied with *her* life, not *theirs*. She had burdened him with her family. Too much older than him--- why wouldn't he run to another younger woman? She was a waitress; she smoked, for God sakes! He said he would never do this to her. He promised. But she had promised things too and didn't come through. She wanted to die, but still wanted to live. She wanted to cry, but had cried all the tears she had. She would finally collapse into a coma for about two hours in the early morning, only to awaken with her heart pounding against her chest and the covers and pillow still in place on his side of the bed.

His friends found him in their little camping trailer at the marina where they kept their boat. He had a gun, and the thought of suicide had crossed his mind. They found him and dragged him to some meetings. He called Nancy at work and told her in a monotone that he had been seeing someone else. She was in a meeting. She whispered "I want you to be at home when I come home tonight" She went back to the meeting stuffing the pain into her blue suit jacket pocket. The actress played her part exceptionally well until, at four-thirty p.m., she walked rubber legged to her car in the parking lot, turned the key, and headed for what she felt was the end of her marriage.

He had taken everything from their bedroom and packed it in boxes. The closet was empty. The pictures of lighthouses and a waterfall were off the wall. The dresser drawers were bare except for a few fuzz balls and torn paper liners. He was sitting on the couch. He looked smaller, angrier, and more sullen than she had ever seen him. She tried to swallow the anger, hurt, fear that was sitting like a lion ready to pounce on him.

"Where have you been? I was worried sick about you! They found a body in the river and I was so afraid it was you! Why did you take everything out of the bedroom? Don't you love me anymore?" Her voice became more pleading with every query.

He said nothing. He just stared ahead and looked at his hands. She reached for one of them. He did not hold her hand back. His was limp and uninterested.

"Honey, you have to talk to me. We have to work out whatever is going on." she begged.

The kids and Sue had retreated to the bedroom. They wanted to come out and help, but this had to be John and Nancy's solution.

"I know it's been difficult these past years with mom and dad and now Sue and the kids. You have been great. I understand how hard it has been for you. I told you that our difference in age would cause some problems someday. I can't believe you found someone else! Is she prettier than me? I'm sure she is younger! You said you would never do that to me! You said you would love me forever!" her voice cracked as she was loosing the control she promised on the drive home she would absolutely keep. The wounds were opening up eager to drain their poison.

He stood up and looked blankly through her to somewhere past the life they had built together out of broken dreams and failed relationships. He stared past the laughter and the pain, the raising kids and healing wounds and mending fences. He stared into a bottomless pit of emptiness. He wanted to run away – to where? It wasn't really to be with someone else, it was to run from his own self, from the dark aloneness that he was feeling. If sex or booze or drugs could help you run faster away from whatever it was that frightened you, so be it. There was no reason-------- just run.

He sat down again and said in a voice she didn't recognize, "I thought you would want me to leave. I don't know what to do. You have gotten us into so much debt. I was so angry with you. I suddenly stopped caring, or feeling. I still love you, but I am not thinking right and need to just go away."

She wanted to scream at the top of my lungs "It's her, isn't it?!! You are running away with *her. That bitch!*" She didn't say it then but she let him have it many times after that. She already was pretty shaky about believing someone could love her and then he brings in another faceless woman!

She did say instead, "I want you to stay ---please put the things back in the bedroom -----please!" There they come, the tears. They were welling up behind her eyes and burning to be released. They poured out onto her hands that he had dropped unceremoniously. He walked to the garage and started to put his clothes away. She never did find out if he was just leaving or leaving with her. It didn't really matter. He was putting his clothes back in their drawer. He did keep a box packed with some things for quite some time. They both went through rigorous counseling, some pretty hairy battles, silences that were louder than any words they could have shouted. They gradually got a relationship back. It was different than it was when they were together in those first ten years. They settled into a friendship again, love making was part of it, but the passion and the overwhelming feeling of excitement of those early years would only seep through occasionally. They had to work hard to forgive, to put that chapter in their lives in a box, not to be totally forgotten, but to be manageable. Amazingly, neither of them reached for a drink. John was placed on medication for depression for several years and Nancy, the all knowing nurse, realized she had learned zilch about the diseases of the mind in her short three months at the psychiatric institution during training. She read books about depression and was amazed by the extent of it in our culture.

Throughout those days of anguish Nancy's kids and sisters were there for her and for John. Friendships they had developed in the AA program continued to be there for them. . Nancy and John may have had some oddities that crept into what was supposed to be a "normal" life, but their friends and families huddled together in the storms of difficult times and offered love that was compassionate and sincere. Every morning when Nancy pulled into the parking garage to face work during those dark days when John was lost, a friend would call her on her cell phone and say, "You can get through this day. This one day. God can help you. Just say a little prayer to him, and he will ----I know it" It worked. It got her through that one day. That friend was lost somewhere. That friend had a mental illness that left her adrift and behaving in a bizarre manner that caused people to run and hide. Nancy prayed for her as she prayed for Nancy during one of the most harrowing times of her life.

Chapter 29

The Quilt

A brand new quilt of many colors, bright and young and gay
Lay on her newly hammered bed the day she wed in May
The freshness of a summer breeze scented every room
It passed across her lovely quilt – the colors how they bloomed!
A tiny baby babbles lying on the quilted fray
For time has made the colors fade into another day
She lifts her to her breast and sings to soothe her hungry cry
He wraps his arms around them both and kisses them good bye
Upon the bed a gentle child sits and talks of beau's
The colors compliment her eyes filled with first love's glow
She holds the quilt around her and wipes the tears away
When life throws stones and challenges and love seems ne'er to stay
The quilt rests on a frame so weak that barely can she see
The faded blues and reds and gelds that rest upon her knee
Suddenly the room is bright with angels--- gone is any fear she felt
As gentle arms would lift her up ---leaving just a quilt

This story is about courage. The special type of courage Nancy
had seen in so many. Men have courage. Yes, amazing courage. But
women have this thing, this ability to heal, to bond, to empathize; the
courage that often makes them appear the less strong of the two sexes.
The strength is not produced by lifting fifty pound weights; it comes
from lifting burdens from others, from the pains of childbirth, from
genuflecting graciously, and putting band-aids on wounds. There
needs to be a name for it, but Nancy tried and tried to invent one for
this book to no avail. It *is* like the tire swing. It encircles the rider and
molds itself as the rider slowly pumps their way through life's ride.
The rope is tied with a slip proof knot to something bigger than itself.
If you go too high, the rope might jerk you back in mid air and you

could fall. If you stop pumping, stop taking a chance on the ride, you may just sit and twirl, making you dizzy. It's a place to go for comfort. You can hear the birds sing and feel the flutter in your stomach when you swing through the air.

She sits under the ancient tree in the park. A quilt covers her long silk blue dress warming her as the cool breeze of late summer and early fall plays tag with the curls falling gently around her shoulders. A book of poems rests on the quilt, open to a page turned down at the corners. The water in the small lake nearby ripples musically as two swans proudly preen their bleach white feathers. The sun moves across the bluest of skies darting occasionally behind a cloud as if it were playing hide and seek with the earth. The rustle of the leaves on the branches of the tree seems to whisper his name over and over in her head. She straightened the pleats on her blouse that flows over her breasts to the tiny waist band of her skirt. Children she felt she knew giggled and tossed a ball on a playground a short distance from where she sat. Some of the children jumped onto a tire swing hung from an ancient tree. She could here them cheer and laugh as the rider was pushed higher and higher toward the tree branches. A part of her wanted to be a child again, in her grandmother's back yard, stealing into the chicken coop to hear the cooing of the birds, eating green apples without the aftermath, and joining those other children for a ride on the tire swing. The other part, the grown up part, was ready to meet with the person who would take her hand and wrap the quilt around her to keep her warm. He would smile gently as he walked beside her. She would close the book leaving the corners turned down on special pages of her life. They would walk through the beautiful park together with no regrets, no pain, and no insecurities.

The children had left the swing to go on with their lives. It twirled in the soft breeze waiting for their return.

Sue, Deb, John, Tom, Erin, and Ali bathed her tiny withered arms tenderly. They put oil on her parched lips and kissed her cool forehead. John pulled the quilt over her thin body and tucked it lovingly around her shoulders.

Many years battling cancer had led her to the other side of patient care. She now was the care receiver not the care giver. The window behind her bed was open and the orioles were playing in the trees outside the window. The cool breeze of summer turning into fall parted the curtains gently.

"We love you," they all said in their own way between sniffles and real tears. "It's alright to go."

The tiniest of smiles curled her parched lips. They glistened with the oil and she whispered "Me too," so softly that she wondered if they heard.

She reached her skinny arm slightly above the quilt as if she were taking someone's hand.

The tire swing hanging from the tree outside the window swung in the breeze ever so slightly.

The Beginning

About the Author

Nancy Jasin Ensley has worked in the healthcare field as a nurse, consultant compliance officer, hospice specialize, legal nurse consultant, coding specialist, teacher and supervisor. Her poems appear in the National Library of Poetry, Ensley has recently authored two more books; a mystery titled *Orphans* and a short story on E-books titled *A Penny for Your Thoughts.* Her husband, John, and she have five children and fourteen grandchildren. They live in rural Michigan.

Would you like to see your manuscript become a book?

CPSIA information can be obtained at www.ICGtesting.com
Printed in the USA
BVOW070317130712

295071BV00002B/20/P

9 781462 667765